Lecture Notes in Computer Science 5017

Commenced Publication in 1973
Founding and Former Series Editors:
Gerhard Goos, Juris Hartmanis, and Jan van Leeuwen

Editorial Board

David Hutchison
Lancaster University, UK

Takeo Kanade
Carnegie Mellon University, Pittsburgh, PA, USA

Josef Kittler
University of Surrey, Guildford, UK

Jon M. Kleinberg
Cornell University, Ithaca, NY, USA

Alfred Kobsa
University of California, Irvine, CA, USA

Friedemann Mattern
ETH Zurich, Switzerland

John C. Mitchell
Stanford University, CA, USA

Moni Naor
Weizmann Institute of Science, Rehovot, Israel

Oscar Nierstrasz
University of Bern, Switzerland

C. Pandu Rangan
Indian Institute of Technology, Madras, India

Bernhard Steffen
University of Dortmund, Germany

Madhu Sudan
Massachusetts Institute of Technology, MA, USA

Demetri Terzopoulos
University of California, Los Angeles, CA, USA

Doug Tygar
University of California, Berkeley, CA, USA

Gerhard Weikum
Max-Planck Institute of Computer Science, Saarbruecken, Germany

Takashi Nanya   Fumihiro Maruyama
András Pataricza   Miroslaw Malek (Eds.)

Service Availability

5th International Service Availability Symposium, ISAS 2008
Tokyo, Japan, May 19-21, 2008
Proceedings

 Springer

Volume Editors

Takashi Nanya
University of Tokyo
Research Center for Advanced Science and Technology
Tokyo 153-8904, Japan
E-mail: nanya@hal.rcast.u-tokyo.ac.jp

Fumihiro Maruyama
Fujitsu Laboratories Ltd.
Software and Solution Laboratories
Kawasaki 211-8588, Japan
E-mail: maruyama.f@jp.fujitsu.com

András Pataricza
Budapest University of Technology and Economics
Department of Measurement and Information Systems
1117 Budapest, Hungary
E-mail: pataric@mit.bme.hu

Miroslaw Malek
Humboldt University Berlin
Department of Computer Science and Engineering
12489 Berlin, Germany
E-mail: malek@informatik.hu-berlin.de

Library of Congress Control Number: 2008926633

CR Subject Classification (1998): C.2, H.4, H.3, I.2.11, D.2, H.5, K.4.4, K.6

LNCS Sublibrary: SL 3 – Information Systems and Application, incl. Internet/Web
and HCI

ISSN   0302-9743
ISBN-10   3-540-68128-0 Springer Berlin Heidelberg New York
ISBN-13   978-3-540-68128-1 Springer Berlin Heidelberg New York

Springer is a part of Springer Science+Business Media

springer.com

© Springer-Verlag Berlin Heidelberg 2008

Typesetting: Camera-ready by author, data conversion by Scientific Publishing Services, Chennai, India
Printed on acid-free paper   SPIN: 12270767   06/3180   5 4 3 2 1 0

General Chair's Message

On behalf of the Organizing Committee, I welcome you to the proceedings of the 5th International Service Availability Symposium (ISAS2008) held in the Research Center for Advanced Science and Technology (RCAST), University of Tokyo, the youngest research institute of the oldest university in Japan.

Service availability is a vital attribute of networked computing systems for the information society to make people confident in being able to trust the services provided in everyday life and societal activities. The objective of the symposium is to bring together researchers and practitioners from different "service" related areas in both industry and academia to discuss various aspects of service availability toward the goal of implementing dependable information societies. The unique tradition of the ISAS series promoting a strong partnership between industry and academia enabled us to organize an extremely high-quality and attractive program and to provide participants with an invaluable forum to achieve our goal. The "Komaba Research Campus" in the University of Tokyo offers an excellent location for this symposium at the heart of Tokyo, one of the largest cosmopolitan cities in the world.

I would like to thank the PC Co-chairs, Fumihiro Maruyama and András Pataricza, as well as all the PC members, including András Kővi, for their excellent job through the entire process of program organization. My special thanks go to Roberto Baldoni, Professor of University of Rome, and Hiroshi Maruyama, Director of IBM Tokyo Research Laboratory, for their kind acceptance to give interesting and useful keynote talks. I also express my sincere gratitude to the two internationally renowned professors, Miroslaw Malek from the Humboldt University, Germany and Kishor Trivedi from Duke University, USA, for voluntarily presenting excellent tutorials to all the participants.

I am especially indebted to Manfred Reitenspieß, the ISAS Steering Committee Chair and the Publicity Chair of this symposium, and all the Steering Committee members including Tadashi Dohi for their constructive suggestions and invaluable advice for the symposium organization.

I am deeply grateful to the Organizing Committee members, Hiroshi Nakamura (Finance Chair), Masashi Imai (Local Arrangement Chair), Masaaki Kondo (Registration Chair), Hiroyuki Okamura (Web Master) and Kazuto Kamiyama, for their dedicated volunteer services that made the symposium possible.

Last but not least, let me express my sincere appreciation to the "Inoue Foundation for Science" and the "International Communications Foundation" for their generous support in organizing the symposium successfully.

May 2008   Takashi Nanya

Program Chairs' Message

ISAS, the International Service Availability Symposium series, took place for the fifth time. ISAS 2008, like each of its predecessors, strongly relied on the tradition of bringing together academic and industrial experts active in the field of service availability.

As services begin to influence more and more our everyday life, their availability becomes a vital factor of society and for business. This year the broad spectrum of submitted papers represented well a continuous trend in searching for holistic views and solutions in assuring the correct functioning of the service-based information backbone for the good of our society and economy.

Continuing the tradition established by the past symposia, ISAS adhered to the core, almost classical, topics while, at the same time, trying to accommodate trends and new themes. ISAS is traditionally open to innovative technical and scientific ideas having a potential future impact on the availability of services.

This year the conference received a total of 28 submissions, each of which was reviewed by at least 3 Program Committee (PC) members. Subsequently, an electronic discussion was carried out among the PC members until we reached a consensus. As result of the selection process, 12 full papers are included in this volume.

In order to promote an important dialogue primarily between industry and academia, several complementary activities were initiated. Papers carrying an important message for the industry but still in the elaboration phase were invited to be presented as short papers.

The program was complemented by two important keynote presentations by Roberto Baldoni and Hiroshi Maruyama.

In addition to the presentations, a panel of the activities of the Service Availability Forum served as a bridge between the academic world, industrial application development and solution providers. Experiences related to service availability enabling technologies were presented in the form of an Industrial Demo Session. The academic foundations of service availability were presented during two excellent tutorials held by Kishor Trivedi and Miroslaw Malek.

Finally, a special session was devoted to an important open research framework entitled Service Innovation Research Initiative.

The organizers express their gratitude to all who provided continuous support in organizing the program. Special thanks should be given to András Kővi, Manfred Reitenspieß, Tadashi Dohi, Miroslaw Malek and Bratislav Milić for their help in organizing the review process, collecting the papers, editing this volume and publicizing this event, as well as to our General Chair, Takashi Nanya, for his continuous support.

Finally, we strongly believe that this year's conference continued the traditions of having a high scientific and technical quality as well as an extensive dialogue on key issues of service availability.

May 2008   Fumihiro Maruyama
                                                                 András Pataricza

Organization

ISAS 2008 was sponsored by the Research Center for Advanced Science and Technology (RCAST), University of Tokyo and Service Availability Forum, in cooperation with IEICE TC on Dependable Computing and GI TC on Dependability and Fault Tolerance.

Organizing Committee

General Chair
Takashi Nanya (University of Tokyo, Japan)

Program Co-chairs
András Pataricza (Budapest University of Technology and Economics, Hungary)
Fumihiro Maruyama (Fujitsu Lab., Japan)

Finance Chair
H. Nakamura (University of Tokyo, Japan)

Local Arrangement Chair
M. Imai (University of Tokyo, Japan)

Registration Chair
M. Kondo (University of Tokyo, Japan)

Publicity Chair
M. Reitenspieß (Fujitsu Siemens Computers, Germany)

Publication Chair
M. Malek (Humboldt University, Germany)

Web Master
H.Okamura (Hiroshima University, Japan)

Steering Committee

M. Reitenspieß (Fujitsu Siemens Computers, Germany)
S. Benlarbi (Alcatel, Canada)
T. Dohi (Hiroshima University, Japan)
M. Malek (Humboldt University, Germany)
D. Penkler (HP, France)
F. Tam (Nokia, Finland)

Program Committee

A. Avritzer (Siemens, USA)
D. Bakken (Washington S., USA)
R. Baldoni (University of Rome, Italy)
G. Chockler (IBM, Israel)
C. Fetzer (TU Dresden, Germany)
F. Fraikin (SDM, Germany)
R. Fricks (Motorola, USA)
M. Funabashi (Hitachi, Japan)
A. Gokhale (Vanderbilt, USA)
K. Hidaka (IBM, Japan)
M. Hiller (Volvo, Sweden)
H. Ichikawa (UEC, Japan)
K. Iwasaki (Tokyo Metropolitan University, Japan)
Z. Kalbarczyk (UIUC, USA)
T. Kikuno (Osaka University, Japan)
A. Kővi (BME+OptXware, Hungary)
S. Kuo (National Taiwan University, Taiwan)
V. Loll (Nokia, Denmark)
M. R. Lyu (Chinese University, Hong Kong)
V. Mendiratta (Lucent, USA)
N. Milanović (TU Berlin, Germany)
A. Moorsel (University of Newcastle, UK)
A. Naseem (GoAhead, USA)
A. Pasic (Atos Origin, Spain)
H. Ramasamy (IBM Zurich, Switzerland)
A. Romanovsky (University of Newcastle, UK)
S. Sekiguchi (AIST, Japan)
P. Sinha (Philips India)
H. Sun (Sun Microsystems, USA)
N. Suri (TU Darmstadt, Germany)
H. Szczerbicka (University of Hannover, Germany)
M. Toeroe (Ericsson, Canada)
K. Trivedi (Duke University, USA)
T. Katsuyama (Fujitsu Labs, Japan)
K. Ueda (University of Tokyo, Japan)
P. Urban (Google, Switzerland)
S. Valcourt (University of New Hampshire, USA)
A. Wolski (Solid Tech., Finland)
S. Yajnik (Avaya, USA)
T. Yamanouchi (NEC, Japan)

Table of Contents

Fifth International Service Availability Symposium ISAS 2008

Keynotes

The Italian *e*-Government Enterprise Architecture: A Comprehensive
Introduction with Focus on the SLA Issue 1
*Roberto Baldoni, Stefano Fuligni, Massimo Mecella, and
Francesco Tortorelli*

Challenges and Opportunities for Computer Science in Services
Science 13
Hiroshi Maruyama

Tutorials

Predictive Algorithms and Technologies for Availability
Enhancement 17
Miroslaw Malek

Achieving and Assuring High Availability 20
*Kishor Trivedi, Gianfranco Ciardo, Balakrishnan Dasarathy,
Michael Grottke, Rivalino Matias, Andy Rindos, and Bart Vashaw*

Enterprise System Dependability

Optimizing Security Measures in an Intrusion Tolerant Database
System 26
Toshikazu Uemura and Tadashi Dohi

The Impact of Unavailability on the Effectiveness of Enterprise
Information Security Technologies 43
Simon Edward Parkin, Rouaa Yassin Kassab, and Aad van Moorsel

Interaction Faults Caused by Third-Party External Systems — A Case
Study and Challenges 59
Bogdan Tomoyuki Nassu and Takashi Nanya

Software Service Availability

User-Perceived Software Service Availability Modeling with Reliability
Growth 75
Koichi Tokuno and Shigeru Yamada

Execution Path Profiling for OS Device Drivers: Viability and
Methodology   90
    Constantin Sârbu, Andréas Johansson, and Neeraj Suri

Analysis of a Software System with Rejuvenation, Restoration and
Checkpointing   110
    Hiroyuki Okamura and Tadashi Dohi

Service Availability Platform

A Platform for Cooperative Server Backups Based on Virtual
Machines   129
    Akiyoshi Sugiki, Kei Yamatozaki, Richard Potter, and Kazuhiko Kato

Platform Management with SA Forum and Its Role to Achieve High
Availability   142
    Ulrich Kleber, Frédéric Herrmann, and Ulrich Horstmann

Automatic Generation of AMF Compliant Configurations   155
    *Ali Kanso, Maria Toeroe, Ferhat Khendek, and
    Abdelwahab Hamou-Lhadj*

Service Dependability Analysis

Dependability Evaluation of a Replication Service for Mobile
Applications in Dynamic Ad-Hoc Networks   171
    *Erling V. Matthiesen, Ossama Hamouda, Mohamed Kaâniche, and
    Hans-Peter Schwefel*

Ten Fallacies of Availability and Reliability Analysis   187
    *Michael Grottke, Hairong Sun, Ricardo M. Fricks, and
    Kishor S. Trivedi*

Analytical Availability Assessment of IT Services   207
    Miroslaw Malek, Bratislav Milic, and Nikola Milanovic

Author Index   225

The Italian *e*-Government Enterprise Architecture: A Comprehensive Introduction with Focus on the SLA Issue

Roberto Baldoni[1], Stefano Fuligni[2],
Massimo Mecella[1], and Francesco Tortorelli[2]

[1] SAPIENZA – Università di Roma, Dipartimento di Informatica e Sistemistica
{baldoni,mecella}@dis.uniroma1.it
[2] CNIPA - Centro Nazionale per l'Informatica nella Pubblica Amministrazione
{s.fuligni,f.tortorelli}@cnipa.it

Abstract. The paper describes the currently ongoing effort for defining and developing a nationwide *e*-Government Enterprise architecture in order to guarantee a flexible approach for integrated application services, respecting local and central administrations' autonomy. An appropriate mixture of organizational initiatives, together with the promulgation of appropriate laws, and the development of innovative technical rules, seems to be the success factor of the approach. From a more technical point of view, the definition *(i)* of semantically-rich service agreements, *(ii)* of a repository more complex than a simple UDDI registry, and *(iii)* of complementary components for dealing with QoS and security, represent the core elements of the infrastructure. Finally the paper discusses the problem related to the monitoring of QoS at the level of the service execution.

1 Introduction

Before 1999, the scenario of the ICT in the Italian public administrations (PAs) was quite disomogeneous: there were sectors of excellence in some central PAs as far as basic and advanced interoperability is concerned, and other central or regional PAs that acted as almost isolated systems. Basic network services (not necessarily Internet-based) were outsourced by each PA to external providers with an explosion of costs and possibly lack of interoperability between basic services of different PAs. In this context, the "Nationwide Cooperative Network" (referred to as RUPA [1]) was established in order to provide security and basic interoperability services (e.g., directory, e-mail, WWW) to the central PAs. But, even if from one hand RUPA created a system's vision (about interoperability) and generated big savings for the central administrations, on the other hand, during the years it became clearer and clearer that basic interoperability is not sufficient, and there was a real need for advanced interoperability and application cooperation/integration between back offices.

The heterogeneity of procedures, data and infrastructures among local and central PAs has been exacerbated from the political viewpoint. The reform of

T. Nanya et al. (Eds.): ISAS 2008, LNCS 5017, pp. 1–12, 2008.

the Italian Constitution in 2001 attributed indeed new possibilities for action to local authorities. Since then, the right to pass laws autonomously represented an increasingly effective means for decentralization with respect to administrative, organizational and also technical aspects. But from an ICT management point of view, this decentralization generated different points of decision, possibly leading to different ICT choices as well as different organizational processes. This can bring rapidly to the proliferation of different interoperability infrastructures (a sort of "spaghetti" connections/middlewares) with the consequent high risk of inefficiency.

Even though this process of decentralization of competencies and diversification of ICT solutions can help in defining and actuating in a rapid way political objectives (defined by laws) at the regional or local level, it will make tremendously difficult the implementation of political objectives at the inter-regional or national level sharing local and central competencies. Many examples of such strategic objectives can be found in the areas of healthcare, employment, register offices, tax offices, etc. If not mastered properly, therefore this process of decentralization, instead of turning out in an advantage for the country, can lead to a lack of interoperability among the PAs.

Given this context, the issue was to set-up an organizational process, together with technical solutions, that would allow the development of nationwide application cooperation/integration between back offices. Even if Web services are the technological instrument enabling the solution, such a solution requires *(i)* a strategic vision, based on a bottom-up process for reaching a shared PA-wide Enterprise Architecture, and for maintaining it, and *(ii)* a deep and comprehensive technical specification.

The aim of this paper is to outline both *(i)* the strategic actions, that at the level of overall governance of the Italian *e*-Government process, have been undertaken, and *(ii)* the enterprise architecture and the innovative technological solutions that have been proposed for the realization of such a nationwide , referred to as SPCOOP - *Sistema Pubblico di Cooperazione* [Public Cooperative System] . Finally, we look at the problems encountered in designing metrics for Service Level Agreements inside the Italian Enterprise Architecture as well as the system to be developed for their monitoring. This is one of the main technical challenges of the entire Enterprise Architecture.

2   Strategic and Governance Actions

In 2003, CNIPA [1] started the coordination of a nationwide bottom-up consensus operation, from basic telecommunication services to advanced application cooperation. Different working groups were started with the participation of over 300 representatives of central and local PAs, universities and research centers

---

[1] The CNIPA (National Centre for IT in Public Administration) is a government agency which depends on the Italian Cabinet (Presidency of the Council of Ministers). CNIPA supports and implements policies delivered by the Minister for reform and innovation in Public administration.

and Italian ICT companies. The outcome has been a set of about 30 documents describing a technical and organizational nationwide system for network, communication, basic interoperability, cooperation and security services among administrations. This system consists of SPC - *Sistema Pubblico di Connettività* [Public Internetworking System] and, on top of it, of SPCOOP for the application cooperation among PAs.

The Legal Interoperability Framework. In parallel to the bottom-up process for the definition of SPC and SPCOOP, the Government issued in February 2005 a Law Decree, namely the digital administration code (CAD) (Law decree n. 82/05), that defined the legal interoperability framework, CAD defines rules regarding the digitalization of the PAs, grouped in the following sectors: (i) The rights of citizens and enterprises on Public Administration (ii) Citizens and enterprises must be placed at centre of PAs services (iii) Digital signatures and legal validity; (iii) Contracts, payments and accounting deeds (iv) Development, acquisition and reuse of software in PAs. Moreover, as far as SPCOOP and SPC is concerned, CAD establishes its scope, the sectors of interest, the governance, the technical rules of the Italian Enterprise Architecture, and the subsidiarity principles among National authorities and local ones. Additionally, CAD establishes two important principles:

- the cooperation among administrations is exclusively carried out on SP-COOP, with its tools and according to its technical rules; it has *legal* value and no further decree or official publication (e.g., on the Gazette) is needed (e.g., when defining standard XML formats for data exchange);
- the public ICT managers need to organize their information systems, including organizational and management aspects, in order to accommodate SPCOOP rules.

The Italian Enterprise Architecture. SPCOOP is not only a software framework, but also a technical and organizational platform whose aim is to create the conditions for a long-lived *legally valid* cooperation among administrations. It is based on four pillars which are leading-edge in terms of technologies, best practices and organization: *(i)* formalization, and successive publication, of *service agreements* between PAs (detailed in Section 3.1); *(ii)* definition of a federated identity management system for access control; *(iii)* definition of the metadata about the effective data to be used for cooperating, of the semantics and of domains' ontologies; *(iv)* open and continuous update of the SPCOOP model, by taking into account the latest progress in technologies and standards.

A first set of documents including *(i)* the overall vision, *(ii)* the SPC network services and the security model were published in 2004 [2]. The starting point of the SPCOOP has been the publishing in 2005 of a set of technical documents [3].

---

[2] http://www.cnipa.gov.it/site/it-it/In_primo_piano/
    Sistema_Pubblico_di_Connettività_(SPC)/
[3] http://www.cnipa.gov.it/site/it-IT/In_primo_piano/
    Sistema_Pubblico_di_Connettività_(SPC)/
    Servizi_di_interoperabilità_evoluta_e_cooperazione_applicativa/

Such documents define the model of cooperation at the application level for national and local administrations and are, under a specific license, freely usable (e.g., for creating methodologies, software, dissemination, education, etc.). Then, during 2006, four public tenders have been launched concerning:

- Network services, including VoIP and ubiquitous connectivity. The contract has been awarded in June 2006 to 4 providers (BT, FASTWEB, WIND and Telecom Italia). Such network services will form the basic communication infrastructure connecting national and local authorities.
- Shared network infrastructures, including services for managing the Service Level Agreements (SLAs) of the SPC providers, the security and the VoIP services; currently a commission is selecting the partners.
- An initial set of interoperability services of SPCoop, including identity management, PA Web site/portals creation and management, Domain Gateways and tools for wrapping back-office applications as SPCoop Web services to be deployed on the Domain Gateways; currently a commission is selecting the partners.
- The effective SPCoop framework, as detailed in the following of the paper; the public tender deadline has been December 2006, and the commission for selecting the partner is expected to conclude its work by Spring 2007.

Accompanying Measures. 56 regional projects on e-Government, focussed on network and interoperability infrastructures, has been launched, for an overall amount of 100MÅ. These projects will provide best practices as well as reference implementations of the different SPC and SPCOOP elements, in order to direct the bottom-up approach. The biggest project is ICAR (Interoperability and Application Cooperation among Regions), started in June 2006 with 17 partners including 16 out of 19 Italian Regions. The expected results from these projects are: the compliance of large horizontal projects with SPCOOP; the complete definition and advertisement of about 50 service agreements, and the beginning of the definition of about another 100 service agreements; the definition of the core of an upper ontology and of two specific domain ontologies; finally the definition of metric for service-level agreement, the design of a SLA monitoring system and the reference implementation of all the components.

Before concluding this section, we would like to point out how the governance and strategic actions presented above represent the success element of this challenge; adopting a common infrastructure for interoperability and cooperation on the basis of solely technical solutions has proved unsuccessful in the past, conversely the use of a community approach to realize evolving versions of the framework and to create a SPCoop "culture" in the PAs seems a better solution. Such a community is expected to be led by administrations, with the active participation of industries and universities. This also constitutes an enabling factor for the overall innovation process of the whole country. The documents published in 2005 represents a technical road-map for such a community towards the effective SPCoop development, whereas typical community tools (e.g., online forums, development community, the continuous evaluation of standards by CNIPA, etc.) will support the process.

3 Overview of SPCoop Enteprise Architecture

The model proposed for SPCoop is based on the following principles:

- The PAs cooperate through the supply and the use of *application services*; these services are offered by the single administration through a unique (logic) element belonging to its own information system called *Domain Gateway*. In this way the complete autonomy of the single administration is guaranteed, as far as it concerns the implementation and management of the provided application services, as they can be based on any application platform, being it pre-existent or new, as long as they are supplied through the Domain Gateway. The fruition of the application services is carried out through the exchange of messages, whose format is formally specified in the Italian standard referred to as *e-Gov Envelop*. Such a standard is basically an extension of SOAP.
- A service works on the basis of an agreement among at least two subjects (supplier and client); such agreements have a technical basis and an institutional/jurisdictional basis. These agreements should be formalized in order to support the development and the life-cycle of services in a (semi-)automatic way. The agreement specification is called *Service Agreement* and is based on the XML language.
- Sets of administrations which need to cooperate in order to provide composite application services form a *Cooperation Domain*; the services supplied

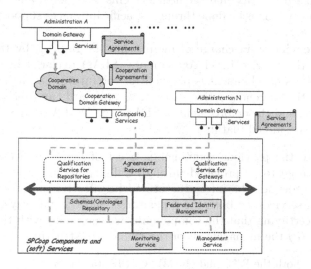

Fig. 1. The components and (soft) services of SPCoop

by such a domain are *externally* described through Service Agreements, and *internally* by a specification describing how the different PAs concur to compose the final service, referred to as *Cooperation Agreement*.

It emerges that the cooperation model of SPCOOP is organized as a Service Oriented Architecture (SOA) [2]; but even if the basic aspects related to a SOA are well defined under a technological point of view, conversely it is necessary to extend the advanced aspects in order to make the architecture suitable to the specific e-Government scenario. The reader should note that all the service architectures [4]/SOAs need a neutral element [5], with the goal to mediate between the different subjects cooperating for the service supply/use; the SPCOOP framework includes a set of infrastructural components to be used to simplify these operations (e.g., retrieving a service trough automatic categorization, managing digital identities, etc). They are represented in Figure 1:

Agreements Repository is the software component used to register and to maintain the Cooperation/Service Agreements. It can be considered as the "database" of the cooperation. This component offers functionalities for the registration, the access, the update and the search of the agreements. The UDDI standard is the core of this component; however this standard does not offer all the required functionalities, therefore it has been extended.

Schemas/Ontologies Repository is the software component offering functionalities to deal with the service and information semantics, in order to find out services that are more suitable to provide required functionalities. This component acts as a structure to store ontologies and conceptual schemas, offering functionalities of registration, access, update and reasoning on them.

Federated Identity Management is used to authorize and control the access to application services over SPCOOP; the federation is needed to reuse the already in-place identity management systems of regional and national authorities. Integration is be done through specific interfaces supporting SAML v2.0.

Monitoring Service is in charge of monitoring the respect, by the different services, of the Service Level Agreements (SLAs) declared in the Service Agreements. Its development is planned for the future (i.e., it has not been included in the currently active tender), as standards and technologies for the definition and the enforcement of SLAs (e.g., WSLA or WS-Agreement) are not yet considered mature.

In addition to the previous components, a set of (soft) services, i.e., functionalities that need to be provided through different tools (either software or managerial) in order for the infrastructure to be effective, have been defined: *(i)* qualification services for both the repositories and the gateways, i.e., coded procedures for certifying that the components are compliant with the SPCOOP technical rules; *(ii)* the management of the whole infrastructure.

---

[4] This is true for both the W3C and ebXML/OASIS standards.

[5] Technically called *service directory*.

In the next sections, some technical details on the most innovative aspects of SPCOOP will be provided.

3.1 Service Agreements

A service agreement is a well-specified XML document that regulates the relationships of an application service between a supplier and a client in the following aspects: *(i)* service interface, *(ii)* conversations admitted by the service, *(iii)* access points, *(v)* Service Level Agreements (SLAs), *(v)* security characteristics and *(vi)* descriptions of the semantics of the service. The formal and well specified nature of the service agreement has been done to support the development and the life-cycle of services in a (semi-)automatic way. Moreover, the public nature of the service agreement makes easier the establishment of domain ontologies that allows to aggregate services with similar semantics. Finally, in the context of a set of public administrations (i.e., a Cooperation Domain), services can be composed and orchestrated, thus generating other services described in turn by service agreements.

The application services are supplied/used through Web service technologies and standards "enforced" by public service agreements.

WSDL can be (and is actually) used to describe the elements *(i)* and *(iii)*. The element *(ii)* is considered as a typical application service requires multiple interactions between the service supplier and the client, and not all the offered operations are invocable in every step during the interaction. Thus, in order to use the service correctly (and therefore to develop *correct* clients), it is important to know in which steps operations can be invoked. This is different from the description of the internal process of a service, i.e., the description of the workflow implemented by the application service to offer such operations; nevertheless such conversational protocol can be obtained from the internal process by making abstractions in order to eliminate the details (internal view) while focusing on those service functionalities that are visible outward (external view) [3,4]. The model that describe the conversation protocol through a Finite State Machine [5], is considered meaningful and simple at the same time. Nowadays it does not exist a standard in the Web Service arena having the characteristics needed to describe this element, and therefore a new language, specifically designed for this purpose, has been introduced, namely WSBL (Web Service Behavioral Language), stemming from previous standard proposals (WSCL - Web Service Conversation Language [6]) and academic ones (WSTL - Web Service Transition Language). When in the future, new standards or existing one will mature and will be appropriate for describing such an element, then the SPCOOP rules will be in turn evolved by incorporating them.

As far as points *(iv)* and *(v)*, their importance is related to the particular scenario: application services that offer to citizens and enterprises operations belonging to the administrative/bureaucratic field, have to declare the supported levels of quality and of security. Again, at the time of this writing, standards in these fields are not mature yet, therefore the filling out of these parts is not

---

[6] http://www.w3.org/TR/wscl10/

mandatory. The accompanying measure project ICAR is currently investigating these issues and more details will be given in Section 4.

The last point (i.e., *(vi)*) is introduced as, in an *e*-Government scenario, many concepts that should be shared and universally accepted, conversely show deep differences of meaning among different cooperating subjects, presenting different descriptions and formats. As a result, the description of the conceptual schemas and the ontologies related to the information carried out by a service, have the same importance of the definition of the interface [6]. Proposals for the description of these aspects are rapidly emerging; but the proposals related to OWL and/or WSML/WSMO (the so called *Semantic Web*) are not yet considered as standards, and their relationship with Web services and the related standards is under investigation. The ambitious aim is to have, in the near future, as few ontologies as possible, through which to describe the semantics of all the application services offered by the different administrations.

3.2   Cooperation Domains and Cooperation Agreements

A Service Agreement describes a *2-party* collaboration/cooperation, with a subject offering a SPCOOP application service and another subject using such a service. A lot of administrative processes do not concern only a single administration, but they involve different subjects.

The *Cooperation Domain* is the formalization of the wish of different subjects to join in order to cooperate for the automation of administrative processes. Inside the Cooperation Domain, a *responsible coordinator* should be identified, it assures the organizational and technical effectiveness and the coordination of all involved subjects and of the set of *composite application services* supplied outward by the Cooperation Domain. The Cooperation Domain is seen outward as a service supplier acting like a normal domain of a single administration; the main difference is in the way its services are designed and deployed: in the Cooperation Domain they are built by composing and integrating simple services offered by the involved administrations; whereas for the single domain the supply of a service is related to applications that are fully under the responsibility of the single administration.

A *Cooperation Agreement* represents the specification of application services offered by a Cooperation Domain. The service supply is characterized by three basic elements:

- application services offered outward by the Cooperation Domain. From the user point of view, these services (*composite services*) are identical to any other service directly offered by a Domain, and like them they are described by a Service Agreement;
- application services used internally by the Cooperation Domain to build the composite services, referred to in the following as *component services*; they are described by their own Service Agreements too;

– the specification of the way the component services are coordinated to build the composite service. This specification, needed for each composite service, can be defined either in terms of orchestration (i.e., from the point of view of the composite service, by describing the process for the composition and coordination of the component services) or in terms of choreography (i.e., by an external point of view, by describing the constraints on the messages exchanged among the different component services). In SPCOOP, the first solution, through the use of WS-BPEL, has been preferred.

Therefore a Cooperation Agreement consists of *(i)* an *institutive document*, expressed in natural language, describing the purposes and the normative or institutional basis of the Cooperation Domain; *(ii)* a set of references to the Service Agreements, describing the composite services offered by the Cooperative Domain; *(iii)* a set of WS-BPEL documents (one for each composite service) describing the coordination processes among component services [7]; such documents can be processed through suitable orchestration engines that are able to automate the coordination and the supply of a composite service; and *(iv)* a set of lists of references to the Service Agreements describing the component services (a set for each composite service).

3.3 Repositories for Agreements and Schemas/Ontologies

SPCOOP provides an infrastructural software component to register and to maintain Service (and Cooperation) Agreements – it can be defined as the "database" of the cooperation. This component offers functionalities for the registration, the access, the update and the search of the Service/Cooperation Agreements. The UDDI standard is the starting point to define and implement this component; but this standard does not offer all the required functionalities, in particular UDDI defines content-unaware queries, while the Repository will offer the capabilities for queries about the content of the Agreements. Therefore, specific software layers have been designed to extend UDDI in order to realize all the envisioned functionalities. From a deployment point of view, the Repository has been organized into two layers, namely General and Local.

In particular, it is organized in a distributed *master-slave architecture with replication of information* with the following structure: *(i)* a singleton instance of the *General Repository* contains all the information needed for the supply of the provided functionalities; *(ii)* N instances of the Repository, referred to as as *Local Repositories*, contain (sub-)sets of information, defined according to different rules (e.g., geographic location, functional relationship, relationship with the supplier): if an information is in a Local Repository, it is surely in the General one, while the viceversa is not always true. Updates can be performed either at the level of General and Local Repositories, and a synchronization mechanism based on Publish&Subscribe technologies has been devised in order to guarantee the correctness of all the Repositories.

---

[7] Further evolutions of the Cooperation Agreement will consider the specification of the documents describing the choreographies.

The Schemas/Ontologies Repository is the software component offering functionalities to deal with service and information semantics, in order to find out services that are more suitable to provide required functionalities. As described in Section 3.1, the "operational" point of view for the provided services is not the only possibility, being sometime better to search a service on the basis of the type of information that it carries on/deals with. The ontologies and the conceptual schemas represent the mechanism to describe this aspect, and suitable technologies, commonly referred to as "semantic" ones, allow the achievement of (semi-)automatic "reasoning" on the basis of such information. Even if the semantic descriptions are part of the Service Agreements, they are more effectively managed as separate elements.

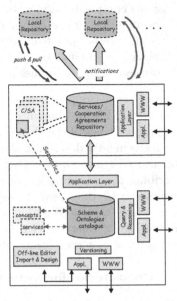

Fig. 2. Repositories in SPCOOP

Therefore the Schemas/Ontologies Repository acts as a structure to store ontologies and conceptual schemas, offering functionalities of registration, access, update and reasoning on them; it is, in fact, the "database" of the ontologies and schemas. Figure 3 shows the complex architecture according to which Agreements Repositories (one General and various Local) and the Schemas/Ontologies Repository (unique in SPCOOP) are arranged in a distributed fashion.

4 Service Level Agreements: A Real Challenge

The definition of metric for measuring the service level agreement (SLA) and the designing of a system for SLAs monitoring are among the most difficult challenges of the entire SPCOOP. This is due to the fact that nowadays, standards with the needed characteristics do not exist: (i) the WSLA (Web Service Level Agreement) proposal did not become a standard and IBM gave up its development, yet showing many interesting conceptual elements and a very detailed description of the possible metrics to be used in a client-server interaction; (ii) WS-Agreement is implied in a process of standardization in the limited context of the Grid Computing, whose final outcome is not yet clear.

The inter-regional Italian project ICAR started to investigate the problem related to metric definition and monitoring system for SPCOOP. From the point of view of SLA metrics, at the time of this writing, there has been a convergence within ICAR to adopt the syntax of WS-Agreement for SLA description and to reuse some of the metric that were defined in WSLA. Specifically, the metrics defined by ICAR are: "response time 5-10" which represents the mean of two averages done on a series of 5 elementary response times of a successful interactions and 10 elementary response times respectively; the average speed of data sent by the supplier to a client computed on a weekly base. The percentage of the successful interactions that executed in less than 1.5 sec. Percentage of unsuccessful interactions done on three-monthly base and, finally, the percentage of unsuccessful operations computed on a fixed number of interactions. According to ICAR findings this is the minimal set of generic metrics that can be helpful for the PA to formally describe a large number of service agreements.

The problem of designing a monitoring system immediately turns out in a decision about the presence (or not) of a trusted third party that executes the monitoring during service execution and assigns penalties. This presence is relatively easy to be integrated in a client-supplier interaction when the number of suppliers is low and the SLA to be monitored is the same at any supplier. This is the typical case of a multiproviders telco system such as SPC. In SPC there are four connectivity providers (BT, FASTWEB, Telecom Italia, WIND) and there is an entity that monitors the SLA guaranteed at the communication level to the PAs. SPCOOP can host potentially thousands of suppliers and each supplier can have a different SLA for each client also considering the same service, therefore the presence of this third party becomes unmanageable. Without the third party, the solution is that client and supplier store in their own the information concerning monitoring of each interaction. This creates problem of validity of the data itself. The solution that ICAR is addressing to create a repository that will be colocated with the service agreement repository and where client and supplier both deposit the information related at each single operations that will be then correlated by ad-hoc software to compute the aggregated SLA metrics.

5 Discussion and Future Work

Many European countries have engaged, in the last years, nationwide e-Government initiatives similar to the one presented in this paper (e.g., [7,8]). As an example, the e-Government Interoperability Framework (eGIF [8]) in UK is mostly focused on the definition of standard XML Schemas to be used for data integration and exchange among different PAs. Currently in Germany (cfr. the IDABC observatory [9]) there is no an overall legal framework for e-Government (i.e., something equivalent CAD Law Decree cited in Section 2), and no nationwide technical framework has been yet established (to the best of author's knowledge). For a complete overview of the various e-Government initiatives at European level, the reader can refer to IDABC [9].

This paper has also focussed on the SLA issue pointing out a clear lack of standards well suited to e-Government frameworks. The situation is different for security and ontologies where standards will soon be ready for answering many of the needs of such frameworks. This makes SLA definition and monitoring one of the hardest points to be faced in the context of a developing of a nationalwide enterprise architecture.

---

[8] http://www.govtalk.gov.uk/schemasstandards/egif_document.asp?docnum=949
[9] http://ec.europa.eu/idabc/en/document/6508/396

In the following months, the SPCOOP framework presented in this paper will start the operative phase, through the assignment of the public tenders and the design and implementation phase – also through open source communities that are already implementing some components [10] , this phase is expected to be concluded within the end of 2007. On the basis of the received feedbacks, and of the continuous update due to the consensus mechanism, it is also expected a major revision of the technical specifications within Summer 2008.

Acknowledgments. The authors would like to thank all the persons involved in the working groups that have contributed to the development of SPCOOP, and in particular the Department "Ufficio Servizi di Interoperabilità Evoluti e Cooperazione Applicativa" of CNIPA. Roberto Baldoni and Massimo Mecella has been partly supported by the European Commission under Contract FP6-2004-IST-4-027517, project SEMANTICGOV, and the Italian MIUR under the Contract no. RBNE0358YR_2, FIRB project EG4M.

References

1. Batini, C., Mecella, M.: Enabling italian e-government through a cooperative architecture. IEEE Computer 34(2) (2001)
2. Alonso, G., Casati, F., Kuno, H., Machiraju, V. (eds.): Web Services. Concepts, Architectures and Applications. Springer, Heidelberg (2004)
3. van der Aalst, W., Weske, M.: The p2p approach to interorganizational workflows. In: Dittrich, K.R., Geppert, A., Norrie, M.C. (eds.) CAiSE 2001. LNCS, vol. 2068, Springer, Heidelberg (2001)
4. Dijkman, R., Dumas, M.: Service oriented design. a multi-viewpoint approach. International Journal of Cooperative Information Systems 13(4) (2004)
5. Benatallah, B., Casati, F., Skogsrud, H., Toumani, F.: Abstracting and enforcing web service protocols. International Journal on Cooperative Information Systems 13(4) (2004)
6. Vetere, G., Lenzerini, M.: Models for Semantic Interoperability in Service-Oriented Architectures. IBM Systems Journal 44(4), 887–904 (2005)
7. Guijarro, L.: Interoperability frameworks and enterprise architectures in e-government initiatives in europe and the united states. Government Information Quarterly 24(1) (2007)
8. Janssen, M., Hjort-Madsen, K.: Analyzing enterprise architecture in national governments: The cases of denmark and the netherlands. In: Proceedings of the 40th Hawaii International Conference on System Sciences (2007)
9. European Commission: Interoperable Delivery of European eGovernment Services to Public Administrations, Businesses and Citizens (IDABC), http://europa.eu.int/idabc/

---

[10] http://www.openspcoop.org is currently implementing open source reference implementation of the Domain Gateway and of the Service Agreements Repository.

Challenges and Opportunities for Computer Science in Services Science

Hiroshi Maruyama

IBM Research, Tokyo Research Laboratory
1624-14 Shimotsuruma, Yamato, Kanagawa, Japan
maruyama@jp.ibm.com
http://www.research.ibm.com/trl/

Abstract. Information technology is playing more vital roles as service businesses increasingly dominate the world's economy. Computer science, which has evolved over the past 50 years, faces new opportunities and challenges to solve critical problems in services science. This presentation discusses these opportunities and challenges from a computer scientist's point of view.

Keywords: Computer Science, Services Science.

1 Introduction

Computer science has evolved in two directions over the past 50 years. The "core" computer science areas such as algorithms and language compilers have been greatly refined, while many new areas, such as bioinformatics, computational physics, and business process modeling, to name a few, have emerged. One of the most promising areas among these "non-core" areas where we can apply techniques and insights developed in the core computer science is "services" science.

2 Emergence of Services Science

The global economy is quickly shifting labor forces to service businesses. In Japan, 70% of the labor force was working in the services sector in 2004. This is in contrast to 25 years earlier, when only 30% of Japan's labor force was in the services sector. Emerging countries such as China and India are also quickly moving to services economies.

Technology companies such as IBM are also shifting their businesses to put more focus on services. In 2007, more than half of IBM's revenue was from IT services, such as consulting, system integration, outsourcing, and maintenance. The participants in the Global Innovation Outlook Version 2.0 [1] agreed that automotive manufacturers are starting to view themselves as services companies, providing services based on the advanced capabilities of their products.

T. Nanya et al. (Eds.): ISAS 2008, LNCS 5017, pp. 13–16, 2008.

Realizing the need for scientific and engineering methodologies for services businesses and students trained with these methodologies, IBM, along with some universities and government institutions, proposed establishing a new scientific descipline called Services Science and Management Engineering (SSME) [2]. SSME is a multi-disciplinary area, intersecting existing disciplines such as computer science, sociology, economics, and management science.

3 Opportunities

There are a number of opportunities for computer science to contribute to enhance the value and efficiency of services. Here are a few examples.

3.1 Model-Driven Approach to Services

Businesses today are becoming more loosely integrated. Industries form very complex value networks to produce their products and services. For example, automotive companies rely heavily on their first- and second-tier suppliers on the supply side and on their networks of dealership on the demand side. They also depend on other companies for non-core business processes such as call centers and site administration. These business processes are provided by external companies as services.

The question is how to design a competitive business by connecting these third-party business processes. The overall business design can become very complex. Methodologies developed in software engineering to cope with very complex designs, such as model-driven methods, should be applicable.

The Component Business Model (CBM) [3] is one of these model-driven approaches. It models the entire enterprise by focusing on the static functionality of the business units, not on their dynamic behaviors. Whether certain function should be owned internally or out-sourced externally is determined during the modeling. Once this is done, the internal business functions are further investigated and implemented using information technology.

3.2 IT Architecture Supporting Services

Businesses are becoming more componentized and reused. Since these componentized business processes are often partially or fully implemented as an information system, it is important that these components be easy to develop, maintain, and reuse. Researchers and developers in computer science have been wrestling with these problems for many years. The Service Oriented Architecture (SOA) [4] is one of the most recent approaches to reusability technology. An SOA defines a common set of interfaces of the components so that the business processes can interoperate and be reused.

The underlying IT infrastructures also need to be maximally utilized. One data center may host a number of business services running on multiple processing nodes. These nodes are virtualized so that they provide maximum flexibility in terms of workload distribution across the nodes. In the *cloud computing* model [5], these computing nodes can be provided as services.

3.3 Analytics and Optimization

As more business processes are implemented as IT-based systems, it is becoming easier to collect data on business behaviors on-line. The data can then be analyzed to determine the key performance indicators (KPIs) of the business. If the business is not performing as expected, the data can be analyzed to discover the root causes. Advances in applied mathematics and computer science, especially in high performance computing, are allowing real time analysis of huge amounts of real world data collected by various business processes and allow for adjusting the business strategies based on the analytic results. Business decision dynamics extend this idea even further. It simulates the external world's reactions (as by consumers and competitors) to several different business strategies and selects the best one according to the simulation. Agent-based simulation is one of the techniques to do the required simulations [6].

4   Challenges

The services economy also poses many technical challenges to computer science. We are focusing on the following two.

4.1   Service Dependability

One immediate challenge is the demand for increased dependability. Dependability can be loosely defined as the state when a system is behaving as expected. The standard security requirements (confidentiality, integrity, and availability) are part of the dependability requirements. In the services economy, one service is often provided as a result of a complex interaction among a large number of component services. In order to guarantee a high level of dependability of the composite service, each component service should maintain an extremely high level of dependability.

   The idea of trusted computing may help establishing trust relationships among remote services. For example, the WS-Attestation developed at IBM's Tokyo Research Laboratory allows verifying the integrity (and associated QoS characteristics) of a remote Web service [7].

4.2   Understanding and Modeling Human Minds

Ultimately services are consumed by human beings and their values are very much subjective relative to the consuming party. Thus, maximizing the value of the service requires understanding the mind of the service-receiving person. This is not an easy task and demands insights from many other disciplines such as cognitive science and sociology.

5   Concluding Remarks – The Changing Roles of Computer Science

As we have seen, computer science (and information technology in general) is filling many critical roles in the services economy in the 21st century. Perhaps the notion of information processing is more pervasive than we may have been thinking. Peter Denning [8] points out that understanding any complex system, be it a natural system consisting of many physical objects, a biological system such as a human being, or a social system such as community of people, requires fundamental notions of information processing. Ideas and techniques we have developed in core computer science will play more important roles in many areas, including SSME.

References

1. IBM: Global Innovation Outlook,
   http://domino.watson.ibm.com/comm/www_innovate.nsf/pages/world.gio.html
2. Hidaka, K.: Trends in Services Sciences in Japan and Abroad. Science & Technology Trends Quarterly Review (2006)
3. IBM Institute for Business Value: Component Business Models. IBM Business Consulting Services
4. Weerawarana, S., Curbera, F., Leymann, F., Storey, T., Ferguson, D.F.: Web Services Platform Architecture: SOAP, WSDL, WS-Policy, WS-Addressing, WS-BPEL, WS-Reliable Messaging and More. Prentice Hall PTR, Upper Saddle River, NJ, USA (2005)
5. Boss, G., Malladi, P., Quan, D., Legregni, L., Hall, H.: Cloud Computing. In: IBM (2007)
6. Mizuta, H., Yamagata, Y.: Agent-based simulation for economic and environmental studies. In: Proceedings of the Joint JSAI 2001 Workshop on New Frontiers in Artificial Intelligence, London, UK, pp. 142–152. Springer, Heidelberg (2001)
7. Yoshihama, S., Ebringer, T., Nakamura, M., Munetoh, S., Maruyama, H.: WS-Attestation: Efficient and Fine-Grained Remote Attestation on Web Services. In: ICWS 2005: Proceedings of the IEEE International Conference on Web Services, Washington, DC, USA, pp. 743–750. IEEE Computer Society, Los Alamitos (2005)
8. Denning, P.J.: Computing is a natural science. Commun. ACM 50, 13–18 (2007)

Predictive Algorithms and Technologies for Availability Enhancement

Miroslaw Malek

Institut für Informatik, Humboldt-Universität zu Berlin
malek@informatik.hu-berlin.de

Predicting the future has fascinated people throughout civilizations but until the 20th century it has been more of a magic than science. Ability to predict the future has a significant impact on wide spectrum of applications ranging from business, communication systems and politics to health monitoring and enviromental protection. It will also become essential in dependability enhancement, security and critical infrastructure protection. With development of machine learning, pattern recognition, data mining and computer technology we seem to be better equipped to tackle the prediction problem with a more science-based, goal-oriented approach.

In this tutorial, we focus on predictive algorithms and technologies which may have a major impact on computer systems availability, security and performance. We first motivate our approach, present the best practice guide for using prediction algorithms and models, then briefly survey short-term prediction techniques, introduce two concrete prediction methods and prediction quality measures, and then demonstrate how the availability of software and hardware systems can be increased by preventive measures which are triggered by short-term failure prediction mechanisms.

Over the past decades computing performance has increased by several orders of magnitude. At the same time, the computer systems dependability due to untamed growth in complexity barely kept up to stay at the same level at best, frequently showing in part unpredictable behavior. Software related failures are now predominant and can be seen as a threat to the benefits computing systems aim to provide. Classical approaches to increase dependability such as testing, formal methods and fault injection are too complex and too rigorous to scale up to enterprise systems. Also, due to dynamicity (frequent configurations, reconfigurations, updates, upgrades and patches) an already tested system can transform into a new untested system and additional faults may be inserted. Furthermore, frequently unpredictable industrial environment makes it difficult to incorporate its behavior into the formal models. New functionality is added in an ad-hoc manner without fully understanding the impact on the entire system. Software and hardware systems tend to be embedded in complex, highly dynamic and frequently decentralized organizations. The support, maintenance and premises of these systems can change frequently which invokes ad-hoc reconfiguration. Additionally, industrial computing systems frequently have significant nonfunctional constraints on their operations. Also, growing connectivity, interoperability and systems proliferation to applications in all domains of human activity makes dependability a key and permanent challenge. It goes without saying that traditional approaches are likely to fail given industrial complexity levels [1].

T. Nanya et al. (Eds.): ISAS 2008, LNCS 5017, pp. 17–19, 2008.

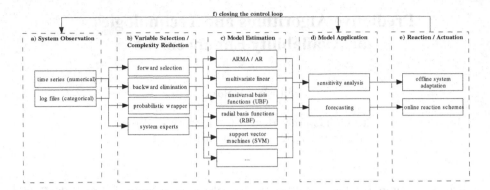

Fig. 1. Building blocks for modeling and forecasting performance variables as well as critical events in complex software systems either during runtime or during off-line testing. System observations (a) include numerical time series data and/or categorical log files. The variable selection process (b) is frequently handled implicitly by system expert's ad-hoc theories or gut feeling, rigorous procedures are applied infrequently. In recent studies attention has been focused on the model estimation process (c). Univariate and multivariate linear regression techniques have been at the center of attention. Some nonlinear regression techniques such as universal basis functions or support vector machines have been applied as well. While forecasting has received a substantial amount of attention, sensitivity analysis (d) of system models has been largely marginalized. Closing the control loop (f) is still in its infancy. Choosing the right reaction scheme (e) as a function of quality of service and cost is nontrivial [1].

In this tutorial, we propose an approach based on runtime monitoring and failure prediction which in combination with preventive techniques may significantly increase dependability while defying system complexity, dynamicity and enviromental changes. We present and evaluate mainly non-parametric techniques which model and predict the occurrence of failures as a function of discrete and continuous measurements of system variables.

We present our best practice guide (see Fig.1) backed by methodology and models for availability enhancement using failure prediction and recovery methods that we have developed [1], [2], [3]. This best practice guide is based on the experience we have gained when investigating these topics in an industrial environment:

- complexity reduction, showing that selecting the most predictive subset of variables contributes more to model quality than selecting a particular linear or nonlinear modeling technique
- information gain of using numerical vs. categorical data: finding that including log file data into the modeling process may degrade model quality for prediction of call availability of a telecommunication system due to increased processing requirements,
- data-based empirical modeling of complex software systems, cross benchmarking of linear and nonlinear modeling techniques, finding nonlinear approaches to be consistently superior than linear approaches, however, not always significantly.

In the tutorial, we introduce this approach in detail. In a nutshell it is a function approximation technique utilising universal basis functions which is a derivative of radial basis functions. The presented modeling method is data driven rather than analytical and can handle large amounts of variables and data. It offers the potential to capture the underlying dynamics of even high-dimensional and noisy systems. Another technique, that will be presented, is based on Hidden Semi-Markov Models and uses error logs with event type and timestamps. The data includes event-based log files and measured system states. Although computationally demanding, this technique produces excellent prediction results.

Both modeling techniques have been applied to real data of a commercial telecommunication platform. We compare the effectiveness of discussed techniques with other methods in terms of precision, recall, F-measure and cumulative cost. The two methods demonstrate largely improved forecasting performance compared to alternative approaches such as linear ARMA models. We also briefly survey other techniques such as Eventset Method and approach used in BlueGene/L supercomputer.

Finally, we present a plethora of preventive measures that can be applied once it is established that a failure appears to be imminent. They range from microreboot to failover.

By using the presented prediction and prevention techniques the system availability may be dramatically improved by up to an order of magnitude.

The current challenges will be introduced and one of them is how to assess service availability at runtime based IT system availability. The first attempt to tackle this challenge is presented in this volume [4].

References

1. Hoffmann, G.A., Trivedi, K.S., Malek, M.: A Best Practice Guide to Resource Forecasting for Computing Systems. IEEE Transactions on Reliability 56(4) (2007)
2. Hoffmann, G.A., Malek, M.: Call Availability Prediction in a Telecommunication System: A Data Driven Empirical Approach. In: IEEE Symposium on Reliable Distributed Systems (SRDS 2006), Leeds, United Kingdom (2006)
3. Salfner, F., Malek, M.: Using Hidden Semi-Markov Models for Effective Online Failure Prediction. In: IEEE Proceedings of the 26th Symposium on Reliable Distributed Systems (SRDS 2007), Beijing, China (2007)
4. Malek, M., Milic, M., Milanovic, N.: Analytical Availability Assessment of IT Services. In: 5017

Achieving and Assuring High Availability

Kishor Trivedi[1], Gianfranco Ciardo[2], Balakrishnan Dasarathy[3], Michael Grottke[4], Rivalino Matias[1], Andy Rindos[5], and Bart Vashaw[5]

[1] Duke University
[2] UC Riverside
[3] Telcordia
[4] University of Erlangen-Nuremberg
[5] IBM

kst@ee.duke.edu, ciardo@cs.ucr.edu, das@research.telcordia.com,
rivalino@ece.duke.edu, michael.grottke@wiso.uni-erlangen.de,
{rindos,vashaw}@us.ibm.com

Abstract. We discuss availability aspects of large software-based systems. We classify faults into Bohrbugs, Mandelbugs and aging-related bugs, and then examine mitigation methods for the last two bug types. We also consider quantitative approaches to availability assurance.

Keywords: High-Availability, Proactive Fault-Tolerance, Software Aging.

1 Overview

Bugs invariably remain when an application is deployed. A good, albeit expensive, development process can reduce the number of residual bugs to the order of 0.1 defects per 1000 lines of code [1]. There are broadly two classes of residual bugs in an application, known as Bohrbugs and Mandelbugs [2]. Bohrbugs are easily isolated and manifest themselves consistently under well-defined sets of conditions; thus, they can be detected and fixed during the software-testing phase, although some of them do remain in production. Preliminary results from investigation of a NASA software project suggest that 52% of residual bugs were Bohrbugs [3]. Mandelbugs instead have complex causes, making their behavior appear chaotic or even non-deterministic (e.g., race conditions), thus are often difficult to catch and correct in the testing phase. Retrying the same operation might not result in a failure manifestation. A third type of bugs has the characteristic that its failure manifestation rate increases with the time of execution. Such faults have been observed in many software systems and have been called aging-related bugs [4], [5], [6]. Memory leaks and round-off errors are examples of aging-related bugs. There are effective approaches to dealing with residual Bohrbugs after a software product has been released. If a failure due to a Bohrbug is detected in production, it can be reproduced in the original testing environment, and a patch correcting the bug or a workaround can be issued. Mandelbugs, however, often cannot be easily fixed, thus techniques to recover from Mandelbugs at run-time are needed. Broadly applicable cost- and time-effective

T. Nanya et al. (Eds.): ISAS 2008, LNCS 5017, pp. 20–25, 2008.

run-time techniques also exist to address aging-related bugs. We focus on Mandel-bugs and aging-related bugs in this tutorial.

In general, there are two ways to improve availability: increase time-to-failure (TTF) and reduce time-to-recovery (TTR). To increase TTF, proactive failure avoidance techniques known as rejuvenation can be used for aging-related bugs. To reduce TTR, we propose instead escalated levels of recovery, so that most failures are fixed by the quickest recovery method and only few by the slowest ones. We are also interested in quantifiable availability assurance.

2 Quantified Availability Assurance

In practice, availability assurance is provided qualitatively by means of verbal arguments or using checklists. Quantitative assurance of availability by means of stochastic availability models constructed based on the structure of the system hardware and software is very much lacking in today's practice [7], [8], [9]. While such analyses are supported by software packages [10], they are not routinely carried out on what are touted as high availability products; there are only islands of such competency even in large companies.

Engineers commonly use reliability block diagrams or fault trees to formulate and solve availability models because of their simplicity and efficiency [10], [11]. But such combinatorial models cannot easily incorporate realistic system behavior such as imperfect coverage, multiple failure modes, or hot swap [7], [9]. In contrast, such dependencies and multiple failure modes can be easily captured by state-space models [11] such as Markov chains, semi-Markov processes, and Markov regenerative processes. However, the construction, storage, and solution of these models can become prohibitive for real systems. The problem of large model construction can be alleviated by using some variation of stochastic Petri nets, but a more practical alternative is to use a hierarchical approach using a judicious combination of state space models and combinatorial models [10]. Such hierarchical models have been successfully used on practical problems including hardware availability prediction [12], OS failures [7], [8] and application software failures [9]. Furthermore, user and service-oriented measures can be computed in addition to system availability. Computational methods for such user-perceived measures are just beginning to be explored [9], [13], [14]. Subsequently, parameter values are needed to solve the models and predict system availability and related measures. Model input parameters can be divided into failure rates of hardware or software components; detection, failover, restart, reboot and repair delays and coverages; and parameters defining the user behavior. Hardware failure rates (actually MTTFs) are generally available from vendors, but software component failure rates are much harder to obtain. One approach is to carry out controlled experiments and estimate software component failure rates. In fact, we are currently performing such experiments for the IBM WAS SIP (WebSphere Application Server Session Initiation Protocol) implementation. Fault-injection experiments can be used to estimate detection, restart, reboot, and repair delays, as in the IBM SIP reliability model [9]. Due to many simplifying assumptions made about the system, its components, and their interactions and due to unavailability of accurate parameter values, the results of the models cannot be taken as a true availability assurance. Monitoring and statistically inferring the observed availability is much more satisfactory assurance of availability. Off-line [16] and on-line [17] monitoring of deployed system availability and related metrics can be carried out. The major difficulty is the amount of time needed to get enough data to obtain statistically significant estimates of availability.

3   Recovery from Failures Caused by Mandelbugs

Reactive recovery from failures caused by Mandelbugs has been used for some time in the context of operating system failures, where reboot is the mitigation method [8]. Restart, failover to a replica, and further escalated levels of recovery such as node reboot and repair are being successfully employed for application failures. Avaya's NT-SwiFT and DOORS systems [18], JPL REE system [19], Alcatel Lucent [15], IBM x-series models [20], and IBM SIP/SLEE cluster [9] are examples where applications or middleware processes are recovered using one or more of these techniques. To support recovery from Mandelbug-caused failures, multiple run-time failure detectors are employed to ensure that detection takes place within a short duration of the failure occurrence. In all but the rarest cases, manual detection is required. As, by definition, failures caused by non-aging-related Mandelbugs cannot be anticipated and must be reacted to, current research is aimed at providing design guidelines as to how fast recovery can be accomplished and obtaining quantitative assurance on the availability of an application.

Stochastic models discussed in the previous section are beginning to be used to provide quantitative availability assurance [9], [18], [19], [20]. Besides system availability, models to compute user-perceived measures such as dropped calls in a switch due to failures are also beginning to be used [9]. Such models can capture the details of user behavior [14] or the details of the call flow [9] and their interactions with failure and recovery behavior of hardware and software resources. Difficulties we encounter in availability modeling are model size and obtaining credible input parameters. To deal with the large size of availability models for real systems, we typically employ a hierarchical approach where the top-level model is combinatorial, such as a fault tree [7], [9], [12] or a reliability block diagram [8]. Lower-level stochastic models for each subsystem in the fault tree model are then built. These submodels are usually continuous-time Markov chains, but if necessary non-Markov models can be employed. Weak interactions between submodels can be dealt with using fixed-point iteration [21]. The key advantage of such an hierarchical approach is that closed-form solution now appears feasible [7], [13] as the Markov submodels are typically small enough to be solved by Mathematica and the fault tree can be solved in closed-form using tools like our own SHARPE software package [10]. Once the closed-form solution is obtained, we can also carry out formal sensitivity analysis to determine bottlenecks and provide feedback for improvement to the designers [13]. We are currently working on interfacing SHARPE with Mathematica to facilitate such closed-form solutions. Errors in these approximate hierarchical models can be studied by comparison with discrete-event simulation or exact stochastic Petri net models solved numerically.

4 Proactive Recovery and Aging-Related Bugs

Aging-related bugs in a system are such that their probability of causing a failure increases with the length of time the system is up and running. For such bugs, besides reactive recovery, proactive recovery to clean the system internal state can effectively reduce the failure rate. This kind of preventive maintenance is known as "software rejuvenation" [2], [22]. Many types of software systems, such as telecommunication software [22], web servers [5], [23], and military systems [6], are known to experience aging. Rejuvenation has been implemented in several kinds of software systems, including telecommunication billing data collection systems [22], spacecraft flight systems [24], and cluster servers [25].

The main advantage of planned preemptive procedures such as rejuvenation is that the consequences of sudden failures (like loss of data and unavailability of the entire system) are postponed or prevented; moreover, administrative measures can be scheduled to take place when the workload is low. However, for each such preemptive action, costs are incurred in the form of scheduled downtime for at least some part of the system. Rejuvenation can be carried out at different granularities: restart a software module, restart an entire application, restart a specific virtual machine in a VMM (Virtual Machine Monitor), perform garbage collection in a node, or reboot a hardware node [23], [26], [27]. A key design question is finding the optimal rejuvenation schedule and granularity. Rejuvenation scheduling can be time-based or condition-based. In the former, rejuvenation is done at fixed time intervals, while, in the latter, the condition of system resources is monitored and prediction algorithms are used to determine an adaptive rejuvenation schedule [4]. A rejuvenation trigger interval, as computed in time-based rejuvenation, can adapt to changing system conditions, but its adaptation rate is slow as it only responds to failures that are expected to be rare. Condition-based rejuvenation instead does not need time to failure inputs; it computes rejuvenation trigger interval by monitoring system resources and predicting the time to exhaustion of resources for the adaptive scheduling of software rejuvenation [4], [25], [28]. Whatever schedule and granularity of rejuvenation is used, the important question is what improvement this implies on system availability, if any. Published results are based on either analytic models [20] or simulations [29]. Early experimental results [26] are very encouraging, where rejuvenation increased the MTTF by a factor of two.

References

1. Holzmann, G.J.: Conquering complexity. IEEE Computer, Los Alamitos (2007)
2. Grottke, M., Trivedi, K.S.: Fighting bugs: Remove, retry, replicate and rejuvenate. IEEE Comp. 40, 107–109 (2007)
3. Grottke, M., Nikora, A., Trivedi, K.S.: Preliminary results from the NASA/JPL investigation - Classifying Software Faults to Improve Fault Detection Effectiveness (2007)
4. Garg, S., van Moorsel, A., Vaidyanathan, K., Trivedi, K.S.: A methodology for detection and estimation of software aging. In: 9th Int'l Symp. on Software Reliability Engineering, pp. 283–292 (1998)

5. Grottke, M., Li, L., Vaidyanathan, K., Trivedi, K.S.: Analysis of software aging in a web server. IEEE Transactions on Reliability 55, 411–420 (2006)
6. Marshall, E.: Fatal error: how Patriot overlooked a Scud. Science 255, 1347 (1992)
7. Smith, W.E., Trivedi, K.S., Tomek, L., Ackeret, J.: Availability analysis of multi-component blade server systems. IBM Systems Journal (to appear, 2008)
8. Trivedi, K.S., Vasireddy, R., Trindade, D., Nathan, S., Castro, R.: Modeling high availability systems. In: Pacific Rim Dependability Conference (2006)
9. Trivedi, K.S., Wang, D., Hunt, J., Rindos, A., Peyravian, M., Pulito, B.: IBM SIP/SLEE cluster reliability model. In: Globecom 2007, D&D Forum, Washington (2007)
10. Sahner, R.A., Trivedi, K.S., Puliafito, A.: Performance and Reliability Analysis of Computer Systems. Kluwer Academic Press, Dordrecht (1996)
11. Trivedi, K.S.: Probability & Statistics with Reliability, Queueing and Computer Science Applications, 2nd edn. John Wiley, New York (2001)
12. Lanus, M., Yin, L., Trivedi, K.S.: Hierarchical composition and aggregation of state-based availability and performability models. IEEE Transactions on Reliability, 44–52 (2003)
13. Sato, N., Nakamura, H., Trivedi, K.S.: Detecting performance and reliability bottlenecks of composite web services. In: ICSOC (2007)
14. Wang, D., Trivedi, K.S.: Modeling user-perceived service availability. In: Malek, M., Nett, E., Suri, N. (eds.) ISAS 2005. LNCS, vol. 3694, Springer, Heidelberg (2005)
15. Mendiratta, V.B., Souza, J.M., Zimmerman, G.: Using software failure data for availability evaluation. In: GLOBECOM 2007, Washington (2007)
16. Garzia, M.: Assessing the Reliability of Windows Servers. In: Int'l Conf. Dependable Systems and Networks (2003)
17. Haberkorn, M., Trivedi, K.S.: Availability monitor for a software based system. In: HASE, Dallas (2007)
18. Garg, S., Huang, Y., Kintala, C.M.R., Trivedi, K.S., Yajnik, S.: Performance and reliability evaluation of passive replication schemes in application level fault tolerance. In: 29th Annual Int'l Symp. on Fault Tolerant Computing, Wisconsin, pp. 15–18 (1999)
19. Chen, D., et al.: Reliability and availability analysis for the JPL remote exploration and experimentation system. In: Int'l Conf. Dependable Systems and Networks, Washington (2002)
20. Vaidyanathan, K., Harper, R.E., Hunter, S.W., Trivedi, K.S.: Analysis and implementation of software rejuvenation in cluster systems. In: ACM SIGMETRICS (2001)
21. Mainkar, V., Trivedi, K.S.: Sufficient conditions for existence of a fixed point in stochastic reward net-based iterative methods. IEEE Transactions on Software Engineering 22, 640–653 (1996)
22. Huang, Y., Kintala, C., Kolettis, N., Fulton, N.: Software rejuvenation: analysis, module and applications. In: 25th Int'l Symp. on Fault-Tolerant Computing, pp. 381–390 (1995)
23. Matias Jr., R., Freitas, P.J.F.: An experimental study on software aging and rejuvenation in web servers. In: 30th IEEE Annual Int'l Computer Software and Applications Conference, Chicago, pp. 189–196 (2006)
24. Tai, A., Chau, S., Alkalaj, L., Hect, H.: On-board preventive maintenance: a design-oriented analytic study for long-life applications. J. Perf. Evaluation 35, 215–232 (1999)
25. Castelli, V., Harper, R.E., Heidelberger, P., Hunter, S.W., Trivedi, K.S., Vaidyanathan, K., Zeggert, W.P.: Proactive management of software aging. IBM Journal of Research and Development 45, 311–332 (2001)
26. Kourai, K., Chiba, S.: A fast rejuvenation technique for server consolidation with virtual machines. In: Int'l Conf. on Dependable Systems and Networks, pp. 245–255 (2007)

27. Xie, W., Hong, Y., Trivedi, K.S.: Analysis of a two-level software rejuvenation policy. Reliability Engineering and System Safety 87, 13–22 (2005)
28. Vaidyanathan, K., Trivedi, K.S.: A comprehensive model for software rejuvenation. IEEE Transactions on Dependable and Secure Computing 2, 124–137 (2005)
29. Dohi, T., Goseva-Popstojanova, K., Trivedi, K.S.: Statistical Non-Parametric Algorithms to Estimate the Optimal Software Rejuvenation Schedule. In: 2000 Pacific Rim Intl. Symp. on Dependable Computing, Los Angeles, pp. 77–84 (2000)

Optimizing Security Measures in an Intrusion Tolerant Database System

Toshikazu Uemura and Tadashi Dohi

Department of Information Engineering, Graduate School of Engineering
Hiroshima University, 1-4-1 Kagamiyama, Higashi-Hiroshima, 739-8527 Japan
dohi@rel.hiroshima-u.ac.jp

Abstract. In this paper we describe the stochastic behavior of an intrusion tolerant database (ITDB) system and quantitatively evaluate its security measures. More specifically, we develop a semi-Markov model and derive three security measures; system availability, system integrity and rewarding availability. By introducing an additional control parameter called the switching time, we develop secure control schemes of the ITDB, which maximize the respective security measures, and show numerically that the security measures can be improved by controlling the switching time.

Keywords: ITDB, dependable and secure service, survivability, system integrity, rewarding availability, optimization, semi-Markov models.

1 Introduction

The use of computer-based systems and Internet has been undergoing dramatic growth in scale, variety and coverage, implying our growing dependence on them for a large number of businesses and day-to-day life services. Unfortunately, the complexity, the heterogeneity and the openness of the supporting infrastructure to uncontrolled users have also given rise to an increasing number of vulnerabilities and malicious threats (viruses, worms, denial of service attacks, fishing attempts, *etc.*). If the access rights are limited, the probability of an intrusion by a malicious attacker will be decreased, but the accessibility and utilization will be reduced. The classical security-related works have traditionally, with a few exceptions, focused on *intrusion avoidance techniques* (vulnerability elimination, strong authentication, *etc.*) and *attack deterrence* (attack tracing, auditing, *etc.*). However, such techniques have proved to be not sufficient to ensure the security of systems connected to networks.

More recently, *intrusion tolerance techniques*, inspired from traditional techniques commonly used for tolerating accidental faults in hardware and/or software systems, have received considerable attention to complement intrusion avoidance techniques, and improve the security of systems connected to the Internet. So far, most efforts in security have been focused on specification, design and implementation issues. In fact several implementation techniques of intrusion

T. Nanya et al. (Eds.): ISAS 2008, LNCS 5017, pp. 26–42, 2008.

tolerance at the architecture level have been developed for real computer-based systems such as distributed systems [3], database systems [12,13], middleware [26,27], server systems [5]. Stroud et al. [24] reported the MAFTIA (Malicious and Accidental Fault Tolerance for Internet Applications) project which was a three-year European research project and explored the techniques to build actual intrusion tolerant systems. The above implementation approaches are based on the redundant design at the architecture level on secure software systems. In other words, since these methods can be categorized by a design diversity technique in secure system design and need much cost for the development, the effect on implementation has to be evaluated carefully and quantitatively.

The quantitative evaluation of information security based on modeling is becoming popular to validate the effectiveness of computer-based systems with intrusion tolerance. Littlewood et al. [11] found the analogy between the information security theory and the traditional reliability theory in assessing the quantitative security of operational software systems, and explored the feasibility of probabilistic quantification on security. Jonsson and Olovsson [10] gave a quantitative method to study the attacker's behavior with the empirical data observed in experiments. Ortalo, Deswarte and Kaaniche [18] applied the privilege graph and the continuous-time Markov chain (CTMC) to evaluate the system vulnerability, and derived the mean effort to security failure. Singh, Cukier and Sanders [22] designed a stochastic activity network model for probabilistic validation of security and performance of several intrusion tolerant architectures. Stevens et al. [23] also proposed probabilistic methods to model the DPASA (Designing Protection and Adaptation into a Survivable Architecture).

On the other hand, it would be quite effective to apply the traditional Markov/ semi-Markov modeling approaches to design the state transition diagram of system security states by incorporating both attacker and system behaviors under uncertainty. Madan et al. [15,16] dealt with an architecture with intrusion tolerance, called SITAR (Scalable Intrusion Tolerant Architecture) and described the stochastic behavior of the system by a discrete-time semi-Markov chain (DTSMC). They also derived analytically the mean time to security failure. Imaizumi, Kimura and Yasui [6] and Uemura and Dohi [25] focused on the typical denial of service attacks for server systems and formulated the optimization problems on the optimal monitoring time and the optimal patch management policy via continuous-time semi-Markov chain (CTSMC) models. Although they mainly considered the expected cost models which are related to the Markov/semi-Markov analyses, the relationship with security attributes was still unclear in modeling.

For the purpose of comprehensive modeling of system-level security quantification, it is actually difficult to model certain security attributes such as *confidentiality* and *integrity* using the probabilistic techniques as well as to quantify the high-level security requirement with different security attributes [17]. Hence, the measurement techniques for model parameterization and validation must be carefully selected in security evaluation. In such a situation, the *survivability* analysis is becoming very common to quantify the computer-based systems under the assumption that failure may occur and that the outcome of the failure negatively impacts a large segment of the subscribers to the IT infrastructure. Such failures may be the result of deliberate, malicious attacks against the infrastructure by an adversary. Survivability has been defined as the *capability* of a system to fulfill its mission in a timely manner, in the presence of attacks, failures, or accidents. Ellison *et al.* [4], Jha *et al.* [7,8] introduced the concept of survivability in network specification and analysis. This idea has been applied to several type of computer-based systems such as wireless communications network [19,20], telephone access network [14], grid resource management system [21], operational software application [1], cluster system [2], cellular network [9].

In this paper we consider the design of an intrusion tolerant database (ITDB) system with a control parameter, and describe the stochastic behavior of an intrusion tolerant database system (ITDB). First, Liu *et al.* [12,13] proposed several ITDB architectures and presented the design and implementation methodologies. While traditional secure database systems rely on preventive controls and are very limited in surviving malicious attacks, the ITDB can detect intrusions and isolate attacks. In addition, it can contain, assess and repair the damage caused by intrusions in a timely manner such that sustained, self-stabilized levels of data integrity and availability can be provided to applications in the face of attacks. With the aim to quantify the ITDB, Yu, Liu and Zang [29] and Wang and Liu [28] developed simple CTMC models to evaluate the survivability of the ITDB. Especially, Wang and Liu [28] formulated two survivability measures; system integrity and rewarding availability[1]. In this paper we extend it to a CTSMC model with non-exponentially distributed transition times, and provide more robust quantitative framework to malicious attacks with a variety of probabilistic patterns.

Further, by introducing an additional control parameter called the *switching time*, we develop secure control schemes of the ITDB, which maximize the security measures; system integrity and rewarding availability, as well as the common system availability. Necessary and sufficient conditions for selecting a unique optimal switching time are derived under not very restrictive parameter assumptions. This is another reason why the underlying CTMC model is extended to a CTSMC model with non-exponentially distributed transitions. These analytical results enable us to maximize the utility of intrusion tolerance in the ITDB. Numerical examples are devoted to examine the dependence of model parameters on the optimal switching time and its associated security measures. Throughout the sensitivity analysis on the model parameters, it is shown numerically that the ITDB should be designed to minimize mission impact by containing both the intrusion and failure. Finally, the paper is concluded with some remarks and future research directions.

---

[1] The *integrity* defined in [28] seems to be somewhat different from the usual qualitative definition as a security attribute. In this paper we call it the *system integrity* which is a quantitative measure, and distinguish from the qualitative measure.

2 Intrusion Tolerant Database System

2.1 Basic Concept

First of all, we give a brief summary on an intrusion tolerant database (ITDB). In the ITDB, once it is damaged from any reason such as infections and attacks, the damaged parts are automatically located, contained and repaired as soon as possible, so that the database can continue being operative with intact intrusion tolerant functions. Figure 1 shows the major components of a comprehensive ITDB, which was introduced in [12,13]. In a fashion similar to the reference [28], we also focus on some significant components; *Mediator*, *Damage containment* and *Damage recovery*, in Fig.1 and describe the stochastic behavior of functions in major components. Mediator subsystem may function as a *proxy* for each user transaction and transaction processing call to the database system, and enables to keep the useful information on user transactions, such as read/write operations. This function is quite important to generate the corresponding logs for damage recovery and containment.

More precisely, in the traditional secure database system, the damage containment can not be made until the data items are identified as damaged ones. In this situation, a significant damage assessment latency may happen, so that the damage caused by attacks or intrusions may propagate to the other data items. In the ITDB, the so-called *multi-phase damage containment* technique is applied as an intrusion tolerant technique [12], where it involves one containing phase and one or more uncontaining phases referred to as *Containment relaxation*. Once an intrusion is detected by *the intrusion detector*, the damage recovery subsystem has the responsibility to do the damage assessment and repair, and retrieves the malicious transaction messages reported from the intrusion detector. Simultaneously, the damage containment subsystem traces the damage propagation by capturing the dependent-upon relationship among transactions.

Hence, the control by the intrusion detector plays an central role to the design of the ITDB. Since the intrusion detector is based on both the trails on the logs and some relevant rules to identify malicious transactions, however, its effect is limited. In other words, it would be impossible to detect all the intrusions automatically in real time. In practice, two control modes can be ready; automatic detection mode and manual detection mode, so that an automatic detection mode can be switched to a manual detection mode if the intrusion detector does return a response during the real time operation. Wang and Liu [28] developed a simple CTMC model with random switching from an automatic detection mode to a manual one, and evaluated the security measures for the ITDB.

2.2 Model Description

Following Wang and Liu [28], we also focus on three components in the ITDB, the mediator, damage recovery and damage containment systems. Suppose that the database system starts operating at time $t = 0$ with *Normal State*; G. If attackers or hackers detect the vulnerability of the database, they try to attack

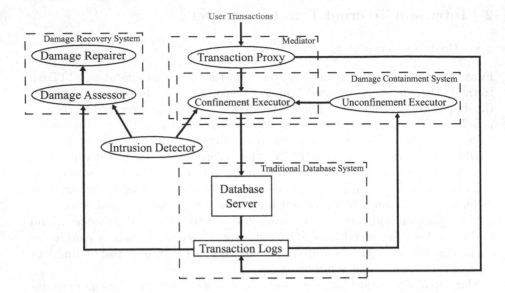

Fig. 1. Basic ITDB architecture

the database and the state may make a transition to *Infection State*; I, where the transition time from G to I has the continuous cumulative distribution function (c.d.f.) $F_{G,I}(t)$ with mean $\mu_{G,I}$ (> 0). Once the malicious attack by an attacker is successful in state I, the intrusion detector begins operating automatically. If the infection of parts or data items is detected in the automatic detection mode, the state makes a transition from I to *Maintenance State*; M, where the transition time from I to M is given by a random variable having the continuous c.d.f. $F_{I,M}(t)$ and mean $\mu_{I,M}$ (> 0). In this phase, when the infected items are identified more specifically through the damage assessor, the corrective recovery operation is triggered in *Recovery State*; R in the damage recovery system. Let the state transition time from M to R be the random variable having the c.d.f. $F_{M.R}(t)$ and mean $\mu_{M,R}$ (> 0). After the completion of recovery operation, the infected parts are fixed and the database system can become as good as new with Normal State, where the completion time to recover the database is given by the non-negative continuous random variable with the c.d.f. $F_{R,G}(t)$ and mean $\mu_{R,G}$ (> 0).

On the other hand it is worth mentioning that identification of infected parts or data items is not always possible only in the automatic detection mode. In other words, the intrusion detection is not always perfect for all possible attacks, so that the system manager or the operator may have to search the infected parts in the manual detection mode. Wang and Liu [28] considered the possibility of switching from the automatic detection mode to the manual detection mode, and assumed that the switching may occur randomly. This corresponds to the switching from the unconfinement executor to the confinement executor. In [28], the associated stochastic model is based on a CTMC with exponentially distribute

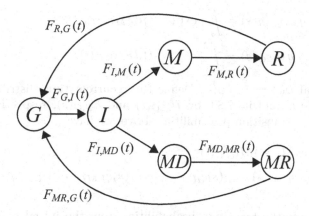

Fig. 2. Semi-Markov transition diagram

transition times. Instead of the exponential switching time, we model the switching time by the non-negative continuous random variable with the c.d.f. $F_{I,MD}(t)$ and mean $\mu_{I,MD}$ (> 0), where *Manual detection state* is denoted by MD, and the damaged parts are contained manually within the ITDB. When the intrusion is detected, the system state makes a transition from MD to MR, and next the recovery operation starts immediately. Finally, when the recovery operation is complete, the state makes a transition from MR to G with Normal state. In this way, the same cycle repeats again and again over an infinite time horizon. Since the underlying stochastic process is a CTSMC, it is noted that our model is an extended version to the CTMC model in [28]. Figure 2 illustrates the state-transition diagram for the CTSMC model.

3   Semi-markov Analysis

Let $Q_{i,j}(t)$ ($i, j \in \{G, I, M, R, MD, MR\}, i \neq j$) be the one-step transition probability from state i to state j for the underlying CTSMC. Also, we define the Laplace-Stieltjes transform (LST) by $q_{i,j}(s) = \int_0^\infty \exp\{-st\}dQ_{i,j}(t)$. From Fig.2 it is immediate to see that

$$q_{G,I}(s) = \int_0^\infty \exp\{-st\}dF_{G,I}(t), \tag{1}$$

$$q_{I,M}(s) = \int_0^\infty \exp\{-st\}\overline{F}_{I,MD}(t)dF_{I,M}(t), \tag{2}$$

$$q_{M,R}(s) = \int_0^\infty \exp\{-st\}dF_{M,R}(t), \tag{3}$$

$$q_{R,G}(s) = \int_0^\infty \exp\{-st\}dF_{R,G}(t), \tag{4}$$

$$q_{I,MD}(s) = \int_0^\infty \exp\{-st\}\overline{F}_{I,M}(t)dF_{I,MD}(t), \tag{5}$$

$$q_{MD,MR}(s) = \int_0^\infty \exp\{-st\}dF_{MD,MR}(t), \tag{6}$$

$$q_{MR,G}(s) = \int_0^\infty \exp\{-st\}dF_{MR,G}(t), \tag{7}$$

where in general $\overline{\psi}(\cdot) = 1 - \psi(\cdot)$. Define the recurrent time distribution from state G to state G and its LST by $H_{G,G}(t)$ and $h_{G,G}(s)$, respectively. Then, from the one-step transition probabilities above, we have

$$\begin{aligned}
h_{G,G}(s) &= \int_0^\infty \exp\{-st\}dH_{G,G}(t) \\
&= q_{G,I}(s)q_{I,M}(s)q_{M,R}(s)q_{R,G}(s) + q_{G,I}(s)q_{I,MD}(s)q_{MD,MR}(s)q_{MR,G}(s).
\end{aligned} \tag{8}$$

Let $P_{G,j}(t)$ denote the transition probabilities from the initial state G to respective states $j \in \{G, I, M, R, MD, MR\}$. Then, the LSTs of the transition probabilities, $p_{G,j}(s) = \int_0^\infty \exp\{-st\}dP_{G,j}(t)$, are given by

$$p_{G,G}(s) = \overline{q}_{G,I}(s)/\overline{h}_{G,G}(s), \tag{9}$$

$$p_{G,I}(s) = q_{G,I}(s)\left\{\overline{q}_{I,M}(s) - q_{I,MD}(s)\right\}/\overline{h}_{G,G}(s), \tag{10}$$

$$p_{G,M}(s) = q_{G,I}(s)q_{I,M}(s)\overline{q}_{M,R}(s)/\overline{h}_{G,G}(s), \tag{11}$$

$$p_{G,R}(s) = q_{G,I}(s)q_{I,M}(s)q_{M,R}(s)\overline{q}_{R,G}(s)/\overline{h}_{G,G}(s), \tag{12}$$

$$p_{G,MD}(s) = q_{G,I}(s)q_{I,MD}(s)\overline{q}_{MD,MR}(s)/\overline{h}_{G,G}(s), \tag{13}$$

$$p_{G,MR}(s) = q_{G,I}(s)q_{I,MD}(s)q_{MD,MR}(s)\overline{q}_{MR,G}(s)/\overline{h}_{G,G}(s). \tag{14}$$

Of our concern here is the derivation of the steady-state probabilities $P_j = \lim_{t\to\infty} P_{G,j}(t)$ $j \in \{G, I, M, R, MD, MR\}$. Based on the above LSTs, $p_{G,j}(s)$, we calculate $P_j = \lim_{t\to\infty} P_{G,i}(t) = \lim_{s\to 0} p_{G,i}(s)$ and, from some algebraic manipulations, obtain

$$P_G = \frac{\mu_{G,I}}{\overline{h}'_{G,G}(0)}, \tag{15}$$

$$P_I = \frac{\int_0^\infty \overline{F}_{I,MD}(t)\overline{F}_{I,M}(t)dt}{\overline{h}'_{G,G}(0)}, \tag{16}$$

$$P_M = \frac{\mu_{M,R} \int_0^\infty \overline{F}_{I,MD}(t)dF_{I,M}(t)}{\overline{h}'_{G,G}(0)}, \tag{17}$$

$$P_R = \frac{\mu_{R,G} \int_0^\infty \overline{F}_{I,MD}(t)dF_{I,M}(t)}{\overline{h}'_{G,G}(0)}, \tag{18}$$

$$P_{MD} = \frac{\mu_{MD,MR} \int_0^\infty \overline{F}_{I,M}(t)dF_{I,MD}(t)}{\overline{h}'_{G,G}(0)}, \tag{19}$$

$$P_{MR} = \frac{\mu_{MR,G} \int_0^\infty \overline{F}_{I,M}(t)dF_{I,MD}(t)}{\overline{h}'_{G,G}(0)}, \tag{20}$$

where

$$\overline{h}'_{G,G}(0) = \lim_{s \to 0} \frac{d\overline{h}_{G,G}(s)}{ds} = \mu_{G,I} + \int_0^\infty \overline{F}_{I,MD}(t)\overline{F}_{I,M}(t)dt$$

$$+(\mu_{M,R} + \mu_{R,G})\int_0^\infty \overline{F}_{I,MD}(t)dF_{I,M}(t)$$

$$+(\mu_{MD,MR} + \mu_{MR,G})\int_0^\infty \overline{F}_{I,M}(t)dF_{I,MD}(t). \qquad (21)$$

In this context, the automatic detection mode is randomly switched to the manual detection mode. Differently from Wang and Liu [28], we introduce the time limit to turn on the manual detection, t_0 ($0 \le t_0 < \infty$), periodically and call it the *switching* time. If the automatic detection is switched to the manual detection, then the system state goes to I from MD. Without any loss of generality, we define the transition probability from I to MD by

$$F_{I,MD}(t) = \begin{cases} 1 & (t \ge t_0) \\ 0 & (t < t_0). \end{cases} \qquad (22)$$

This means that the detection mode can be switched from the automatic mode to the manual model at every t_0 time unit. Then the steady-state probabilities in Eqs.(15)-(20) are represented as functions of t_0 by

$$P_G = \frac{\mu_{G,I}}{T(t_0)}, \qquad (23)$$

$$P_I = \frac{\int_0^{t_0} \overline{F}_{I,M}(t)dt}{T(t_0)}, \qquad (24)$$

$$P_M = \frac{\mu_{M,R}F_{I,M}(t_0)}{T(t_0)}, \qquad (25)$$

$$P_R = \frac{\mu_{R,G}F_{I,M}(t_0)}{T(t_0)}, \qquad (26)$$

$$P_{MD} = \frac{\mu_{MD,MR}\overline{F}_{I,M}(t_0)}{T(t_0)}, \qquad (27)$$

$$P_{MR} = \frac{\mu_{MR,G}\overline{F}_{I,M}(t_0)}{T(t_0)}, \qquad (28)$$

where

$$T(t_0) = \mu_{G,I} + \int_0^{t_0} \overline{F}_{I,M}(t)dt + (\mu_{M,R} + \mu_{R,G})F_{I,M}(t_0)$$

$$+(\mu_{MD,MR} + \mu_{MR,G})\overline{F}_{I,M}(t_0) \qquad (29)$$

is the mean recurrent time from state G to state G and denotes the mean time length of one cycle in the recurrent CTSMC.

4 Security Measures

4.1 System Availability

The most popular quantitative measure among system-level dependability and security measures would be the system availability, which is defined as the probability that the ITDB is operative in the steady state. From the result in Section 3, since the operative state for the system is only state G in Fig.2, the system availability is given by $AV(t_0) = \mu_{G,I}/T(t_0)$ as a fraction of time when the ITDB is operative in the steady state, from its renewal structure. Then, the problem is to derive the optimal switching time t_0^* maximizing $AV(t_0)$. For the purpose, we make the following parametric assumption:

(A-1) $\mu_{MR,G} > \mu_{M,R} + \mu_{R,G}.$

In (A-1), it is assumed that the time length to detect an intrusion automatically is strictly shorter than that by the manual detection. This seems to be intuitively validated from the viewpoint of the utility in automatic detection.

Proposition 1: (1) Suppose that the c.d.f. $F_{I,M}(t)$ is strictly DHR (decreasing hazard rate) under (A-1), *i.e.*, the hazard rate

$$r_{I,M}(t) = \frac{f_{I,M}(t)}{\overline{F}_{I,M}(t)} \tag{30}$$

is strictly decreasing in t, where $f_{I,M}(t) = dF_{I,M}(t)/dt$. Define the function:

$$q_{AV}(t_0) = -\mu_{G,I}\left[1 + \left\{(\mu_{M,R} + \mu_{R,G}) - (\mu_{MD,MR} + \mu_{MR,G})\right\}r_{I,M}(t_0)\right]. \tag{31}$$

(i) If $q_{AV}(0) > 0$ and $q_{AV}(\infty) < 0$, then there exists a finite and unique optimal switching time t_0^* $(0 < t_0^* < \infty)$ satisfying $q_{AV}(t_0^*) = 0$.

(ii) If $q_{AV}(0) \leq 0$, then $t_0^* = 0$, *i.e.*, the manual detection is always optimal and the corresponding system availability is given by

$$AV(0) = \frac{\mu_{G,I}}{\mu_{G,I} + \mu_{MD,MR} + \mu_{MR,G}}. \tag{32}$$

(iii) If $q_{AV}(\infty) \geq 0$, then $t_0^* \to \infty$, *i.e.*, the automatic detection is always optimal and the corresponding system availability is given by

$$AV(\infty) = \frac{\mu_{G,I}}{\mu_{G,I} + \mu_{I,M} + \mu_{M,R} + \mu_{R,G}}. \tag{33}$$

(2) Suppose that the c.d.f. $F_{I,M}(t)$ is IHR (increasing hazard rate) under (A-1), *i.e.*, the function $r_{I,M}(t)$ is increasing in t. If $AV(0) > AV(\infty)$, then $t_0^* = 0$ otherwise $t_0^* \to \infty$.

Proof: Taking the differantiation of $AV(t_0)$ with respect to t_0 and setting it equal to zero 0 imply $q_{AV}(t_0) = 0$. Further, we have

$$\frac{dq_{AV}(t_0)}{dt_0} = -\frac{dr_{I,M}(t_0)}{dt}\mu_{I,M}\{(\mu_{M,R} + \mu_{R,G}) - (\mu_{MD,MR} + \mu_{MR,G})\}. (34)$$

In the strictly DHR case, the right-hand side of Eq.(34) takes a negative value under (A-1) and the function $q_{AV}(t_0)$ is strictly decreasing in t_0. That is, the function $AV(t_0)$ is a quasi-convex function of t_0. If $q_{AV}(0) > 0$ and $q_{AV}(\infty) < 0$, then the function $q_{AV}(t_0)$ crosses the zero level once, and there exists a finite and unique optimal switching time t_0^* ($0 < t_0^* < \infty$) satisfying $q_{AV}(t_0^*) = 0$. If $q_{AV}(0) \leq (\geq) 0$, then the function $q_{AV}(t_0)$ takes a negative (positive) value, and the optimal switching time should be $t_0^* = 0$ ($t_0^* \to \infty$). On the othet hand, in the IHR case, the result is trivial. Q.E.D.

Although the system availability is one of significant dependability and security measures, it does not take account of the quality of data in the ITDB. In the security profile for database systems, it is more important to keep all accessible data clean rather than increasing the fraction of operative time. In other words, it is not sufficient to consider only the system availability in designing the system security for the ITDB.

4.2 System Integrity

Wang and Liu [28] defined the system integrity as a fraction of time when all accessible data items in the database are clean. As mentioned previously in Section 1, the integrity is regarded as one of the most typical security attributes in addition to authentication and non-repudiation. When the integrity is high, the ITDS can serve the users by utilizing the good or clean data with high probability. In Fig. 2, all data items in the ITDB are clean and accessible in state G. When attacks occur, some data items will be affected and the part of accessible data items in state I may be *dirty*. After the intrusion is identified, the ITDB can contain all the damaged data until it finishes the repair process. In this situation, the ITDB carries out the selective containment and repair, and is still available, so that the accessible data items are clean during the containment, damage assessment and repair process. In Fig. 2, since the system states under consideration are G, M, R and MR, the system integrity is defined by $IN(t_0) = U_{IN}(t_0)/T(t_0)$, where

$$U_{IN}(t_0) = \mu_{G,I} + (\mu_{M,R} + \mu_{R,G})F_{I,M}(t_0) + \mu_{MR,G}\overline{F}_{I,M}(t_0). \quad (35)$$

The following result can characterize the optimal switching time maximizing the system integrity.

Proposition 2: (1) Suppose that the c.d.f. $F_{I,M}(t)$ is strictly DHR under (A-1). Define the function:

$$q_{IN}(t_0) = (\mu_{M,R} + \mu_{R,G} - \mu_{MR,G})r_{I,M}(t_0)T_{IN}(t_0) - \Big[1 + \{(\mu_{M,R}$$
$$+\mu_{R,G}) - (\mu_{MD,MR} + \mu_{MR,G})\}r_{I,M}(t_0)\Big]U_{IN}(t_0). \qquad (36)$$

(i) If $q_{IN}(0) > 0$ and $q_{IN}(\infty) < 0$, then there exists a finite and unique optimal switching time t_0^* $(0 < t_0^* < \infty)$ satisfying $q_{IN}(t_0^*) = 0$ and the corresponding system integrity is given by

$$IN(t_0^*) = \frac{(\mu_{M,R} + \mu_{R,G} - \mu_{MR,G})r_{I,M}(t_0^*)}{1 + \{(\mu_{M,R} + \mu_{R,G}) - (\mu_{MD,MR} + \mu_{MR,G})\}r_{I,M}(t_0^*)}. \qquad (37)$$

(ii) If $q_{IN}(0) \leq 0$, then $t_0^* = 0$ and the corresponding system integrity is given by

$$IN(0) = \frac{\mu_{G,I} + \mu_{MR,G}}{\mu_{G,I} + \mu_{MD,MR} + \mu_{MR,G}}. \qquad (38)$$

(iii) If $q_{IN}(\infty) \geq 0$, then $t_0^* \to \infty$ and the corresponding system integrity is given by

$$IN(\infty) = \frac{\mu_{G,I} + \mu_{M,R} + \mu_{R,G}}{\mu_{G,I} + \mu_{I,M} + \mu_{M,R} + \mu_{R,G}}. \qquad (39)$$

(2) Suppose that the c.d.f. $F_{I,M}(t)$ is IHR under (A-1). If $IN(0) > IN(\infty)$, then $t_0^* = 0$ otherwise $t_0^* \to \infty$.

The proof is omitted from the similarity to Proposition 1. For the actual management of database systems, it is more significant to keep the clean and accessible data. So, when the quality of data is considered, the system integrity should be the more attractive security measure than the system availability.

4.3   Rewarding Availability

The system availability is defined as a fraction of time when the ITDB is providing services to its users, and does not care the quality of data. Since the ITDB performs the on-the-fly repair and will not stop its service faced by attacks, it can be expected that the corresponding system availability is nearly 100% in almost all cases. For better evaluation of the security attribute in the ITDB, Wang and Liu [28] considered another type of availability, called *rewarding availability*, which is defined as a fraction of time when all the clean data items are accessible. If the clean data can not be accessed in the ITDB, it can be regarded as a serious loss of service to users. Dissimilar to the system integrity, since the system states under consideration are G, R and MR, the rewarding availability is defined by $RA(t_0) = U_{RA}(t_0)/T(t_0)$, where

$$U_{RA}(t_0) = \mu_{G,I} + \mu_{R,G}F_{I,M}(t_0) + \mu_{MR,G}\overline{F}_{I,M}(t_0). \qquad (40)$$

We give the characterization result on the optimal switching time maximizing the rewarding availability without the proof.

Proposition 3: (1) Suppose that the c.d.f. $F_{I,M}(t)$ is strictly DHR under (A-1). Define the function:

$$q_{RA}(t_0) = (\mu_{R,G} - \mu_{MR,G})r_{I,M}(t_0)T(t_0) - \Big[1 + \{(\mu_{M,R} + \mu_{R,G})$$
$$-(\mu_{MD,MR} + \mu_{MR,G})\}r_{I,M}(t_0)\Big]U_{RA}(t_0). \tag{41}$$

(i) If $q_{RA}(0) > 0$ and $q_{RA}(\infty) < 0$, then there exists a finite and unique optimal switching time t_0^* $(0 < t_0^* < \infty)$ satisfying $q_{RA}(t_0^*) = 0$ and the corresponding rewarding availability is given by

$$RA(t_0^*) = \frac{(\mu_{R,G} - \mu_{MR,G})r_{I,M}(t_0^*)}{1 + \{(\mu_{M,R} + \mu_{R,G}) - (\mu_{MD,MR} + \mu_{MR,G})\}r_{I,M}(t_0^*)}. \tag{42}$$

(ii) If $q_{RA}(0) \leq 0$, then $t_0^* = 0$ and the corresponding rewarding availability is given by

$$RA(0) = \frac{\mu_{G,I} + \mu_{MR,G}}{\mu_{G,I} + \mu_{MD,MR} + \mu_{MR,G}}. \tag{43}$$

(iii) If $q_{RA}(\infty) \geq 0$, then $t_0^* \to \infty$ and the corresponding rewarding availability is given by

$$RA(\infty) = \frac{\mu_{G,I} + \mu_{R,G}}{\mu_{G,I} + \mu_{I,M} + \mu_{M,R} + \mu_{R,G}}. \tag{44}$$

(2) Suppose that the c.d.f. $F_{I,M}(t)$ is IHR under (A-1). If $RA(0) > RA(\infty)$, then $t_0^* = 0$ otherwise $t_0^* \to \infty$.

In this section, we optimized the three security measures for the ITDB and derived the optimal switching times for respective quantitative criteria. In the following section, we will give some numerical examples, and calculate the optimal switching policies and their associated security measures.

5   Numerical Illustrations

5.1   Parameter Set

We focus on both the system integrity and the rewarding availability, and treat the database management system with Oracle 9i server in [28]. Although the security model in [28] was based on a simple CTMC, we here assume that the c.d.f. $F_{I,M}(t)$ is given by the Weibull distribution with scale parameter η and shape parameter m:

$$F_{I,M}(t) = 1 - \exp\{-(t/\eta)^m\}. \tag{45}$$

This assumption implies that the transition time from an intrusion to the containment sate is DHR $(m \leq 1)$ or IHR $(m \geq 1)$, and can represent the more general transition phenomena. When $m = 1$, it reduces to the exponential distribution with constant hazard rate. The other transition rates from state i to state

Table 1. Model parameters

Parameters	Values
attack hitting rate (λ_a)	0.5 (low); 1 (moderate); 5 (heavy)
detection rate ($\lambda_{I,M}$)	10 (slow); 15 (medium); 20 (fast)
marking rate ($\lambda_{M,R}$)	27
repair rate ($\lambda_{R,G}$)	22
manual detection rate ($\lambda_{MD,MR}$)	0.02
manual repair rate ($\lambda_{MR,G}$)	0.02
false alarm rate (α)	10%, 20%, 50%

j are assumed to constant, i.e., $1/\mu_{i,j} = \lambda_{i,j}$ ($i,j \in \{G, I, M, R, MD, MR\}$, $i \neq j$), except for $(i,j) = (I, M)$. In particular, we introduce the attack hitting rate λ_a and the false alarm rate α as Wang and Liu [28] did so. It should be noted that the intrusion detector in Fig. 1 will warn the system user of malicious attacks/intrusions as well as the system failure in case of a false alarm. Let T_a and T_{fa} be the intrusion time and the system failure time measured from time $t = 0$ in state G, and be the exponentially distributed random variables with parameters λ_a and α, respectively. Then the function $F_{G,I}(t)$ is regarded as the c.d.f. of the random variable $\min\{T_a, T_{fa}\}$ and is the exponential c.d.f. with parameter $\lambda_a + \alpha$. Table 1 presents the model parameters used in this example, where they are almost same in [28]. We set $m = 0.2$, and choose η so as to satisfy $\mu_{I,M} = \eta \Gamma(1 + 1/m)$.

5.2 System Integrity

Table 2 presents the maximized system integrity for varying model parameters, where $t_0 \to \infty$ implies the non-manual detection policy. From this table, it is seen that the optimal control of the switching time to the manual detection mode leads to the 2.8% $\sim$ 35.5% improvement of system integrity. In this numerical example, it can be observed that the periodic control of the switching to the manual detection mode and the rapid containment/repair from the damage due to attacks or intrusions are quite important factors to increase the system integrity. On the mean reaction time $\mu_{MD,MR} + \mu_{MR,G}$ in the manual detection mode, when it increases monotonically, the resulting switching time t_0^* also increases so far. In Fig.3, we plot the behavior of the system integrity with respect to the attack hitting rate and the false alarm rate. From this result, it can be seen that the system integrity increases to 0.2% $\sim$ 1.4% ($1.3 \times 10^{-2}\% \sim 0.16\%$) when the attack hitting rate (false alarm rate) decreases. This result can be explained in the following; the system integrity can increase when the total operation time of the ITDB becomes longer with the lower attack hitting rate or when the ITDB tends to become more robust with the lower false alarm rate.

5.3 Rewarding Availability

Similar to Subsection 5.2, we examine the dependence of model parameters on the optimal switching time and its associated rewarding availability in Table 3.

Table 2. Maximizing system integrity for varying model parameters

$(\lambda_{I,M}, \lambda_a, \alpha)$	$t_0 \to \infty$	t_0^*	$IN(t_0^*)$	increment (%)
(10,0.5,10)	0.9459	104.3340	0.9975	5.4505
(10,0.5,20)	0.9379	104.2810	0.9971	6.3067
(10,0.5,50)	0.9154	104.1290	0.9959	8.7926
(10,1.0,10)	0.9084	104.0800	0.9955	9.5949
(10,1.0,20)	0.9016	104.0310	0.9952	10.3845
(10,1.0,50)	0.8822	103.8900	0.9941	12.6801
(10,5.0,10)	0.7358	102.5530	0.9841	33.7328
(10,5.0,20)	0.7332	102.5240	0.9839	34.1875
(10,5.0,50)	0.7255	102.4370	0.9832	35.5193
(15,0.5,10)	0.9633	115.7010	0.9991	3.7195
(15,0.5,20)	0.9577	115.6810	0.9990	4.3050
(15,0.5,50)	0.9420	115.6220	0.9986	6.0068
(15,1.0,10)	0.9370	115.6030	0.9984	6.5567
(15,1.0,20)	0.9321	115.5850	0.9983	7.0981
(15,1.0,50)	0.9183	115.5300	0.9979	8.6738
(15,5.0,10)	0.8069	115.0200	0.9944	23.2411
(15,5.0,20)	0.8048	115.0080	0.9944	23.5581
(15,5.0,50)	0.7986	114.9760	0.9941	24.4872
(20,0.5,10)	0.9722	124.4060	0.9996	2.8182
(20,0.5,20)	0.9680	124.3960	0.9995	3.2620
(20,0.5,50)	0.9559	124.3680	0.9994	4.5527
(20,1.0,10)	0.9520	124.3590	0.9993	4.9698
(20,1.0,20)	0.9482	124.3500	0.9993	5.3805
(20,1.0,50)	0.9374	124.3240	0.9991	6.5764
(20,5.0,10)	0.8478	124.0820	0.9975	17.6578
(20,5.0,20)	0.8461	124.0770	0.9975	17.8994
(20,5.0,50)	0.8409	124.0620	0.9974	18.6079

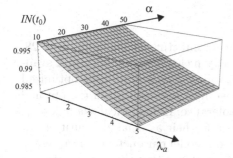

Fig. 3. Behavior of system integrity with respect to λ_a and α

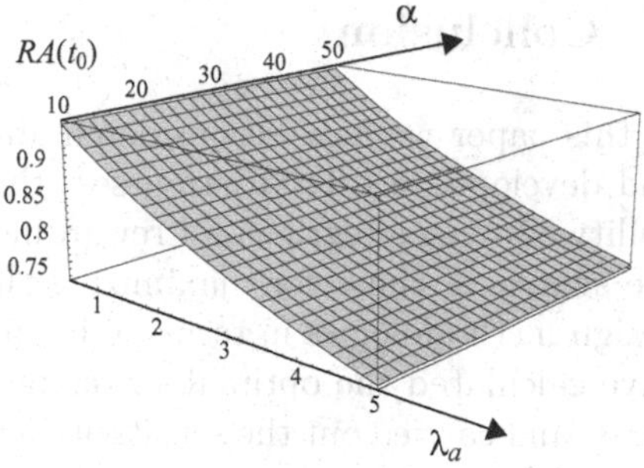

Fig. 4. Behavior of rewarding availability with respect to λ_a and α

From this table, it can be found that the periodic control of the switching to the manual detection mode enables us to increase the rewarding availability up to $0.2\% \sim 12.3\%$. As the detection speed becomes faster, it can be increased to $0.3\% \sim 3.9\%$. Figure 4 shows the behavior of rewarding availability on the attack hitting rate and the false alarm, where the rewarding availability varies in the ranges of $27.2\% \sim 32.8\%$ and $1.7\% \sim 3.2\%$ for α and λ_α, respectively. Thus, the attack hitting rate is more sensitive than the false alarm rate not only for the system integrity but also for the rewarding availability.

Table 3. Maximizing rewarding availability for varying model parameters

$(\lambda_{I,M}, \lambda_a, \alpha)$	$t_0 \to \infty$	t_0^*	$RA(t_0^*)$	increment (%)
(10,0.5,10)	97.8264	0.9506	0.9259	2.6735
(10,0.5,20)	96.7376	0.9431	0.9149	3.0743
(10,0.5,50)	93.5265	0.9213	0.8841	4.2076
(10,1.0,10)	92.4741	0.9144	0.8745	4.5635
(10,1.0,20)	91.4302	0.9076	0.8651	4.9089
(10,1.0,50)	88.3487	0.8880	0.8386	5.8857
(10,5.0,10)	55.5619	0.7158	0.6380	12.1884
(10,5.0,20)	54.7108	0.7120	0.6344	12.2378
(10,5.0,50)	52.1533	0.7008	0.6238	12.3416
(15,0.5,10)	108.6100	0.9529	0.9429	1.0565
(15,0.5,20)	107.4660	0.9456	0.9343	1.2155
(15,0.5,50)	104.1020	0.9249	0.9098	1.6660
(15,1.0,10)	103.0030	0.9183	0.9020	1.8078
(15,1.0,20)	101.9140	0.9119	0.8944	1.9456
(15,1.0,50)	98.7091	0.8933	0.8729	2.3364
(15,5.0,10)	66.1144	0.7347	0.6996	5.0182
(15,5.0,20)	65.3302	0.7315	0.6963	5.0498
(15,5.0,50)	63.0064	0.7219	0.6867	5.1321
(20,0.5,10)	116.8210	0.9535	0.9516	0.1983
(20,0.5,20)	115.6110	0.9464	0.9442	0.2274
(20,0.5,50)	112.0580	0.9260	0.9231	0.3088
(20,1.0,10)	110.8970	0.9195	0.9164	0.3340
(20,1.0,20)	109.7490	0.9131	0.9099	0.3583
(20,1.0,50)	106.3720	0.8949	0.8911	0.4257
(20,5.0,10)	72.5066	0.7404	0.7351	0.7254
(20,5.0,20)	71.7090	0.7373	0.7320	0.7217
(20,5.0,50)	69.3535	0.7282	0.7231	0.7069

6   Conclusion

In this paper we have reconsidered an ITDB architecture of Wang and Liu [28] and developed a CTSMC to assess the security measures such as system availability, system integrity and rewarding availability. Further, we have optimized the switching times for maximizing the above measures and given the optimal design methodologies in terms of intrusion tolerance. In numerical examples, we have calculated the optimal switching times and their associated security measures, and carried out the sensitivity analysis on model parameters. As the lesson learned from the numerical examples, it has been shown that the system integrity and the rewarding availability could be improved by controlling appropriately the switching times to the manual detection mode.

In the on-going research, we will evaluate quantitatively the other measures in survivability in the ITDB. Since the survivability can be evaluated in the same framework as performability [9,17], the CTSMC model developed in this paper can still be useful for the analysis with different measures. Also, though we focused on only the mediator subsystem as a proxy for each user transaction and transaction processing call to the database system, the other part on dynamic transaction processing such as the database system itself may be included for modeling from the macroscopic point of view. Such an integrated model should be developed by applying the semi-Markov analysis in the future.

References

1. Aung, K.M.M.: The optimum time to perform software rejuvenation for survivability. In: Proceedings of 7th IASTED International Conference on Software Engineering, pp. 292–296. ACTA Press (2004)
2. Aung, K.M.M., Park, K., Park, J.S.: A survivability model for cluster system. In: Hobbs, M., Goscinski, A.M., Zhou, W. (eds.) ICA3PP 2005. LNCS, vol. 3719, pp. 73–82. Springer, Heidelberg (2005)
3. Deswarte, Y., Blain, L., Fabre, J.C.: Intrusion tolerance in distributed computing systems. In: Proceedings of 1991 IEEE Symposium on Research in Security and Privacy, pp. 110–121. IEEE CS Press, Los Alamitos (1991)
4. Ellison, R., Linger, R., Longstaff, T., Mead, M.: Survivability network system analysis: a case study. IEEE Software 16(4), 70–77 (1999)
5. Guputa, V., Lam, V., Ramasamy, H.V., Sanders, W.H., Singh, S.: Dependability and performance evaluation of intrusion-tolerant server architectures. In: de Lemos, R., Weber, T.S., Camargo Jr., J.B. (eds.) LADC 2003. LNCS, vol. 2847, pp. 81–101. Springer, Heidelberg (2003)
6. Imaizumi, M., Kimura, M., Yasui, K.: Reliability analysis of a network server system with illegal access. In: Yun, W.Y., Dohi, T. (eds.) Advanced Reliability Modeling II, pp. 40–47. World Scientific, Singapore (2006)
7. Jha, S., Wing, J., Linger, R., Longstaff, T.: Survivability analysis of network specifications. In: Proceedings of 30th Annual IEEE/IFIP International Conference on Dependable Systems and Networks, DSN 2000, pp. 613–622. IEEE CS Press, Los Alamitos (2000)
8. Jha, S., Wing, J.M.: Survivability analysis of network systems. In: Proceedings of the 23rd International Conference on Software Engineering, ICSE-2001, pp. 307–317. IEEE CS Press, Los Alamitos (2001)
9. Jindal, V., Dharmaraja, S., Trivedi, K.S.: Analytical survivability model for fault tolerant cellular networks supporting multiple services. In: Proceedings of International Symposium on Performance Evaluation of Computer and Telecommunication Systems, SPECTS 2006, pp. 505–512. IEEE Press, Los Alamitos (2006)
10. Jonsson, E., Olovsson, T.: A quantitative model of the security intrusion process based on attacker behavior. IEEE Transactions on Software Engineering 23(4), 235–245 (1997)
11. Littlewood, B., Brocklehurst, S., Fenton, N., Mellor, P., Page, S., Wright, D., Doboson, J., McDermid, J., Gollmann, D.: Towards operational measures of computer security. Journal of Computer Security 2(2/3), 211–229 (1993)
12. Liu, P.: Architectures for intrusion tolerant database systems. In: Proceedings of 18th Annual Computer Security Applications Conference, ACSAC 2002, pp. 311–320. IEEE CS Press, Los Alamitos (2002)
13. Liu, P., Jing, J., Luenam, P., Wang, Y., Li, L., Ingsriswang, S.: The design and implementation of a self-healing database system. Journal of Intelligent Information Systems 23(3), 247–269 (2004)
14. Liu, Y., Mendiratta, V.B., Trivedi, K.: Survivability analysis of telephone access network. In: Proceedings of 15th International Symposium on Software Reliability Engineering (ISSRE 2004), pp. 367–377. IEEE CS Press, Los Alamitos (2004)
15. Madan, B.B., Goseva-Popstojanova, K., Vaidyanathan, K., Trivedi, K.S.: Modeling and quantification of security attributes of software systems. In: Proceedings of 32nd Annual IEEE/IFIP International Conference on Dependable Systems and Networks (DSN 2002), pp. 505–514. IEEE CS Press, Los Alamitos (2002)

16. Madan, B.B., Goseva-Popstojanova, K., Vaidyanathan, K., Trivedi, K.S.: A method for modeling and quantifying the security attributes of intrusion tolerant systems. Performance Evaluation 56(1/4), 167–186 (2004)
17. Nikol, D.M., Sanders, W.H., Trivedi, K.S.: Model-based evaluation: from dependability to security. IEEE Transactions on Dependability and Secure Computing 1(1), 48–65 (2004)
18. Ortalo, R., Deswarte, Y., Kaaniche, M.: Experimenting with quantitative evaluation tools for monitoring operational security. IEEE Transactions on Software Engineering 25(5), 633–650 (1999)
19. Park, J.S., Aung, K.M.M.: Transient time analysis of network security survivability using DEVS. In: Kim, T.G. (ed.) AIS 2004. LNCS (LNAI), vol. 3397, pp. 607–616. Springer, Heidelberg (2005)
20. Paul, K., Choudhuri, R.R., Bandyopadhyay, S.: Survivability analysis of ad hoc wireless network architecture mobile and wireless communications networks. In: Omidyar, C.G. (ed.) MWCN 2000 and NETWORKING-WS 2000. LNCS, vol. 1818, pp. 31–46. Springer, Heidelberg (2000)
21. Qu, Y., Lin, C., Li, Y., Shan, Z.: Survivability analysis of grid resource management system topology. In: Zhuge, H., Fox, G.C. (eds.) GCC 2005. LNCS, vol. 3795, pp. 738–743. Springer, Heidelberg (2005)
22. Singh, S., Cukier, M., Sanders, W.H.: Probabilistic validation of an intrusion tolerant replication system. In: Proceedings of 33rd Annual IEEE/IFIP International Conference on Dependable Systems and Networks (DSN 2003), pp. 615–624. IEEE CS Press, Los Alamitos (2003)
23. Stevens, F., Courtney, T., Singh, S., Agbaria, A., Meyer, J.F., Sanders, W.H., Pal, P.: Model-based validation of an intrusion-tolerant information system. In: Proceedings of 23rd IEEE Reliable Distributed Systems Symposium (SRDS 2004), pp. 184–194. IEEE CS Press, Los Alamitos (2004)
24. Stroud, R., Welch, I., Warne, J., Ryan, P.: A qualitative analysis of the intrusion-tolerant capabilities of the MAFTIA architecture. In: Proceedings of 34th Annual IEEE/IFIP International Conference on Dependable Systems and Networks (DSN 2004), pp. 453–461. IEEE CS Press, Los Alamitos (2004)
25. Uemura, T., Dohi, T.: Quantitative evaluation of intrusion tolerant systems subject to DoS attacks via semi-Markov cost models. In: Denko, M.K., Shih, C.-s., Li, K.-C., Tsao, S.-L., Zeng, Q.-A., Park, S.H., Ko, Y.-B., Hung, S.-H., Park, J.H. (eds.) EUC-WS 2007. LNCS, vol. 4809, pp. 31–42. Springer, Heidelberg (2007)
26. Verissimo, P.E., Neves, N.F., Correia, M.: Intrusion-tolerant architectures: concepts and design. In: de Lemos, R., Gacek, C., Romanovsky, A. (eds.) Architecting Dependable Systems. LNCS, vol. 2677, pp. 3–36. Springer, Heidelberg (2003)
27. Verissimo, P.E., Neves, N.F., Cachin, C., Poritz, J., Powell, D., Deswarte, Y., Stroud, R., Welch, I.: Intrusion-tolerant middleware. IEEE Security and Privacy 4(4), 54–62 (2006)
28. Wang, H., Liu, P.: Modeling and evaluating the survivability of an intrusion tolerant database system. In: Gollmann, D., Meier, J., Sabelfeld, A. (eds.) ESORICS 2006. LNCS, vol. 4189, pp. 207–224. Springer, Heidelberg (2006)
29. Yu, M., Liu, P., Zang, W.: Self-healing workflow systems under attacks. In: Proceedings of 24th International Conference on Distributed Computing Systems (ICDCS 2004), pp. 418–425. IEEE CS Press, Los Alamitos (2004)

The Impact of Unavailability on the Effectiveness of Enterprise Information Security Technologies⋆

Simon Edward Parkin, Rouaa Yassin Kassab, and Aad van Moorsel

School of Computing, Newcastle University
Claremont Tower, NE1 7RU, Newcastle upon Tyne
{s.e.parkin,rouaa.yassin-kassab,aad.vanmoorsel}@newcastle.ac.uk

Abstract. This paper surveys existing enterprise technologies that control access to confidential digital data, and analyzes the impact of system and staff unavailability on the obtained security. The researched technologies allow restrictions to be placed on copying, editing, viewing and printing from within various software applications, provide auditing options and prevent outsider access through encryption. We discuss USB access control solutions, digital rights management software, disk encryption techniques and operating system solutions, respectively. An interesting aspect of the various technologies is their reliance on the cooperation of various people and system components, thus making it vulnerable to unavailability of these people and components. Two opposite effects (security risk and productivity loss) determine the effectiveness of information security technologies, and we analyze the impact of unavailability of resources on both these metrics.

1 Introduction

Recently published data suggests that some of the most serious IT threats organizations face relate to the theft and careless distribution of data by employees. [9] suggests that the greatest information security threats within an organization are leakage of confidential information and distortion of sensitive information. These threats have the potential to damage company reputations and impact upon the potential customer base [9], as well as inviting sanctions by industrial regulatory bodies [9]. One of the contributing factors is the ease with which data can be copied and carried. By 2006 at least two-thirds of office workers [2,4] owned a removable storage device (e.g. USB memory stick, media player etc.), and some 70% of workers connected a removable storage device to a company PC on a daily basis [2]. Portable storage devices are one of the major conduits of

---

⋆ Supported in part by: UK Department of Trade and Industry, grant nr. P0007E ('Trust Economics'), UK EPSRC platform grant EP/D037743/1 ('Networked Computing in Inter-Organisation Settings'), EU network of excellence 026764 ('ReSIST: Resilience for Survivability in IST') and EU coordination action 216295 ('AMBER: Assessing, Measuring, and Benchmarking Resilience').

T. Nanya et al. (Eds.): ISAS 2008, LNCS 5017, pp. 43–58, 2008.

data leakage within Europe [9]. Following from this, 70% of all security breaches originate from inside company networks [2], with 60% of incidents caused by human error [2]. Furthermore, it is estimated that two-thirds of USB sticks are lost by their owners, with 20% of these devices containing sensitive information [2]. Over 50% of IT professionals feel that EU legislation should require businesses to protect any personal data they retain from threats internal to the company. Proposed solutions include the deployment of consistent internal security policies and tools to realize such policies.

Although the above numbers should be considered with care (the publishing source may be biased, and/or the data is reported in a way that does not lend itself to scientific validation), the above suggests a growing security problem. Recent news items, such as the loss of CDs with personal data of millions of UK citizens further illustrate the risks [27]. The following example of an employee using a removable USB storage device illustrates key points relating to enterprise information security. It is feasible to imagine the use, by operations staff, of USB memory sticks to store company/confidential data whilst outside of the company's environment. A typical problem might be that a staff member buys a memory stick from a high-street store, saves confidential or sensitive data onto it on Friday afternoon, and reloads the data to the system on Monday morning. Over the weekend, the stick may have been exposed to a range of highly insecure, potentially corrupted environments.

This previous use case alludes to requirements both within and outside the associated working environment. Access control measures must be taken to limit the risks to enterprises and the public, but the danger exists that such measures may negatively influence the productivity of employees. If an access control solution proves to be less than transparent, it may influence the behavior patterns of those users that it directly affects. For example, access to a secured device may be restricted to environments operating the same company-controlled access control software, which may make 'working from home' infeasible. In this paper we analyze this trade-off between security improvement and productivity loss, in particular with respect to the reliability of the chosen access control measures.

In this paper we first survey current information security technologies. These technologies are all available as industrial products, using well-established software security and management solutions. By putting these technologies into perspective we can analyze their respective strengths and weaknesses. We note that this survey is a synopsis of a more detailed Newcastle University technical report [19]. We focus here on the main technologies that we believe will remain valid for considerable time to come, leaving out most of the product comparisons and pricing schemes one can find in [19].

From our survey, it will become clear that the discussed information security technologies can be quite involved, requiring systems such as directories and client applets to be deployed, protected devices to be networked, and administrative staff to be present to deal with policy exceptions. From the perspective of the IT administrators, information security is offered as a service to the users within an enterprise, with requirements for the reliability and availability of various components as well as the help desk. From the user perspective, the service may potentially be regarded as a hindrance, and almost per definition introduces overhead in many routine work-related activities. Thus, a trade-off between security improvement and productivity loss must be considered when introducing such technologies into the enterprise. In this paper we study the influence of component and people unavailability on this trade-off decision. We believe that the proposed analysis may present a useful tool when making investment decisions about reliability improvements and help desk staffing.

This paper is organized as follows. We survey technologies in four categories: USB access control solutions in Section 2, digital rights management solutions (Section 3), disk encryption solutions (Section 4) and operating system solutions (Section 5). Section 6 summarizes the capabilities of the technologies visited in the preceding sections, while discussing outstanding and introduced vulnerabilities. Section 7 then provides the unavailability impact analysis on the effectiveness of information security solutions.

2   USB Access Control Solutions

USB access control software is primarily concerned with how removable data-storage devices interact with the computer network operated by an organization, and how the associated physical connection endpoints can be secured and brought under control of the organization. Using these technologies users of an enterprise network and the company data therein should adhere to a unified device access policy dictated from within the organization, thereby providing predictable, manageable behavior amongst the associated workforce.

The principal driving factor of the considered technologies is prevention of data theft from within an organization [5,22,25]. This is closely coupled with preventing the injection of unsolicited content into the network (as promoted by [8]). Compliance with regulatory standards and copyright laws is also highlighted [20,22,24]. [10] also promotes endpoint access control as a means of limiting the maintenance overhead introduced by unauthorized devices. Coverage is provided to control access to other USB device endpoints (such as Firewire and writeable CD drives), and remote-communication channels such as WiFi and Bluetooth.

The considered technologies install from a centralized security station, sending client-side installations directly to user workstations. Most products suggest that they actively attempt to deploy as little logic as possible upon user workstations [3,8,10]. Deployment in this way assumes that all computers connected to an organization network are centrally managed. There is also an assumption that corporations have dedicated IT security staff available at all times. Control of access permissions by IT personnel is centralized (typically through a dedicated software-based management console). If this central management system were to fail, company-wide data security policies may become inconsistent or inoperable.

The timely deployment of per-user or per-device access controls relies upon the availability of specialized staff. However, one can automate access policies applicable to groups of users and known device types. Common (i.e. predictable)

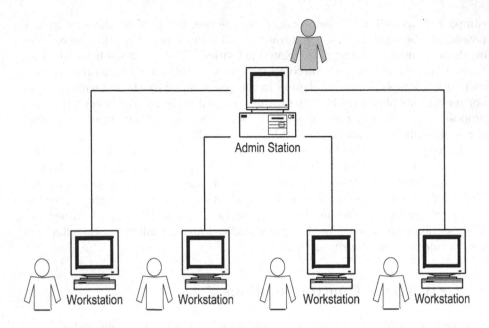

Fig. 1. Centralized administration of end-user workstations

working practices, with static user access permissions, can be controlled in this way without intervention from administrative staff. Policy exceptions (e.g. a need to correct improper policy clauses or to add a new device type upon request) would however require action by the appropriate IT personnel.

Many products employ 'white-list' and 'black-list' approaches to device access (Fig. 2), which can respectively be used to explicitly include or exclude devices within an organization's device access schemes. This allows access policies to be reused across different user accounts or user groups. Administrative personnel are however required to maintain these lists.

A number of USB access control solutions [5,10,11,20,22,24] incorporate file-type filtering techniques to limit the types of files that can be transferred to removable media. Filtering schemes are defined by administrators and enacted at user workstations local to the access endpoints. These technologies can prohibit executable files or 'autorun' programs from being copied to or executed from removable storage devices. Such precautions are prudent in the face of threats to the company network from malicious software, but if managed inappropriately may not accommodate legitimate use of a program from a device (e.g. an in-house prototype application).

The USB access restriction technologies deal with the possibility that employees will try to exploit the enterprise network from within, regardless of whether they hold the appropriate access permissions. End users may also unintentionally access files that they should not have been able to. If recorded, these events can be analyzed and prevented from reoccurring. As such, audit trails of device and file access are generated, such as which devices were connected to which

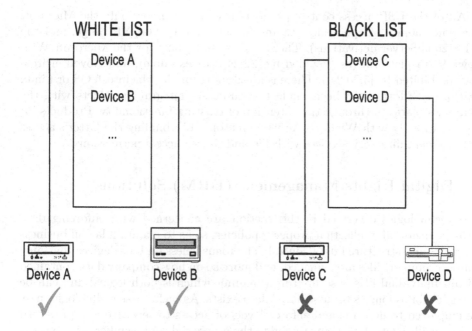

Fig. 2. 'White list' and 'black list' device access control

ports, and which files were accessed by which users. Duplications of copied data are also retained, should they be needed as evidence against employees during any subsequent legal action against them.

Facilities to encrypt data before it is transferred to removable storage devices (either automatically or after prompting end users) are also being used, and often even facilitate access to encrypted data outside of the work environment [3,5,20,24]. Use of encryption essentially extends the reach of the enterprise, securing data in such a way that it can only be accessed in accordance with an organization's data access policies.

Most technologies provide for employees needing to gain legitimate, temporary access to a device otherwise prohibited by their assigned access rights, or gain access to a protected device from a machine that is outside of the control of the organization. With the latter it is assumed that the central policy server can be contacted from the subject machine through a network connection. Products offer distinct methods for achieving offline access to secured devices. For instance [3] and [25] permit temporary access to secured devices through phone conversations with IT administrators (to obtain an access code). This relies on the availability of administrative staff, and is not directly integrated with enterprise-wide access management; it is not clear whether the details of phone conversations are synchronized with device access logs. Others [22] provide offline device access through a specialized utility carried with data when a device is encrypted, essentially re-appropriating the device as a self-enclosed, encrypted store.

All of the USB access control products reviewed support only the Microsoft Windows family of operating systems (generally the 2000/XP range, and the NT4/2003 Server derivations). There is limited support for the Microsoft Windows Vista platform (as provided by [22,24], for example), and Novell eDirectory (exhibited by [5,20,24]). There is no support for the Macintosh OS or Linux platforms. Efforts have been made to seamlessly integrate products with the Windows platform through the extension of existing functionality. Products integrate directly with Windows Active Directory [13], binding the latter's access management directory services with file and device access permissions.

3   Digital Rights Management (DRM) Solutions

The technologies described in this section are concerned with enforcing data management and intellectual property policies, so as to maintain lawful business practices and structured data control. The focus is less on how devices that may contain company files are managed, and more so on how company data contained within individual files is secured in a manner which is both logical and can be persisted for as long as the associated data exists. As such, these technologies may be employed to describe and enforce levels of access to sensitive and protected company file content that correspond to the access rights of members or groups of staff. They are aimed at securing specific types of electronic documents, and are intended for use by those subsets of employees working with 'office' documents (e.g. word processor or spreadsheet files).

The technologies in this section aim to ensure that the content of confidential files is only available to those persons that have the correct privileges. Centralized access rights are associated with company files. Access schemes for individual files persist with those files regardless of whether they reside within the enterprise network, on a removable data storage device, or on a computer that is not controlled by the organization. [18] extends the applicability of document security by including capabilities to track the use of sensitive enterprise data both within and outside the company network. [1] provides content integrity as a means to manage intellectual property, adding document signing and watermarking capabilities.

As with the USB access control solutions, all of the products described in this section are centrally managed. All of the permissions associated with a particular document are stored in a centralized location within the organization. With an emphasis on data security, the technologies [18,28] audit end user access to protected files. Audited information includes details of successful and attempted file access events, including the identified user, the time of the event, the application that was used, and the location of the accessed file.

Content control products are primarily concerned with restricting the editing, copying, storage, and printing of protected file contents. All these technologies provide role based access schemes, and incorporate encryption as a means of securing the contents of confidential files. Some, such as [18], require users to 'log in' to protected files, either with a dedicated password or automatically with their Windows user account information. Others, such as [1], provide extensive authentication capabilities, including the ability to associate digital certificates or watermarking attributes to encrypted files. Emphasis is placed on how security policies remain associated with the subject file, with an expectation that files will be transferred between secure and insecure locations. With [18] access identities have configurable and enforceable offline periods, thereby accommodating the mobility of employees. Sealed documents can be created and accessed through use of dedicated creation and reader applications. [1] integrates authentication measures directly into a protected document, with the expectation that secured files may be transferred across different storage devices and across different realms of authority. [1] can also create 'secure teams' of employees, allowing collaboration with external companies regarding file content.

4 Disk Encryption Solutions

Disk encryption solutions protect the contents of hard drives from unauthorized users while also ensuring that contents are not compromised and transported to external storage devices.

There exist several variations of disk encryption technologies. [26] is a disk encryption solution with the capability to encrypt an entire hard disk partition or a storage device such as a USB flash drive. [7] is a hard disk encryption application which automatically encrypts and decrypts data as it moves to and from an encrypted drive. [23] concentrates on securing confidential data as it travels between individuals. The argument here is that data is only at risk when it is being transported, be that via removable media (such as USB storage devices or CDs) or e-mails.

[7] and [23] provide role based access schemes, whereas with [26] users are prompted for access passwords or key files whenever they mount a protected drive. [23] encrypts files in a self-contained manner, so no additional software is required to access the file at a later date. [7] incorporates features such as secure data wiping, and management of the programs permitted to access secured data. For example, employees may be granted access to a file, but without the ability to simultaneously run file copying programs.

With [26] if there is a need to access a TrueCrypt volume simultaneously from multiple operating systems, an encrypted volume can either be mounted or dismounted on a single computer (e.g. a server), to allow decrypted or encrypted shared access to drive contents respectively, as appropriate. Options are available in [23] to create self-extracting secured files, which are then associated with an integrated password authentication application. [26] can run in so-called 'traveler' mode, so that it does not have to be directly installed on the platform under which it is run. [7] provides USB disk portability, in that it can be used with USB storage drives, DVDs, portable media players etc.

5   Operating System Solutions

It is worth investigating whether any of the access control or digital rights management functionality (as discussed in Sections 2 and 3) is available within current operating systems. If it were it would be possible that the features required by a company may be integrated into the operating system they already use, negating the purchase and maintenance of additional applications.

Microsoft Windows Vista. The latest version of the Microsoft Windows operating system, Windows Vista [14], provides additional functionality for the control of both copyrighted material and stored data. It is the belief of Microsoft that next generation multimedia content such as BluRay will see greater adoption over the next few years [21]. Windows Vista incorporates what is called the Protected Media Path (PMP) to ensure that protected (i.e. copyright-controlled) content can be accessed correctly. Documentation states that high definition content is "valuable content that needs to be protected from stealing", and that as such "each content type has its own particular policy that defines what the user can and cannot do with it".

Windows Vista provides group policy settings to define end user access permissions for removable storage devices (e.g. USB and other removable media, CD/DVD drives) [16]. An administrator can apply policies to control whether users are able to read from or write to removable storage devices.

Microsoft Windows Vista enterprise and Ultimate editions include BitLocker drive encryption [17]. With BitLocker the entire Windows volume is encrypted to prevent unauthorized users from gaining access to hard drive contents. The Encrypting File System can also be used to encrypt files and folders to protect data from unauthorized access. Although not a part of the Windows Vista operating system, the Microsoft Windows Office 2003 suite of applications provides features for information rights management [15]. Office 2003 documents (specifically files created in Microsoft Word 2003, Microsoft Excel 2003 or Microsoft Powerpoint 2003) can have restrictions associated with them to control the actions that particular users can enact on protected files.

Microsoft Windows XP also incorporates Encrypting File System. Windows XP can also be augmented with the Windows Rights Management Service [12], allowing centrally managed permissions to be associated with Microsoft Office documents.

Other Operating Platforms. Similar functionality to that described in Microsoft Windows Vista (i.e. centralized document access control, device access control, off-line drive protection etc.) is not immediately available on the Macintosh OS or Linux platforms.

6   Discussion of Technologies

The main features of the various information security technologies we have reviewed can be found in Table 1. We now close our survey of technologies by

Table 1. Summary of features offered for different information security solutions

	Operating Platform	Adminis-tration	Coverage	Monitoring	Encryption
Access Control	Windows	Central	Devices, Programs	Audit Trails	Files, Portable Drives
DRM	Windows	Central	Files, File Content	Audit Trails	Files
Disk Encryption	Windows, Linux	Local	Fixed Disks, Portable Disks	None	Drives
Operating System	Windows	Central, Local	Files, Devices, Programs	None	Drives

discussing particular complications that may arise from introducing any of the discussed technologies into an enterprise network. These complications have the potential to restrict employee productivity or otherwise leave existing vulnerabilities in conventional working practices unresolved.

Centralized Administration. All of the access control solutions that were examined follow a model of centralized control, wherein access policies are recorded at a single location from which they are pushed to end users whenever they interact with the network. This approach maintains consistent, manageable security policies, but in itself can create problems. It is assumed that all workstations with access to secured company data are accessible from any location within the company network. Where employees are working with sensitive files, it is assumed those files can be secured from a remote location without consultation with the end user.

Local Agents. There is the potential for locally deployed security software agents on end user workstations to fail. 'Failure' may be regarded as the product interacting with the local software platform in an unpredictable manner, or otherwise not providing a level of adaptability that the end user is comfortable with (for instance if they regularly require atypical security permissions).

Centralized Policy Management. Although centralized policy management provides for a consistent data security environment, it limits the control that end users have with regards to their own access rights. If an employee has a genuine and legitimate requirement for a specific access permission not already associated with their user account, they must rely on IT personnel to accurately provide the relevant permissions in a timely manner. Even the most expedient procedures could not achieve this without causing some delay to the end user.

In what follows, we will analyze the impact of these issues (particularly component failure and staff unavailability) on the effectiveness of information security solutions.

7   Unavailability Impact Analysis

7.1   Trade-Offs

The software solutions described in this document purport to solve a variety of data protection problems in the workplace. These include prohibiting improper use of USB (and other) endpoints, securing confidential document content, and securing data at rest within the company network. If an organization is to consider purchasing products to resolve the latter issues, there are associated factors that must be assessed.

System and Support.   The great majority of products require that user profiles and resources within a company network be centrally managed. In order to ensure timely deployment and management of access permissions amongst employees, it is necessary to have appropriate numbers of IT staff to regulate user access rights and permissions relating to new and differing storage media or file content. To further ensure that a central management system is kept functional and responsive, it may be necessary to incorporate some level of redundancy into the company network. Without this, if parts of the network were to cease functioning correctly, employee productivity may be limited or inconsistencies in the network-wide access control scheme may be introduced.

Productivity Loss. Employee productivity may be hindered by deployment of a chosen software solution. End users may find that their normal work routines need to be altered, or that completely new ways of interacting with the network need to be developed. Adapting to new network procedures may take time away from other areas of work, or could potentially sway employees away from their normal work routines entirely.

In what follows, we first quantify productivity loss, and look at how unavailability of system and support influences the productivity loss metrics. Then we discuss the trade-off between increased security and productivity loss. In both cases, we use probabilistic/stochastic modelling to describe the interactions between technologies, users and staff, relying on the Möbius software [6] to create and solve the models.

7.2   Productivity Loss

Fig. 3 shows a model representing access control technologies as discussed in Section 2 and Section 3. For ease of explanation, Fig. 3 shows the simplest model we used; more complicated versions of the depicted stochastic activity network (a formalism used in [6]) were necessary to derive the results in the next subsection. The flow of the users can easily be understood from Fig. 3 when following the arcs. There exist a number of active users ('Active_Users'), which exercise the local PC protection software ('LocalSW') at a certain frequency (given by 'Security_Check'). It takes some time to do the local software check (given by the time taken by 'Searching_Success1'), and after completion two

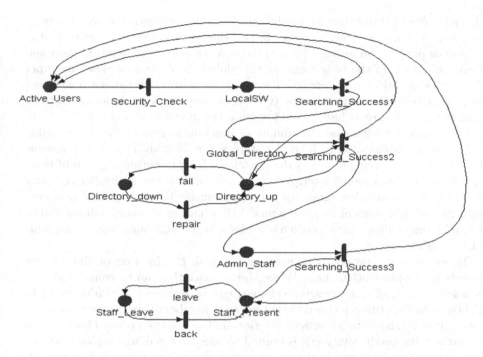

Fig. 3. Stochastic Activity Network of USB access control (base scenario)

things can happen. When the check was resolved correctly, the user returns to the active mode, while if the check was not resolved correctly, the global directory ('Global_Directory') is called. Some time is taken to perform the check at the global directory (activity 'Searching_Success2'), after which again two things may happen. When the check is resolved correctly at the global directory, the user returns to the active user mode, while if the check is not resolved correctly, the administrative staff has to be contacted ('Admin_Staff'). There again the user spends some time, but we assume in the base model that success is then guaranteed, and the user can return to active user mode (in the next section we relax that assumption). The model also accounts for failures and repairs of the global directory (activities 'fail' and 'repair' between the places 'Directory_up' and 'Directory_down') and the presence and absence of staff (activities 'leave' and 'back' between the places 'Staff_Present' and 'Staff_leave').

The time scale of the model is in minutes. We assume that each user interacts with the access control technologies once every 10 minutes on average and the software spends about 5 seconds doing the local check. In one percent of the cases, we assume the global directory is called; this number may vary a lot depending on the specific product, see Section 2. At the global directory about one minute is spent on average to determine execution rights. Again, one percent of requests is not resolved at the global directory, at which time administrative staff is called. The staff is assumed to spend 30 minutes on an average call. Note that the above implies that only one in ten thousand interactions with the access control solution end up at administrative staff, and that each individual user calls staff only once per year on average (to be precise, once every one hundred thousand active minutes). In the base scenario, the global database goes down once per three working days for an average of ten minutes, while staff takes a break once every four hours for thirty minutes. (Of course, all parameter choices need to be adjusted for the case at hand when applying the model in practice.)

In our model we increase the number of users up to tens of thousands, using a discrete approximation to keep the state space limited. That is, we assume 100 active users circle around in the model, each representing a group of users as determined by a model multiplier. By incorporating the multiplier correctly in the various transition rates, we can approximate the behavior of a system with tens of thousands of users by a model that has less than one million states. Arguably, one million states is still a considerable amount, but easily manageable with tools such as [6].

To measure the productivity loss, we compute the fraction of time a user spends in any place other than 'Active_Users', since this can be considered time 'wasted' because of access control technologies. Fig. 4 shows the results, for up to 25,000 employees (users). One sees that once the number of employees rises above two thousand, the system starts to deteriorate. For less than several hundreds of employees, the productivity loss is limited to one percent of an employee's time. For a company with 1000 employees, the productivity loss is about two percent, while for 3000 users the productivity loss rises above ten percent, and continues increasing when the number of users increases further.

Some back-of-the-envelope calculations based on above mentioned rates reveal that the staff presence is the bottleneck once the number of employees increases

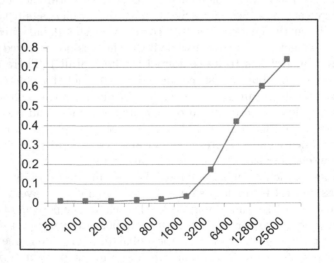

Fig. 4. Number of Employees (x-axis) versus Productivity Loss as a Fraction of Work Time (y-axis)

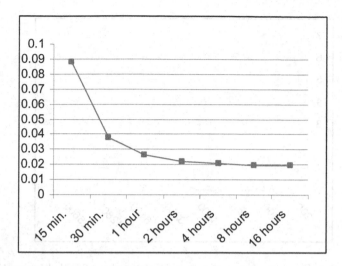

Fig. 5. Time between Staff Leaving (x-axis) versus Productivity Loss as a Fraction of Work Time (y-axis)

beyond one or two thousand. In our second experiment, we set the number of users to one thousand, and look at the sensitivity of employee productivity to the availability of staff to help when called. Note that one thousand employees amounts to less than one staff involvement per hour. Fig. 5 plots the productivity loss depending on the frequency with which staff leaves (and is absent for about 30 minutes); that is, the left-most data point in the graph depicts a staff member departing every 15 minutes. We see in Fig. 5 that as soon as staff members are interrupted every two hours or less, productivity starts to degrade for this particular scenario. In a similar way, results for multiple staff members can be derived, and decisions about the right number of staff members for an enterprise can be derived.

7.3   Departing Users

In the second model we assume that users are not as patient as in the above base model. In the above model, no matter how long the requests are queued in the global directory, or how long the administrative staff is on leave, the user waits for the access control solution to take a decision. In this subsection, we assume that when resources are unavailable (i.e. down or occupied), users leave the access control system; in such a case, the interesting question is what could or should happen with the task the employee wanted to carry out. At the one extreme, such failed interactions with the access control solution result in the employee not being able to do their task, thus seriously impairing the productivity of an employee. At the other extreme, the user is allowed to complete the task, thus seriously impairing security. In between these two extremes, the employee may be given the power to decide for him or herself; in some settings, this may be

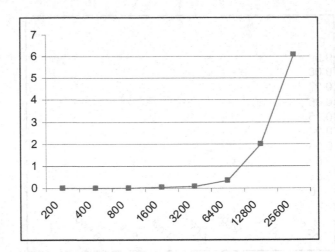

Fig. 6. Number of Employees (x-axis) versus total Number of Failed Interactions with the Access Control System per minute (y-axis)

an appropriate corporate strategy, best balancing the trade-off between security improvement and productivity loss.

To quantify the trade-off between productivity loss because of terminating requests, we consider each individual interaction with the access control system, and determine if it completes or fails. We show in Fig. 6 the number of instances per time unit in which the interaction with the access control solution fails, and the employee either cannot complete its work, or must make a decision him or herself. The question thus becomes, for an enterprise with 25 thousand employees, how important are these 6 uncompleted interactions every minute, and how much damage can they potential do if we let the employee make the decision what to do next. As a rule, the employee should not decide if for an average interaction the expected cost c_p because of productivity loss is less than the expected cost c_s because of security impairment. So, if p is the probability that an employee makes the right decision when forced to do so, then one should allow the employee to make that decision if $c_p < (1-p).c_s$. It should be noted that the access control system is introduced exactly because the probability p is in general not believed to be high enough. In other words, assuming the introduction of the access control system was a financially appropriate decision, allowing employees to make individual decisions makes sense only if employees make more careful decisions in the remaining cases in which the system delegates the decision-making to the user. Note furthermore that the trade-off between security enhancements and productivity loss can be decided yet better if attack modes and attack mode probabilities are known, and if the risk c_s can be identified for all these different attack modes.

8   Conclusion

A variety of enterprise information technologies have emerged over recent years, 'productized' by many different vendors. It seems therefore appropriate at this time to survey the available access control solutions, and evaluate their strengths and weaknesses. This paper does so. Since the great majority of the technologies examined in this document use centralized administration models to consistently manage role and group based access to critical company data, these solutions depend on the availability of computing and people resources. We built a probabilistic model and illustrated how the model can be used to determine the impact of system and staffing availability on the achieved security as well as the loss of productivity. It can also be used to improve staffing decisions as well as IT resource decisions.

Acknowledgements

Comments and feedback from our partners in the 'Trust Economics' project (UK Department of Trade and Industry, grant nr. P0007E) has substantially contributed to the technical report [19] on which this paper is based.

References

1. Avoco Secure Limited, Secure2Trust (as viewed 09/05/07),
   www.avocosecure.com/html_pages/products/secure2trust.html
2. Centennial Software, Gone in Sixty Seconds: The Executive Guide to Internal Data Theft (2006) (as viewed 29/07/07),
   www.centennial-software.com/resources/whitepapers/?product=2
3. Centennial Software, DeviceWall Product Info (as viewed 09/05/07),
   www.devicewall.com/pro/
4. Charlesworth, A.: Data theft by employees 'commonplace' (as viewed 29/07/07),
   www.vnunet.com/vnunet/news/2165309/theft-employees-commonplace
5. Check Point Software Technologies Inc., Pointsec Protector (as viewed 10/05/07),
   www.checkpoint.com/products/datasecurity/protector/index.html
6. Clark, G., Courtney, T., Daly, D., Deavours, D., Derisavi, S., Doyle, J.M., Sanders, W.H., Webster, P.: The Möbius Modeling Tool. In: Proceedings of the 9th International Workshop on Petri Nets and Performance Models, Aachen, Germany, September 11-14, 2001, pp. 241–250 (2001)
7. Dekart, Private Disk (as viewed 20/06/07),
   www.dekart.com/products/encryption/private_disk/
8. GFI Software, GFI EndPoint Security (as viewed 09/05/07),
   http://www.gfi.com/endpointsecurity/
9. Infowatch, Internal IT Threats in Europe 2006 (as viewed 29/07/07),
   www.infowatch.com/threats?chapter=162971949\&id=207784668
10. Layton Technology, DeviceShield (as viewed 20/06/07),
    www.laytontechnology.com/pages/deviceshield.asp
11. McAfee Inc., McAfee Data Loss Prevention (as viewed 20/06/07),
    www.mcafee.com/us/enterprise/products/data_loss_prevention/
    data_loss_prevention.html

12. Microsoft Corporation, Windows Rights Management Services (as viewed 20/06/07), www.microsoft.com/windowsserver2003/technologies/rightsmgmt/ default.mspx
13. Microsoft Corporation, Windows Server 2003 Active Directory (as viewed 02/06/07), www.microsoft.com/windowsserver2003/technologies/directory/ activedirectory/default.mspx
14. Microsoft Corporation, Windows Vista Home Page (as viewed 18/07/07), www.microsoft.com/windows/products/windowsvista/default.mspx
15. Microsoft Corporation, About Information Rights Management (as viewed 20/06/07), office.microsoft.com/en-us/help/HP062208591033.aspx
16. Microsoft Corporation, Step-By-Step Guide to Controlling Device Installation and Usage with Group Policy (as viewed 20/06/07), www.microsoft.com/technet/ windowsvista/library/9fe5bf05-a4a9-44e2-a0c3-b4b4eaaa37f3.mspx
17. Microsoft Corporation, Windows Vista Security Guide Chapter 3: Protect Sensitive Data (as viewed 20/06/07), http://www.microsoft.com/technet/windowsvista/ security/protect_sensitive_data.mspx
18. Oracle Corporation, Oracle Information Rights Management (as viewed 09/05/07), www.oracle.com/products/middleware/content-management/ information-rights-management.html
19. Parkin, S.E., van Moorsel, A.: A Trust-economic Perspective on Information Security Technologies, Technical Report CS-TR:1056, School of Computing Science, Newcastle University (October 2007)
20. Reflex Magnetics, Reflex Magnetics Disknet Pro (as viewed 09/05/07), www.reflex-magnetics.co.uk/products/disknetpro/
21. Russinovich, M.: Windows Administration: Inside the Windows Vista Kernel: Part 3 (as viewed 18/07/07), www.microsoft.com/technet/technetmag/issues/ 2007/04/VistaKernel/default.aspx
22. Safend Ltd., Safend Protector (as viewed 10/05/07), www.safend.com/65-en/Safend%20Protector.aspx
23. SafeNet Inc., SafeNet ProtectPack (as viewed 09/05/07), www.safenet-inc.com/products/data_at_rest_protection/ProtectPack.asp
24. SecureWave, SecureWave Sanctuary Device Control (as viewed 09/05/07), www.securewave.com/usb_security.jsp
25. Smartline Inc., DeviceLock (as viewed 09/05/07), www.protect-me.com/dl/
26. TrueCrypt Foundation, TrueCrypt (as viewed 20/06/07), www.truecrypt.org/
27. Wattanajantra, A.: Data Thefts and Losses in the UK-Timeline (as viewed January 25, 2008), www.itpro.co.uk/news/158184/ data-thefts-and-losses-in-the-uk-timeline.html
28. Workshare Inc., Workshare Protect (as viewed 09/05/07), www.workshare.com/products/wsprotect/default.aspx

Interaction Faults Caused by Third-Party External Systems — A Case Study and Challenges

Bogdan Tomoyuki Nassu and Takashi Nanya

Research Center for Advanced Science and Technology (RCAST)
The University of Tokyo
4-6-1 Komaba, Meguro-ku, Tokyo 153-8904, Japan
{bogdan,nanya}@hal.rcast.u-tokyo.ac.jp

Abstract. Interaction faults caused by a flawed external system designed by a third party are a major issue faced by interconnected systems. In this paper, we define a scenario where this type of problem occurs, and describe some fault cases observed in real systems. We also discuss the most important challenges faced in this scenario, focusing on error detection. The problem is divided in several sub-problems, some of which can be addressed by traditional or simple techniques, and some of which are complex problems by themselves. The purpose of this paper is not to present ad hoc solutions to specific sub-problems, but to introduce a new scenario and give general approaches to address each sub-problem. That includes a detailed insight on important concepts, such as implicit redundancies. With this, we lay down the foundations for a wide range of future work.

Keywords: Interaction Faults, Error Detection, Case Study, Communication Protocols, Fault Model.

1 Introduction

More and more, networked systems built from interconnected sub-systems become widespread. The Internet reach is already worldwide, and consumer electronics companies now aim at devices which connect to each other to form ubiquitous systems [1,2]. Networked systems like these are not monolithic blocks, and sub-systems may be designed by independent parties. Communication is achieved by the means of standards, which must be implemented by all the sub-systems. However, as these standards become more complex, problems such as misinterpreted specifications or insufficient testing may result in a sub-system being released with an incorrect or incomplete implementation of a communication standard. When communicating, these flawed sub-systems may cause *interaction faults*, hindering or halting system services.

One common solution used in this situation is designing more robust communication standards, to be implemented by future systems. Though this is very important, it only affects future systems, and current faulty sub-systems remain

T. Nanya et al. (Eds.): ISAS 2008, LNCS 5017, pp. 59–74, 2008.

faulty. Besides that, the new communication standards may also be badly implemented — leaving the problem unsolved. Another common solution is replacing or fixing the faulty sub-system. However, this is not always feasible in practice, as the sub-systems may be designed and controlled by different parties. Furthermore, consumers are not always willing or able to replace the sub-systems.

Therefore, a sub-system must be designed so that it is able to deal with interaction faults originated from third-party external systems. It must be at least protected so that interaction faults do not cause data loss or other hazardous effects. Ideally, the faults should be detected, or even tolerated, so that they do not affect the system's services from a user's point of view. Fault tolerance in this scenario must cope with some restrictions: the fault-tolerant sub-system cannot rely on cooperation from an external sub-system which does not implement its expected function, and must tolerate faults without changing the standard or the faulty sub-system itself.

In this paper, we detail a scenario where interaction faults are caused by a third-party external system, and describe some fault cases observed in real systems. We also discuss the most important challenges to be addressed, with special focus on error detection. The problem is divided in several sub-problems, shown in figure 1. Though some of these sub-problems can be addressed by existing techniques, others are complex problems by themselves. The purpose of this paper is not to present ad hoc solutions to specific sub-problems, but to introduce a new scenario and give general ideas about how to deal with each sub-problem. Special attention is given to new sub-problems that cannot be fully solved by existing techniques, as well as important concepts, such as implicit redundancies. With this, we lay down the foundations for a wide range of future work. A preliminary version of this work has appeared in [3].

The remainder of this paper is organized as follows. In section 2, the system and fault models are defined, and a case study is described. In section 3, we discuss the challenges for error detection in our scenario. Section 4 concludes the paper.

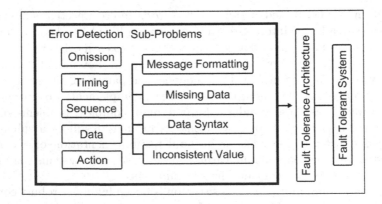

Fig. 1. Error detection sub-problems

2   Scenario Description and a Case Study

In this section, the considered system and fault models are defined. We also illustrate the scenario by describing a case study based on actual field data.

2.1   System Model

We consider a networked system built from sub-systems, or units, which use a communication standard to interact. Interaction occurs with the exchange of a' sequence of *messages*, each containing a set of data *fields*. Each field contains data of a certain *type* (string, positive integer, monetary value, etc.); and is identified by a *name* ("Action", "Connections", "Price", etc.). A field can be delimited by headers, tags, position, etc., depending on the standard.

A system in its simplest form consists of two units, one of which is a third-party *external unit*. The other system is ideally designed to tolerate faults, and is called the *adaptable unit*. We assume that no faults are originated from the adaptable unit — our focus is on faults caused by an external unit, and designing a unit capable of tolerating its own faults is a different problem. To further isolate the problem, we restrict faults to a single standard, which can be in any level above the physical layer. Any protocols below the considered standard are abstracted as a fault-free "communication interface". Note, however, that faults can propagate to higher layers. Figure 2 illustrates the system model.

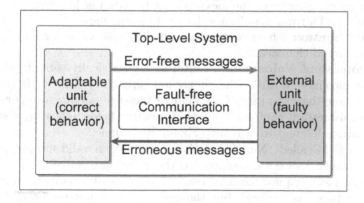

Fig. 2. System model

2.2   Errors Caused by Interaction Faults

In our scenario, faults manifest themselves when the external unit exhibits a behavior that deviates from the specification of the standard (which is assumed to be correct); or when it sends a message containing incorrect data. As we assume the standard runs over a fault-free communication interface, we do not consider faults caused by transmission errors in the physical layer. That means, for example, messages are not corrupted or lost in the communication channel, but are indeed generated containing incorrect data or are not sent.

Following the classification from reference [4], we deal with interaction faults, as they are originated from an external unit. As these faults are usually caused by a flawed implementation of the standard, they could be mistakenly seen as design faults. Indeed, if only the external unit is considered, they are design faults, but they make the external unit fail in operation time, becoming the cause of interaction faults in the top-level system. The faults can also be considered permanent — a fixed external unit is seen as a different unit.

Interaction faults may result in several types of errors. As the adaptable unit does not have direct access to the flawed implementation of the standard, the errors are described in terms of what can be observed outside the external unit, i.e. the messages it sends (or fails to send). Most error types are well-known, as they are also caused by other types of faults. We define the following classification for the errors:

- **Omission:** the external unit does not send a message it was expected to send.
- **Timing:** the external unit sends a message out of expected timing constraints.
- **Sequence:** the external unit sends a message out of the expected sequence.
- **Data Errors:** occur if a message is correctly received, but contain errors. There are four types of data errors:
  - **Message Formatting:** the message is not properly formatted. This type of error refers to the message, not to data inside fields.
  - **Missing Data:** a mandatory data field is missing.
  - **Data Syntax:** a field contains an unacceptable value for its data type (e.g. invalid characters).
  - **Inconsistent Value:** a field contains a syntactically correct value, but it is inconsistent with what it should represent — i.e. it is incorrect regarding the semantics of the field. A message may be also considered inconsistent if it contains correctly formatted fields indicating a state or situation different from reality. Examples include:
    * A field called "Number of Users" contains a valid integer, but the integer does not correspond to the actual number of users.
    * A query request for a variable is issued, and a correctly formatted response is received, but the response does not correspond to the requested variable.
    * A correctly formatted error message is received, but the described error did not occur.
- **Action Error:** this general category is used for errors that cannot be observed in the messages sent by the external unit. In fact, every error can be seen as the result of an incorrect action, but this category is used when all the messages are correctly received and contain correct data.

Note that these types of errors may occur in protocols in any layer of the communication, though they have different characteristics. For example, timing

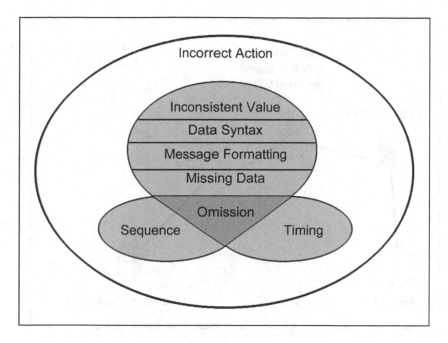

Fig. 3. Errors grouped by category

constraints are usually more strict in lower layers, but timing errors may occur even in the application level. Another example: inconsistent values in lower layers may be represented by inverted bits, but in the application layer, they are represented by arbitrary strings, or even incorrect images or audio data. Depending on the specific standard, some error types occur more frequently than others, and some will never occur — for example, in some standards there is no distinction between timing and omission errors.

Figure 3 show the error categories and how they relate. Omission is a special case of timing error (infinite delay), sequence error (the sequence is not respected) and missing data (all data is missing).

2.3   A Case Study

A good way of validating a fault model is checking how well it can represent a large base of real fault cases [5,6]. Unfortunately, obtaining a large number of real fault cases is also difficult in some scenarios. In this work, we do not validate the fault model by comparing it to field data in a large amount — this remains as an open problem to be addressed in the future. Even so, we have analyzed a number of real fault cases in order to get some insight on particularities of our scenario[1].

The analyzed data consists of reports of faults found during the design phase of some devices, including captured communication logs in pcap [7] format. The

---

[1] This data was gently provided by Matsushita Electric Industrial Co., Ltd.

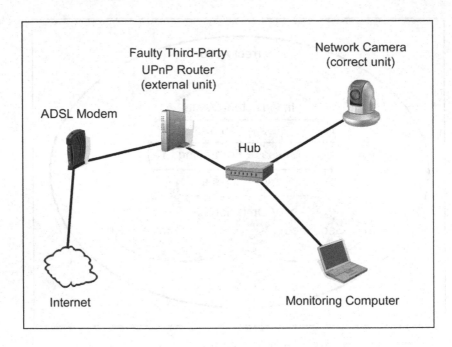

Fig. 4. Typical fault case setting

devices communicate using Universal Plug-and-Play (UPnP) [8,2] — an architecture for service exchange between electronic devices; based on well-known protocols, such as IP, HTTP and XML, as well as some specialized protocols. In the fault cases, devices such as a network camera, a printer or a television interact with commercially available UPnP internet routers, specified in reference [9]. These third-party routers exhibited a faulty behavior when interacting with the other devices, and are the external units in our system model. Figure 4 shows a typical fault case setting.

We have analyzed 14 fault cases which resulted in 6 omissions and 17 inconsistent values — several errors may occur in a same fault case. Below, we summarize the characteristics of the observed errors. For space reasons, the details of the analysis are not included. Descriptions 1–3 refer to the omission cases, the remaining descriptions refer to inconsistent values.

1. In 2 fault cases, the adaptable unit sends a search message and receives an error message in the ICMP layer. However, the described errors are caused by the external unit, and not by a bad request. If the considered protocol was in the lower-level layer, the error would be an inconsistent value. As the message never reaches the UPnP layer, it is considered an omission.
2. In 3 fault cases, the adaptable unit sends a search message, but does not receive any response.
3. In 1 fault case, the adaptable unit sends an action request, but does not receive any response.

4. In 1 fault case, the external unit has a valid external IP address, but all the requests for a `GetExternalIPAddress` action receive the value "0.0.0.0" in the response field.
5. In 5 fault cases, an `AddPortMapping` action is requested, and an error message is received, indicating a conflict between the requested port mapping and an existing mapping, or invalid arguments in the request. Though the error message is correct itself, it indicates a conflict when there is no conflict at all, or invalid arguments event though the request is correct. It can be considered that all the fields indicating the error status are inconsistent with the real state of the external unit or with the issued request.
6. In 4 fault cases, the actions received expected error messages as responses. These error messages were expected because they correctly indicated the actions could not be performed considering the internal state of the external unit. However, the error messages contained error codes and/or descriptions which were not suitable for the requested actions. In one case, the error description actually seems to be only a sequence of meaningless arbitrary characters.
7. In 2 fault cases, a port mapping is requested and added. However, a later request for the `GetSpecificPortMappingEntry` action returns an error message or a different mapping than the one which was added — i.e. the response is inconsistent with the real mapping.
8. In 4 fault cases, a field contains a numeric value outside the specified range.
9. In 1 fault case, a meaningless string is received in the HTTP `CONTENT-TYPE` header.

Even though the number of analyzed cases is quite small, some preliminary conclusions can be taken from this analysis:

- First and foremost, inconsistent values seem to be rather common in practice, at least in this particular system instance (considering UPnP routers). On the other hand, besides omissions, other error types were not observed.
- An error in a lower-level layer may result in another error of a different type in an upper layer. Even if each standard is considered independent from the lower layers, when an adaptable unit is designed, all the layers must be individually considered.
- Several errors do not lead to failures that affect service availability in the system — this is specially true for some descriptive fields that are not used by the correct unit and for some out-of-range values that are used without testing.
- All the errors are repeated if a specific external unit receives the same sequence of messages. In some cases, different correct units try to perform the same actions, and the same errors occur — i.e. an error is repeated if certain conditions are repeated. That observation is compatible with the idea that interaction faults may be caused by design faults in the external unit.

3   Challenges for Error Detection

The problem of detecting errors caused by interaction faults was previously addressed mainly aiming at specific faults or applications, in an ad hoc manner. In this paper, we seek general principles that can be used to detect errors, instead of focusing on such ad hoc solutions. Another common way of dealing with this problem is designing more robust (or safer, if the faults are malicious) protocols, or simply fixing or replacing the faulty unit. However, updating or fixing the standard in existing systems is often not feasible, for economic and practical reasons; and users are not always willing or able to replace the unit.

Before anything, it is necessary to ensure the adaptable unit is correct itself. To this purpose, techniques such as interoperability testing [10], as well as any other software engineering technique used to guarantee a protocol is implemented as specified, are of vital importance. More than this, the adaptable unit must be protected from incorrect inputs that may cause data loss or other hazardous effects. This is a well-known problem, and several techniques for defensive programming are already used in practice [11]. However, these techniques aim at removing design faults (bugs) and vulnerabilities from a system. Our work aim at a different problem: assuming a system correctly implements its specification and is protected from harmful inputs, how can it detect errors originated from a faulty external system?

Before any mechanism for error detection is specified, it is important to observe some restrictions imposed by the system model's characteristics. These restrictions limit the choice of mechanisms for error detection, and some traditional techniques [12] cannot be used, such as unit duplication, temporal redundancy (retries), or offline test phases.

- *The communication standard and the external unit cannot be changed.* This restriction exists because the standard has been already specified and is (incorrectly) implemented by the external unit.
- *Errors must be detected at runtime.* This occurs because the external unit is not part of the system being designed. Thus, the designer of the adaptable unit has no control over the faulty implementation of the standard, and the specific external unit is not known while the adaptable unit is being designed.
- *The adaptable unit must rely on information locally available or provided by the external unit.* This occurs because in real settings, several interactions occur only between a pair of units. Furthermore, protocols often do not have any mechanism for voting or group communication — of course, if such mechanisms are available, they may be used.

It is also important to notice that most standards already incorporate receiver-based robustness techniques, which provide some degree of fault tolerance. For example, TCP [13] uses timeouts and sliding windows to deal with omission and sequence errors. Another example: in real-time transmission of voice over the Internet [14], a unit can use buffers to deal with variable delays and generate substitutions for lost packets. The schemes here described are to be employed in addition to these techniques, to cover areas not addressed by the standard itself — specially because we assume the implementation is flawed in the external unit. Even if it is not possible to tolerate every single fault, a reasonable detection/correction coverage may prove valuable.

In the next subsections, several ideas for error detection are discussed. We divide the error detection problem in several sub-problems, according to the types of errors. Some sub-problems can be addressed by traditional or fairly simple techniques, while others are more complex, and require further investigation following the directions presented in this paper. Figure 5 lists the identified error detection sub-problems and summarizes the schemes to be employed, adding more ramifications to the simplified view presented earlier in figure 1. The most important challenges that must be addressed in the future are underlined. Before discussing those schemes, we describe a concept that is of vital importance to our work: *implicit redundancies*.

Omission: timers, *implicit redundancies*

Timing: timers, *implicit redundancies*

Sequence: test fields with sequential behavior

Data Errors

    Message Formatting

      Low Level: undetectable

      High Level: parsers, pattern matching, auxiliary rules

    Missing Data: simple tests based on the specification

    Data Syntax

      Numbers: undetectable

      Strings: implicit redundancies (grammar inference)

      Other Types: ad hoc

    Inconsistent Value: implicit redundancies

      Sequence-Independent: history

        Numbers: range / distribution

        Strings: dictionaries

        Other Types: ad hoc

      Sequence-Dependent: Temporal Data Mining

    Action: ad hoc

Fig. 5. Error detection sub-problems

3.1 Implicit Redundancies

Several communication standards incorporate error detection mechanisms based on explicit redundancies, which are specified and used as such. However, some protocols, specially complex high-level ones, also include "entropic" information, in the form of seemingly unrelated events or data fields, but which are in fact related to each other. In other words, sometimes a value received in a field gives a "hint" about what can be expected in other fields, or in the same field during other stages of the communication. This concept is not entirely new: implicit redundancies are used to describe entropic information which can be extrapolated to decode an encrypted message [15,16]. Implicit redundancies encode knowledge about the communication standard and the type of data exchanged by the units, and can be used to aid error detection, as well as error correction when replacements for incorrect or missing data fields are needed.

Before implicit redundancies can be used, they must be located. The most natural approach to this purpose is simply using the designer's knowledge about the problem domain. That approach is actually the same as the commonplace practice of addressing error detection case-by-case: the designer writes error detection functions based on relations he is aware of.

A way of enhancing this approach would be defining an intermediate, semi-structured format to describe the communication standard. With this format, the designer would be able to add his own knowledge about the problem to the existing specification — e.g. by describing each field as a function of other fields. However, this approach has several limitations. Converting the standard to a semi-structured format is a complex job, and the designer may be unable to describe the standard and all the fields correctly. Locating all the existing relations is also difficult, specially if the communication standard has many different types of messages and data fields — for example, a single UPnP device may deal with more than 250 different data fields [17]. Choosing only the most "important" fields would result in an ad hoc solution.

Given those problems, approaches for automatically locating implicit redundancies, based on examples of communications, are highly desirable. These approaches should be based on specific patterns that define relations between fields, and are among the most important challenges to be faced before error detection can be achieved in the proposed scenario.

3.2   Omissions and Timing Errors

Timing errors are traditionally detected by timers: a timer is triggered whenever a message is expected, and if the message is not received before a given timeout, the error is detected. Omission errors are detected the same way as timing errors, but usually with larger timeouts. It is a known fact that, if unbounded communication delays are assumed, late and omitted messages are indistinguishable, and some standards consider them to be the same, specially if there are strict real time requirements.

In some cases, the adaptable unit cannot tell if a message must be received — for example, the omitted search responses from the fault cases in section 2.3. In these cases, the error is undetectable unless an ad hoc solution or at least more information is provided by some implicit redundancy — e.g. user inputs or specific patterns such as repeated searches, indicating a message should be received.

3.3   Sequence Errors

Sequence errors are traditionally detected by comparing the order of the messages with an expected communication pattern, or checking fields having sequential behavior, such as counters or sequence numbers.

3.4   Message Formatting Errors

Message formats fall in two major categories: low level (e.g. TCP, IP), with rigid, bit level descriptions for the format, and high level (e.g. XML, HTML), with the fields being delimited by tags or special characters. Low level formatting errors are only detectable if the number of bits in the message is different from the expected, in which case error detection is straightforward. Otherwise, as there are no special delimiters for the fields, the error cannot be detected. In that case, a formatting error can result in a data syntax or inconsistent value error, and must be detected as such. High level message formats can be described by context-free grammars [18] and similar rules. In these cases, errors are traditionally detected by format parsers, pattern matching and auxiliary rules (e.g. XML schemas).

3.5   Missing Data

A correct and complete specification of the standard, which we assume to be the case, must state which fields are expected in each message. For low-level identification schemes (e.g. if the fields have a fixed number of bits), a missing field may result in a message with incorrect size. If the fields are delimited by identifiers (e.g. XML tags), missing data can be detected by simple tests which look for the expected tags. If the missing field is optional, the error is addressed as an inconsistent value error — missing data refers only to required fields.

3.6   Data Syntax Errors

Data syntax errors are detected based on each data type. There are three basic data types from which every type is derived from: numbers, strings and "others".

Syntax Errors in Numbers. Numbers include signed and unsigned integers, floating-point values, some representations for date and time, etc. We consider only bit-level number representations, such as the two's complement representation for signed integers — numbers represented as strings containing digits and separators are addressed the same way as other strings. Error detection for bit level number representations is impossible in most cases: usually, a field generated with the incorrect syntax will still contain a syntactically correct, but inconsistent, value. These errors should be addressed as inconsistent values.

Syntax Errors in Strings. Strings include any data type described by a sequence of characters, including names, IP addresses, URLs, text in natural language, or even numbers. The syntax for string types can be described by reference rules, and data syntax errors can be detected by comparing the received data with the appropriate rules. However, in several cases, the specification of syntax rules is not formal, being written in natural language; or is implicit or ignored, based on the assumption that the type is well known. Besides that, even though implementation of these syntax rules is usually not hard by itself, the number of different data types in a single communication standard may be very large — for example, a single UPnP device may deal with over 100 types of strings [17].

For the reasons above, in several occasions, designers are not able to success-fully obtain syntax rules for every single type of data. In several real implemen-tations, some subtleties are ignored, and the syntax is checked only in a very basic level, for example, looking for invalid characters. In other cases, only the most "important" types of data are addressed, resulting in an ad hoc solution to the problem.

This problem may benefit from automatic methods for defining models to rep-resent syntax rules. This is a type of implicit redundancy: the syntax is implicit in the received data, and can be learned from examples. The learned syntax rules may be given as a grammar, regular expression, pattern or even a non-human-friendly model, such as an artificial neural network. This process of learning may occur in design-time, involving only examples of data from each type, and not necessarily communication examples.

This type of problem have been studied for several years by the grammar infer-ence community [19], and has a solid theoretical foundation. Though traditional and formal models have some disappointing or limited theoretical results [20,21], this problem can be also addressed by other machine learning approaches, which have been employed successfully for problems such as the identification of pat-terns for sequences of genes [22]. As the general principles of grammar inference are independent from the domain, they can also be used for identifying syntax rules for string data types.

Other Syntax Errors. Though numbers and strings are the most common types of data, there is a multitude of other formats used for audio, video, pictures, etc. If the syntax for each type is defined, the rules for data syntax error detection can be derived from the specification. Each particular type is specified in a different manner, and though some types could benefit from the same techniques used by strings, there is no single universal mechanism able to deal with these differences.

3.7   Inconsistent Values

All the types of errors discussed so far share a characteristic: they can be detected using exclusively information available in the specification of the communication standard or data type. It is always specified when a message is expected, what are the timing requirements and the sequence to be followed by the messages, which is their format, and which fields and types of data are present. Inconsistent values are different from other types of error because they are not detectable using only information directly available from the specification: they include values that are accepted by the standard in a normal situation. That can make inconsistent values very hard to detect.

To exemplify this situation, suppose an adaptable unit receives in a message a field containing a value for international money remittance, named "amount to send". Suppose the minimum tax for international remittance is US$100.00, and that the external unit sends a message with the (incorrect) value "US$2.00" in this field. Though it is very unlikely that someone would make a money remittance of US$2.00 and pay US$100.00 in taxes, the received value is syntactically correct. The only way of detecting such an error is resorting to the semantics of the task (international money remittance), data type (monetary value), field (amount to send) and how it is associated with the concept of taxation.

An error detector for inconsistent values must incorporate knowledge about the semantics of each task, data type and field. This knowledge is external, not directly available from the specification, and it is common practice to address this type of error in a case-by-case basis. In the money remittance example above, the designer could deem that an amount is incorrect if it is below the tax (note this is a naive solution).

To better explore external knowledge, error detectors for inconsistent values may employ implicit redundancies. An error detector for inconsistent values must have a set of functions that relate a given field with data observed in the past. These relations may depend not only on the semantics of the performed task and data types, but also on the context each value is received. There are two types of relations that may be used to detect inconsistent values. The first type occurs when a field is related to previously observed values, independent of the exact sequence they appear. The second type occurs when a field is related with the sequence of values received before it. The general approaches to identify these types of implicit redundancies are described below.

To locate sequence-independent relations, the general principle is keeping a history of data received earlier, from the same unit, from other units, or during a design-time learning process. The values in the history are then used as a model for expected values to be received in the future. When a new value is received, it is compared to data in the history which has the same meaning. An error is detected if the received data differs from what is expected, given a suitable difference measure. This approach can become way more effective if each field is further divided in smaller particles, or terms. In that case, instead of relating only fields, the adaptable unit may also relate particles with the same meaning. The learning process for numbers, strings and other types of data is as follows:

- **Numbers:** the adaptable unit uses data received previously to determine, for each field, the expected value ranges and possibly the distribution of the values. If a received value is outside the learned range or is very different from the expected distribution (i.e. is an outlier), an error may be detected. In the money remittance example presented earlier, the error could be detected if no value as low as US$2.00 was ever received in the "amount to send" field during previous communications. Numeric particles from string types may also be addressed by this scheme.

– **Strings:** the adaptable unit uses data received previously to build a "dictionary" containing known values for each field. Errors are detected if a value is similar, but different, from a value present in the dictionary. If the relations are between particles, the problem becomes very similar to detecting spelling errors in search engines [23]. For example, suppose the adaptable unit receives a field called "web page", with value "www.hal.rcast. u-tokyo.ac.jp", and later receives the "e-mail" field, containing the inconsistent value "nanya@hal.rcas.u-tokyo.ac.jp". Based on the syntax of these data types (web address and e-mail address), the words "rcast" and "rcas" can be regarded as isolated terms with the same meaning, and the error may be detected.
– **Other Types:** it is very hard to generalize the learning process to other types of data, as this depends on their format, properties and meaning. Relations involving other types of data must be located in an ad hoc manner.

Locating relations of the second type, where the sequence is relevant, is essentially a temporal data mining [24] problem. That may include techniques based on time series (for numeric values) or in a more general sense, discovery of frequent episodes and rules [25]. Learning methods for sequences have some known issues, especially the difficulty of locating complex relations involving several fields, and the possibility of finding relations where they do not exist. These issues must be carefully considered when these techniques are used for learning implicit redundancies that will be employed for error detection.

Given the semantic nature of inconsistent values, detection of this type of error carries some degree of uncertainty, and in some cases the learned redundancies may not be enough to tell for sure if a value is inconsistent or not. Depending on how it is defined, an inconsistent value detector may have different degrees of confidence in its response: some values will be very far from the acceptable (e.g. out of range) and can be easily considered inconsistent, but sometimes the value is acceptable, but is suspicious. Thus, the output from some inconsistent value detectors will not be binary (i.e. present or absent), but indicate a "level of suspicion" for a given value. Sometimes, depending on the affected fields, the adaptable unit may have to resort to further action, in order to determine whether a suspect value is inconsistent or not. Furthermore, some errors occurring during one task may remain undetected until later, when another task fails because of the inconsistent data.

3.8 Action Errors

As said in section 2.2, this category includes errors that cannot be directly observed in the messages the external unit sends or fails to send. That makes this type of error very difficult, or even impossible, to detect. Action errors can only be detected if the external exhibits specific patterns of behavior, such as cycles or repetitions. Given their general nature, these errors must be addressed in a case-by-case (ad hoc) manner — i.e. specialized solutions for known faults which may occur.

4   Conclusions and Future Work

In this paper, we have summarized the most important challenges faced when designing a system able to detect errors caused by interaction faults. In the considered scenario, interaction faults result from a flawed external system, designed by a third party. Existing work aim at specific applications instead of a general model, and at the design of more robust protocols — usually a better solution in the technical sense, but not always feasible in practice. Furthermore, the assumption that the external unit may be badly implemented is a real issue often ignored in existing work.

We have defined the system and fault models for this scenario, and divided the problem in several sub-problems — some of which can be addressed by simple or traditional schemes, and some of which are complex problems themselves. Our aim was not to present ad hoc solutions to specific sub-problems, but to introduce a new scenario and give general approaches to each sub-problem. Though we did not present detailed schemes for detecting all the possible types of errors, we have proposed general mechanisms and showed when traditional schemes can be employed. We have also discussed implicit redundancies — an important concept that can be explored when tolerating interaction faults.

This paper lays down the foundations for a wide range of future work. The complex sub-problems we have identified must be addressed individually. That includes the inference of patterns/grammars to detect syntax errors in strings; a methodology to assist a designer to locate implicit redundancies in the specification of the standard; and specially automatic location of implicit redundancies, through techniques such as statistical analysis of previous data, dictionaries and data mining. Other future work include ways of exploring the notion of implicit redundancies to correct errors, and the creation of a single architecture joining all the schemes for error detection and correction.

Finally, it can be noted that the some of the identified sub-problems are very general, and the same principles used to solve them may also be extended to other types of problems sharing the same characteristics. For example, in several instances, a human user may be seen as an external system — and schemes employing implicit redundancies may be useful, for example, in the design of dependable systems which interact with humans or detect intrusions.

References

1. Weiser, M.: The World is not a Desktop. Interactions 1(1), 7–8 (1994)
2. Digital Living Network Alliance: DLNA Home Page, www.dlna.org
3. Nassu, B.T., Nanya, T.: Tolerating Interaction Faults Originated From External Systems. IEICE Technical Report 106(292), 7–12 (2006)
4. Avizienis, A., et al.: Basic Concepts and Taxonomy of Dependable and Secure Computing. IEEE Transactions on Dependable and Secure Computing 1(1), 11–33 (2004)

5. Jarboui, T., Arlat, J., Crouzet, Y., Kanoun, K., Marteau, T.: Analysis of the Effects of Real and Injected Software Faults: Linux as a Case Study. In: PRCD 2002: Proceedings of the 2002 Pacific Rim International Symposium on Dependable Computing, Tsukuba, Japan, pp. 51–58 (2002)
6. Duraes, J.A., Madeira, H.S.: Emulation of Software Faults: A Field Data Study and a Practical Approach. IEEE Transactions on Software Engineering 32(11), 849–867 (2006)
7. Duraes, J.A., Madeira, H.S.: TCPDUMP Public Repository, http://www.tcpdump.org
8. Contributing Members of the UPnP Forum: UPnP Device Architecture 1.0 (2003)
9. Contributing Members of the UPnP Forum: InternetGatewayDevice:1 Device Template Version 1.01 (2001)
10. Lai, R.: A Survey of Communication Protocol Testing. Journal of Systems and Software 62(1), 21–46 (2002)
11. Dowd, M., McDonald, J., Schuh, J.: The Art of Software Security Assessment: Identifying and Preventing Software Vulnerabilities. Addison-Wesley Professional, Reading (2006)
12. Siewiorek, D.P., Swarz, R.S.: Reliable Computer Systems — Design and Evaluation, 3rd edn. AK Peters, Ltd. (1998)
13. Postel, J. (ed.): Transmission control protocol (1981) DARPA Internet Program. Transmission Control Protocol. In: RFC 793 (1981)
14. Kostas, T.J., Borella, M.S., Sidhu, I., Schuster, G.M., Grabiec, J., Mahler, J.: Real-Time Voice Over Packet-Switched Networks. IEEE Network 12(1), 18–27 (1998)
15. Grangetto, M., Cosman, P.: MAP Decoding of Arithmetic Codes With a Forbidden Symbol. In: ACIVS 2002: Advanced Concepts for Intelligent Vision Systems, Belgium (2002)
16. Gong, L.: A Note on Redundancy in Encrypted Messages. ACM SIGCOMM Computer Communication Review 20(5), 18–22 (1990)
17. Contributing Members of the UPnP Forum: UPnP AV Architecture: 0.83 (2002)
18. Sipser, M.: Introduction to the Theory of Computation, 2nd edn. Course Technology (2005)
19. Gold, E.M.: Language Identification in the Limit. Information and Control 10(5), 447–474 (1967)
20. Haussler, D.: Probably Approximately Correct Learning. In: National Conference on Artificial Intelligence, pp. 1101–1108 (1990)
21. Case, J., Jain, S., Reischuk, R., Stephan, F., Zeugmann, T.: A Polynomial Time Learner for a Subclass of Regular Patterns. Electronic Colloquium on Computational Complexity (ECCC) (38) (2004)
22. Chan, S.C., Wong, A.K.C.: Synthesis and Recognition of Sequences. IEEE Transactions on Pattern Analysis and Machine Intelligence 13(12), 1245–1255 (1991)
23. Martins, B., Silva, M.J.: Spelling Correction for Search Engine Queries. In: EsTAL: Advances in Natural Language Processing, Springer, Spain (2004)
24. Antunes, C.M., Oliveira, A.L.: Temporal Data Mining: An Overview. In: Workshop on Temporal Data Mining, Conference on Knowledge Discovery and Data Mining (KDD 2001), USA, pp. 1–13 (2001)
25. Mannila, H., Toivonen, H., Verkamo, A.I.: Discovery of Frequent Episodes in Event Sequences. Data Mining and Knowledge Discovery 1(3), 259–289 (1997)

User-Perceived Software Service Availability Modeling with Reliability Growth

Koichi Tokuno and Shigeru Yamada

Department of Social Systems Engineering,
Faculty of Engineering, Tottori University
4-101, Koyama, Tottori-shi, 680-8552 Japan
{toku,yamada}@sse.tottori-u.ac.jp

Abstract. Most of conventional software availability models often assume only up and down state for the time-dependent behavior of a software-intensive system. In this paper, we develop a plausible software service availability model considering the degradation of system service performance and the software reliability growth process in operation. We assume that the software system has two operational states from the viewpoint of the end user: one is providing with service performance according to specification and the other is with degraded service performance. The time-dependent behavior of the system alternating between up and down state is described by a Markov process. This model can derive instantaneous software service availability defined as the expected value of possible service processing quantity per unit time at a specified time point. Finally, we show several numerical examples of the measures to analyze the relationship between the service availability evaluation and software reliability growth characteristic.

Keywords: software service availability, service capacity, Markov process, software reliability growth.

1 Introduction

It has been established that the outages of computing systems are caused due to software faults in most cases [1]. Furthermore, it has been increasingly important to evaluate not only the inherent quality characteristics of the computing systems but also the quality of service created by the use of the systems. Recently, **service reliability theory** or **service reliability engineering** have a growing attention; these consider the situations, behaviors, and satisfaction of the users receiving services by the operation of systems as well and are more comprehensive frameworks than the conventional reliability engineering. Tortorella [2,3] has described the basic concepts and the methods of the service reliability engineering; this aims to establish quantitative evaluation methods for the quality of service created by the use of the artificial industrial products as well as the inherent quality of the products. Considering the software systems are just the industrial products to provide the services for the users, especially in computer

T. Nanya et al. (Eds.): ISAS 2008, LNCS 5017, pp. 75–89, 2008.
© Springer-Verlag Berlin Heidelberg 2008

network systems, it is meaningful to discuss the performance evaluation methods for software systems oriented to the service reliability engineering.

The studies on performance evaluation methods for computing systems have much been discussed from the viewpoint of the hardware configuration. For example, Beaudry [4] has proposed the performance-related measures such as the computation reliability, the mean computation between failures, the computation thresholds, the computation availability, and the capacity threshold and demonstrated the analytical solutions of these measures for typical gracefully degrading computing systems. Meyer [5] has introduced the concept of performability taking account of accomplishment levels from customer's viewpoint. Nakamura and Osaki [6] have discussed the performance evaluation for a multi-processor system considering the demand of jobs. They have applied the Markov renewal process and the queueing theory to the exact and approximate analyses of several performance-related reliability measures. Sols [7] has introduced the concept of degraded availability. These studies have considered that computing systems have several different performance or service levels.

Recently, on the other hand, software-conscious approaches to performance/ reliability evaluation of computing systems have increased. In particular, studies on the optimal schedule of software preventive maintenance, referred to as software rejuvenation, have much been conducted. Pfening *et al.* [8] and Garg *et al.* [9] have considered the situation where the system performance (i.e., service rate) gradually degrades with time due to the software aging, referred to as a soft failure, and discussed the determination problem of the optimal software rejuvenation time. Eto and Dohi [10] have treated the multiple degradation levels of the software system which consists of one operating system and multiple applications and derived the optimal preventive rejuvenation schedule maximizing the steady-state service availability. There exist another approaches aiming at the software fault-tolerant architecture. Kimura *et al.* [11,12] have regarded the N-version programming software system [13] and the recovery block software system [14] as responsive systems [15], which combine the fault-tolerant architecture and real-time requirement, and derived the reliability-related performance measures such as responsiveness defined as the probability that the system outputs a correct result within a stipulated response time, and the mean response time. Furthermore, for a fault-tolerant software system with two-version redundant structure, Rinsaka and Dohi [16] have modeled the stochastic behavior of the system with rejuvenation and analyzed the steady-state system availability and the mean time to failure; the framework of this analysis has followed the study of Huang *et al.* [17].

The above software-conscious approaches are discussed on the basis of performance measures in steady states and assume that the probabilistic or stochastic characteristics in system failure or restoration do not alter even though the system is restored or refreshed, i.e., the system returns to the initial state, neither better nor worse states. As to this point, the analytical framework in the above studies is basically similar to that from the aspect of the hardware configuration even though these studies are software-oriented. Traditional stochastic software reliability modeling often considers the dynamic reliability/performance growth process; Musa [18] says that this is one of main differences from the modeling for the hardware system. As the studies considering the dynamic characteristics peculiar to software systems mentioned above, Tokuno and Yamada [19] have developed the stochastic model for performance evaluation of the multi-task processing software system, considering the dynamic software reliability growth process and the upward tendency of difficulty in debugging. They have applied the infinite server queueing theory [20] to the description of the stochastic behavior of the cumulative number of tasks whose processes are complete successfully and derived several quantitative performance measures. Subsequently to [19], Tokuno *et al.* [21] have considered the real-time property defined as the attribute that the system can complete the task within the stipulated deadline [22] and analyzed the more generalized case where the task arrival process follows a non-homogeneous Poisson process. The performance measures have been given as the functions of time and the number of debugging activities.

In this paper, we develop a stochastic software service availability model considering the dynamic software reliability growth by extending the model of Tokuno and Yamada [23]. Most of traditional software availability models [24,25,26] often assume only up and down states and provide the probabilistic measures such as the instantaneous availability defined as the probability that the system is operating at a given time point; this value does not reflect the operational service levels. Recently, it is often that the traditional measures, however, are not appropriate from the viewpoint of end users. As mentioned in [8,9], software-intensive systems could not always display their peak performance or service, or some internal parts of systems might be unfavorable states even though they are available or do not seem to fall into operation stoppage outwardly in actual operational environment. For instance, the system is capable of decreasing throughput due to not only software aging but also the concentration of loads into some specified system resources. In the web-based service system, end users may often perceive the performance degradation due to congestion of the network. As another case, some parts of system functions are unavailable due to maintenance of the corresponding software subcomponents [10]. We assume that there are two user-perceived operational states: one is providing with service performance according to specification, i.e., a desirable operational state, and the other is with degraded service performance. The time-dependent behavior of the software system alternating between up and down states is described by a Markov process. In this model, several analytical solutions of system performance measures are derived. In particular, we propose **instantaneous software service availability** defined as the expected value of possible service processing quantity per unit time at a specified time point. This measure takes account of reliability and service performance simultaneously and is given as the function of time and the number of debuggings.

The organization of the rest of this paper is as follow. Section 2 states the model description and the notion of service processing. Section 3 shows the derivation of software service availability measures. Section 4 analyzes the relationship between the service availability evaluation and the inherent software failure/restoration characteristics by illustrating several numerical examples of measures derived in the paper. Finally, Section 5 summarizes the results obtained in the paper and the future works.

2 Model Description

Based on [23], the following assumptions are made for extension to service-oriented software availability modeling:

A1. When the software system is operating, the time-interval of operation with service performance according to specification, T_{ss}, and the holding time of service performance degradation, T_{sd}, follow the exponential distributions with means $1/\theta$ and $1/\eta$, respectively.

A2. The software system breaks down and starts to be restored as soon as a software failure occurs, and the system cannot operate until the restoration action completes.

A3. The restoration action includes the debugging activity and software reliability growth occurs if a debugging activity is perfect.

A4. Consider the imperfect debugging environment where the debugging activity may fail, i.e., it is probabilistic whether the debugging activity succeeds or fails. The debugging activity is perfect with perfect debugging probability a $(0 < a < 1)$, while imperfect with probability $b(= 1-a)$. A perfect debugging activity corrects and removes one fault from the system.

A5. When n faults have been corrected, the next software failure-occurrence time-interval and the restoration time follow the exponential distributions with means $1/\lambda_n$ and $1/\mu_n$, respectively.

We define the service capacity as system's possible service processing quantity per unit time; this term is referred by Pfening *et al.* [8] and the basic notion of service capacity is similar to that of the computation capacity defined by Beaudry [4]. For example, instructions/second or packets/second are adequate as the units of the service capacity for the web-based systems. It is also assumed that the service capacities of the system are $C(> 0)$ and $C\delta$ $(0 < \delta < 1)$ when the system is operating with service performance according to specification and degraded service performance, respectively. We call δ the decreasing ratio of the service capacity. Furthermore, we refer to the treatment of the probabilistic characteristics of T_{ss} and T_{sd} in this paper. As mentioned in the previous section, there exist various causes of service performance degradation, for example, not only the internal factors such as software aging or temporal suspension of some services due to restoration but also the external factors such as the congestion of the network or the concentration of the access to some system resources. From the viewpoint of end users, the phenomenon of the service performance degradation is one of interesting issues, but users hardly care about the causes of service performance degradation. Since we pay attention to the user-perceived modeling, it is assumed that both of the occurrence of service performance degradation and the retrieval from the performance degradation arise randomly.

We introduce a stochastic process $\{X(t),\, t \geq 0\}$ representing the user-perceived state of the software system at the time point t. The state space of the process $\{X(t),\, t \geq 0\}$ is defined as follows:

$\boldsymbol{W} = \{W_n : n = 0, 1, 2, \ldots\}$: the system is operating with service performance according to specification (desirable operational state),

$\boldsymbol{L} = \{L_n : n = 0, 1, 2, \ldots\}$: the system is operating with degraded service performance,

$\boldsymbol{R} = \{R_n : n = 0, 1, 2, \ldots\}$: the system is utterly inoperable and restored,

where $n = 0,\ 1,\ 2,\ \ldots$ denotes the cumulative number of corrected faults. Figure 1 illustrates the sample state transition diagram of $X(t)$. Let $Q_{A,B}(\tau)$ $(A,\ B \in \{\boldsymbol{W},\ \boldsymbol{L},\ \boldsymbol{R}\})$ denote the one-step transition probability that after making a transition into state A, the process $\{X(t),\, t \geq 0\}$ makes a transition into state B by time τ. The expressions for $Q_{A,B}(\tau)$'s are given as follows:

$$Q_{W_n,L_n}(\tau) = \frac{\theta}{\lambda_n + \theta}[1 - e^{-(\lambda_n + \theta)\tau}], \tag{1}$$

$$Q_{W_n,R_n}(\tau) = \frac{\lambda_n}{\lambda_n + \theta}[1 - e^{-(\lambda_n + \theta)\tau}], \tag{2}$$

$$Q_{L_n,W_n}(\tau) = \frac{\eta}{\lambda_n + \eta}[1 - e^{-(\lambda_n + \eta)\tau}], \tag{3}$$

$$Q_{L_n,R_n}(\tau) = \frac{\lambda_n}{\lambda_n + \eta}[1 - e^{-(\lambda_n + \eta)\tau}], \tag{4}$$

$$Q_{R_n,W_{n+1}}(\tau) = a(1 - e^{-\mu_n \tau}), \tag{5}$$

$$Q_{R_n,W_n}(\tau) = b(1 - e^{-\mu_n \tau}). \tag{6}$$

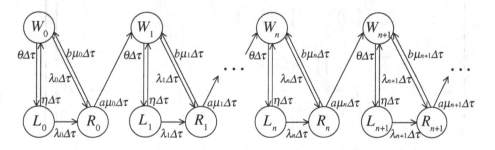

Fig. 1. Sample state transition diagram of $X(t)$

3   Model Analysis

3.1   Distribution of Transition Time of $X(t)$ between State W

We first consider the random variable $S_{i,n}$ representing the transition time of $X(t)$ from state W_i to state W_n $(i \leq n)$ and Let $G_{i,n}(t)$ be the distribution function of $S_{i,n}$. Then the renewal equation of $G_{i,n}(t)$ is obtained as

$$
\left.\begin{array}{l}
G_{i,n}(t) = H_{W_i,R_i} * Q_{R_i,W_{i+1}} * G_{i+1,n}(t) + H_{W_i,R_i} * Q_{R_i,W_i} * G_{i,n}(t) \\
H_{W_i,R_i}(t) = Q_{W_i,R_i}(t) + Q_{W_i,L_i} * Q_{L_i,R_i}(t) \\
\qquad\qquad + Q_{W_i,L_i} * Q_{L_i,W_i} * H_{W_i,R_i}(t) \\
\qquad (i, n = 0,\ 1,\ 2,\ \ldots;\ i \le n)
\end{array}\right\},
$$
(7)

where $*$ denotes the Stieltjes convolution and $H_{W_i,R_i}(t)$ represents the probability that the process $X(t)$ makes a transition from state W_i to state R_i in an amount of time less than or equal to t. We apply the Laplace-Stieltjes (L-S) transforms [27] to solve Eq. (7) and the L-S transform of $G_{i,n}(t)$ is given by

$$
\begin{aligned}
\widetilde{G}_{i,n}(s) &= \prod_{m=i}^{n-1} \frac{d_m^1 d_m^2}{(s + d_m^1)(s + d_m^2)} \\
&= \sum_{m=i}^{n-1} \left(\frac{A_{i,n}^1(m) d_m^1}{s + d_m^1} + \frac{A_{i,n}^2(m) d_m^2}{s + d_m^2} \right).
\end{aligned}
$$
(8)

By inverting Eq. (8), we have the distribution function of $S_{i,n}$, $G_{i,n}(t)$ as

$$
\left.\begin{array}{l}
G_{i,n}(t) \equiv \Pr\{S_{i,n} \le t\} = 1 - \displaystyle\sum_{m=i}^{n-1} \left[A_{i,n}^1(m) e^{-d_m^1 t} + A_{i,n}^2(m) e^{-d_m^2 t} \right] \\
\qquad (i, n = 0,\ 1,\ 2,\ \ldots;\ i \le n) \\
\left.\begin{array}{l} d_i^1 \\ d_i^2 \end{array}\right\} = \dfrac{1}{2}\left[(\lambda_i + \mu_i) \pm \sqrt{(\lambda_i + \mu_i)^2 - 4a\lambda_i\mu_i} \right] \\
\qquad \text{(double signs in same order)} \\
A_{i,n}^1(m) = \dfrac{\displaystyle\prod_{j=i}^{n-1} d_j^1 d_j^2}{d_m^1 \displaystyle\prod_{\substack{j=i \\ j \ne m}}^{n-1} (d_j^1 - d_m^1) \prod_{j=i}^{n-1} (d_j^2 - d_m^1)} \quad (m = i,\ i+1,\ \ldots,\ n-1) \\
A_{i,n}^2(m) = \dfrac{\displaystyle\prod_{j=i}^{n-1} d_j^1 d_j^2}{d_m^2 \displaystyle\prod_{\substack{j=i \\ j \ne m}}^{n-1} (d_j^2 - d_m^2) \prod_{j=i}^{n-1} (d_j^1 - d_m^2)} \quad (m = i,\ i+1,\ \ldots,\ n-1)
\end{array}\right\},
$$
(9)

where $A_{i,n}^1(m)$ and $A_{i,n}^2(m)$ hold the following relation:

$$
\sum_{m=i}^{n-1} \left[A_{i,n}^1(m) + A_{i,n}^2(m) \right] = 1.
$$
(10)

3.2 State Occupancy Probability

Let $P_{A,B}(t)$ be the state occupancy probabilities, that is,

$$
P_{A,B}(t) \equiv \Pr\{X(t) = B \mid X(0) = A\} \quad (A,\ B \in \{W,\ L,\ R\}).
$$
(11)

We have the following renewal equation of $P_{W_i,W_n}(t)$:

$$\left.\begin{aligned}
P_{W_i,W_n}(t) &= G_{i,n} * P_{W_n,W_n}(t) \\
P_{W_n,W_n}(t) &= e^{-(\theta+\lambda_n)t} + Q_{W_n,R_n} * Q_{R_n,W_n} * P_{W_n,W_n}(t) \\
&\quad + Q_{W_n,L_n} * Q_{L_n,W_n} * P_{W_n,W_n}(t) \\
&\quad + Q_{W_n,L_n} * Q_{L_n,R_n} * Q_{R_n,W_n} * P_{W_n,W_n}(t)
\end{aligned}\right\}. \tag{12}$$

The L-S transform of $P_{W_i,W_n}(t)$ is obtained as

$$\tilde{P}_{W_i,W_n}(s) = \frac{s(s+\lambda_n+\eta)(s+\mu_n)}{(s+\lambda_n+\theta+\eta)(s+d_n^1)(s+d_n^2)} \cdot \prod_{m=i}^{n-1} \frac{d_m^1 d_m^2}{(s+d_m^1)(s+d_m^2)}$$

$$= s \cdot \left[\frac{B_{i,n}^0}{s+\lambda_n+\theta+\eta} + \sum_{m=i}^{n} \left(\frac{B_{i,n}^1(m)}{s+d_m^1} + \frac{B_{i,n}^2(m)}{s+d_m^2} \right) \right]. \tag{13}$$

By inverting Eq. (13), we have $P_{W_i,W_n}(t)$ as

$$P_{W_i,W_n}(t) \equiv \Pr\{X(t) = W_n | X(0) = W_i\}$$
$$= B_{i,n}^0 e^{-(\lambda_n+\theta+\eta)t} + \sum_{m=i}^{n} \left[B_{i,n}^1(m)e^{-d_m^1 t} + B_{i,n}^2(m)e^{-d_m^2 t} \right]$$
$$(i, n = 0, 1, 2, \ldots; \ i \le n)$$

$$\left.\begin{aligned}
B_{i,n}^0 &= \frac{-\theta(\mu_n - \lambda_n - \theta - \eta)\displaystyle\prod_{j=i}^{n-1} d_j^1 d_j^2}{\displaystyle\prod_{j=i}^{n}(d_j^1 - \lambda_n - \theta - \eta)(d_j^2 - \lambda_n - \theta - \eta)} \\
&\quad (i, n = 0, 1, 2, \ldots; \ i \le n) \\[2ex]
B_{i,n}^1(m) &= \frac{(\lambda_n + \eta - d_m^1)(\mu_n - d_m^1)\displaystyle\prod_{j=i}^{n-1} d_j^1 d_j^2}{(\lambda_n + \theta + \eta - d_m^1)\displaystyle\prod_{\substack{j=i \\ j\ne m}}^{n}(d_j^1 - d_m^1)\displaystyle\prod_{j=i}^{n}(d_j^2 - d_m^1)} \\
&\quad (m = i, i+1, \ldots, n) \\[2ex]
B_{i,n}^2(m) &= \frac{(\lambda_n + \eta - d_m^2)(\mu_n - d_m^2)\displaystyle\prod_{j=i}^{n-1} d_j^1 d_j^2}{(\lambda_n + \theta + \eta - d_m^2)\displaystyle\prod_{\substack{j=i \\ j\ne m}}^{n}(d_j^2 - d_m^2)\displaystyle\prod_{j=i}^{n}(d_j^1 - d_m^2)} \\
&\quad (m = i, i+1, \ldots, n)
\end{aligned}\right\}, \tag{14}$$

where $B_{i,n}^0$, $B_{i,n}^1(m)$, and $B_{i,n}^2(m)$ hold the following relations:

$$\left.\begin{aligned}
B_{i,i}^0 + B_{i,i}^1(i) + B_{i,i}^2(i) &= 1 \quad (i = n) \\
B_{i,n}^0 + \sum_{m=i}^{n} \left[B_{i,n}^1(m) + B_{i,n}^2(m) \right] &= 0 \quad (i < n)
\end{aligned}\right\}. \tag{15}$$

Similarly, we have the following renewal equation of $P_{W_i,R_n}(t)$:

$$\left.\begin{array}{l} P_{W_i,R_n}(t) = G_{i,n} * H_{W_n,R_n} * P_{R_n,R_n}(t) \\ P_{R_n,R_n}(t) = e^{-\mu_n t} + Q_{R_n,W_n} * H_{W_n,R_n} * P_{R_n,R_n}(t) \end{array}\right\}, \qquad (16)$$

where $H_{W_n,R_n}(t)$ has appeared in Eq. (7). The L-S transform of $P_{W_i,R_n}(t)$ is obtained as

$$\begin{aligned} \widetilde{P}_{W_i,R_n}(s) &= \frac{s}{a\mu_n} \cdot \frac{a\lambda_n\mu_n}{(s+d_n^1)(s+d_n^2)} \cdot \widetilde{G}_{i,n}(s) \\ &= \frac{s}{a\mu_n}\widetilde{G}_{i,n+1}(s), \end{aligned} \qquad (17)$$

where $d_n^1 d_n^2 = a\lambda_n\mu_n$ from Eq. (9). By inverting Eq. (17), we obtain $P_{W_i,R_n}(t)$ as

$$\begin{aligned} P_{W_i,R_n}(t) &\equiv \Pr\{X(t) = R_n | X(0) = W_i\} \\ &= \frac{g_{i,n+1}(t)}{a\mu_n} \quad (i, n = 0,\ 1,\ 2,\ \ldots;\ i \le n), \end{aligned} \qquad (18)$$

where $g_{i,n}(t) \equiv dG_{i,n}(t)/dt$ is the density function of $S_{i,n}$. We note that $P_{W_i,R_n}(t)$ has no bearing on the parameters θ and η.

Let $\{Y(t), t \ge 0\}$ be the counting process representing the cumulative number of faults corrected at the time point t. Then we have the following relationship:

$$\begin{aligned} \{Y(t) = n | X(0) = W_i\} &\Longleftrightarrow \\ \{X(t) = W_n | X(0) = W_i\} \cup \{X(t) = R_n | X(0) = W_i\} &\cup \{X(t) = U_n | X(0) = W_i\} \\ &(i \le n). \qquad (19) \end{aligned}$$

Furthermore, the probability mass function of $\{Y(t), t \ge 0\}$ is given by

$$\Pr\{Y(t) = n | X(0) = W_i\} = G_{i,n}(t) - G_{i,n+1}(t). \qquad (20)$$

Accordingly, $P_{W_i,L_n}(t)$ is given by

$$\begin{aligned} P_{W_i,L_n}(t) &\equiv \Pr\{X(t) = L_n | X(0) = W_i\} \\ &= G_{i,n}(t) - G_{i,n+1}(t) - P_{W_i,W_n}(t) - P_{W_i,R_n}(t) \\ &(i, n = 0,\ 1,\ 2,\ \ldots;\ i \le n), \qquad (21) \end{aligned}$$

since the events $\{X(t) = W_n | X(0) = W_i\}$, $\{X(t) = R_n | X(0) = W_i\}$, and $\{X(t) = L_n | X(0) = W_i\}$ are mutually exclusive.

3.3 Software Service Availability Measures

Hereafter, we set the time point where the i-th fault-removal is complete at the time origin $t = 0$.

The instantaneous software availability is defined as

$$A_{(i)}(t) \equiv \sum_{n=i}^{\infty} [P_{W_i,W_n}(t) + P_{W_i,L_n}(t)]$$

$$= 1 - \sum_{n=i}^{\infty} P_{W_i,R_n}(t), \qquad (22)$$

which represents the probability that the software system is operable at the time point t. This value does not consider the service performance level.

Here we consider the stochastic process $\{Z(t),\ t \geq 0\}$ representing the service level of the system (i.e., service performance capacity) at the time point t; this possible values are C, $C\delta$, and 0. We define the instantaneous software service availability as the expected value of service performance capacity at the time point t and this measure is given by

$$A_{s(i)}(t) \equiv \mathrm{E}[Z(t)|X(0) = W_i]$$
$$= C \cdot \mathrm{Pr}\{X(t) \in \boldsymbol{W}|X(0) = W_i\} + C\delta \cdot \mathrm{Pr}\{X(t) \in \boldsymbol{L}|X(0) = W_i\}$$
$$+ 0 \cdot \mathrm{Pr}\{X(t) \in \boldsymbol{R}|X(0) = W_i\}$$

$$= C \sum_{n=i}^{\infty} [P_{W_i,W_n}(t) + \delta P_{W_i,L_n}(t)]. \qquad (23)$$

The notion of the instantaneous software service availability is based on that of the computation availability proposed by Beaudry [4].

We should note that the cumulative number of faults corrected at the time origin, i.e., integer i cannot be observed immediately since this model assumes the imperfect debugging environment. However, we can easily observe the number of debugging activities and the cumulative number of faults corrected after the completion of the l-th debugging, N_l, is distributed with the probability mass function $\mathrm{Pr}\{N_l = i\} = \binom{l}{i}a^i b^{l-i}$. Therefore, we can convert Eqs. (22) and (23) into the functions of the number of debuggings, l, as

$$A(t; l) = \sum_{i=0}^{l} \binom{l}{i} a^i b^{l-i} A_{(i)}(t) \quad (l = 0,\ 1,\ 2,\ \ldots), \qquad (24)$$

$$A_s(t; l) = \sum_{i=0}^{l} \binom{l}{i} a^i b^{l-i} A_{s(i)}(t) \quad (l = 0,\ 1,\ 2,\ \ldots), \qquad (25)$$

respectively. Equations (24) and (25) represent the instantaneous software availability and the instantaneous software service availability, given that the l-th debugging was complete at time point $t = 0$, respectively. We note that Eq. (24) is identical with one derived in [23].

4   Numerical Examples

Using the model discussed above, we present several numerical illustrations of software service availability assessment, where we apply $\lambda_n \equiv Dc^n$ $(D > 0,\ 0 <$

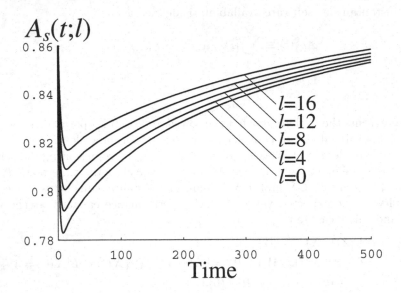

Fig. 2. $A_s(t;l)$ for various number of debuggings, l ($\theta = 5.0$, $\eta = 48.0$, $C = 1.0$, $\delta = 0.5$)

$c < 1$) and $\mu_n \equiv E r^n$ ($E > 0$, $0 < r \leq 1$) to the hazard and the restoration rates, respectively [28].

We cite the estimates of the parameters associated with λ_n and μ_n from Ref. [19], i.e., we use the following values:

$$\widehat{D} = 0.246, \ \widehat{c} = 0.940, \ \widehat{E} = 1.114, \ \widehat{r} = 0.960,$$

where we set $a = 0.8$. These values have been estimated based on the simulated data set generated from data cited by Goel and Okumoto [29]; this consists of 26 software failure-occurrence time-interval data and the unit of time is day. The detail of parameter estimation of λ_n and μ_n is described in [19].

Figure 2 shows the instantaneous software service availability, $A_s(t;l)$, in Eq. (25) for various number of debuggings, l, in the case where the system service degradation occurs five times a day on average ($\theta = 5.0$) and the mean service degradation time is 30 minutes (E$[T_{sd}] = 1/\eta = 1/48.0$) and the degraded service performance level is half of desirable level, i.e., $C = 1.0$ and $\delta = 0.5$. This figure displays that software service availability improves as the debugging process progresses (i.e., the inherent software reliability growth occurs).

Hereafter, we show evaluation examples after the completion of the 26th debugging activity.

Without software failure-occurrence, we might consider only two states; operational states with desirable service performance, denoted as state W, and with

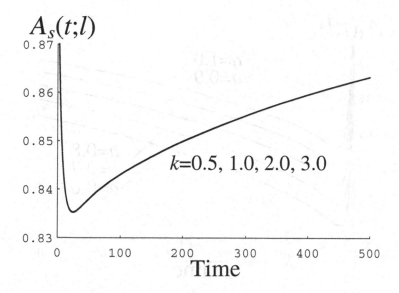

Fig. 3. $A_s(t;l)$ for various values of θ and η, given $\theta/\eta = 5/48$ ($l = 26$; $C = 1.0$, $\delta = 0.5$)

degraded service performance, denoted as state L. Then the state occupancy probabilities are given by

$$P_{W,W}(t) \equiv \Pr\{X(t) = W | X(0) = W\}$$

$$= \frac{\eta}{\theta + \eta} + \frac{\theta}{\theta + \eta} e^{-(\theta + \eta)t}$$

$$= \frac{1}{\nu + 1} + \frac{\nu}{\nu + 1} e^{-\eta(\nu + 1)t}, \tag{26}$$

$$P_{W,L}(t) \equiv \Pr\{X(t) = L | X(0) = W\}$$

$$= \frac{\theta}{\theta + \eta}\left[1 - e^{-(\theta + \eta)t}\right]$$

$$= \frac{\nu}{\nu + 1}\left[1 - e^{-\eta(\nu + 1)t}\right], \tag{27}$$

respectively, where we denote $\nu \equiv \theta/\eta$, and the limiting software service availability is obtained as

$$A_s \equiv \lim_{t \to \infty} C[P_{W,W}(t) + \delta P_{W,L}(t)]$$

$$= \frac{C(1 + \delta\nu)}{\nu + 1}. \tag{28}$$

Equations (26), (27), and (28) imply that the limiting software service availability depends on the ratio of θ and η, rather than individual values of θ and η, and that the larger values of both of θ and η with their ratio constant, in other words,

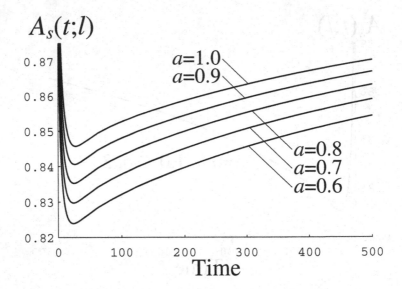

Fig. 4. $A_s(t; l)$ for various values of perfect debugging probability, a ($l = 26$; $\theta = 5.0$, $\eta = 48.0$, $C = 1.0$, $\delta = 0.5$)

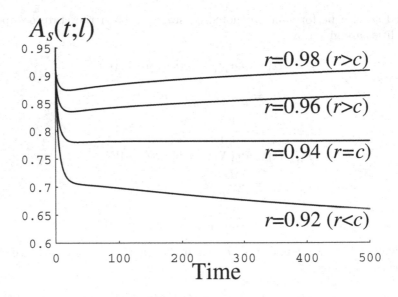

Fig. 5. $A_s(t; l)$ for various values of decreasing ratio of restoration rate, r ($l = 26$; $\theta = 5.0$, $\eta = 48.0$, $C = 1.0$, $\delta = 0.5$)

the situation where the cycle between state W and state L becomes shorter converge the software service availability to A_s faster. However, the evaluation considering software failure-occurrence in this paper is different from the above mention. Figure 3 shows the dependence of $A_s(t;l)$ on the values of k, given θ/η is constant, where we set $\theta_0 = 5.0$ and $\eta_0 = 48.0$, then $\theta = k\theta_0$ and $\eta = k\eta_0$. In the case without software failure-occurrence, we can see that the larger value of k converges to A_s faster from the form of Eqs. (26) and (27). On the other hand, Fig. 3 displays that the behavior of $A_s(t;l)$ is almost same in any case of k; this tells us that the the software service availability almost depends on only the value of θ/η, not individual values of θ and η.

Figure 4 shows the dependence of $A_s(t;l)$ on the values of perfect debugging probability, a. This figure indicates that the higher debugging ability contributes to faster improvement of software service availability.

Figure 5 shows the dependence of $A_s(t;l)$ on the value of r, representing the decreasing ratio of the restoration rate, μ_n. According to [23], the behavior of the maintenance factor, $\rho_n \equiv \lambda_n/\mu_n$ $(n = 0, 1, 2, \ldots)$, decides whether the instantaneous software availability given by Eq. (24) or the average software availability improve or degrade with time, i.e., the traditional software availability improves (degrades) if ρ_n is a decreasing (increasing) function of the cumulative number of corrected faults, n. From Fig. 5, we can see that ρ_n has a similar impact on software service performance evaluation. In the case of $r = c$, the traditional software availability converges to $1/(\rho_0 + 1) = 1/[(D/E) + 1]$, while the software service availability converges to

$$A_{s0} = \frac{A_s}{\rho_0 + 1}, \tag{29}$$

which is different value from A_s in Eq. (28).

5 Concluding Remarks

In this paper, we have discussed the service-oriented software availability modeling with two different operational levels; one is the desirable operational state providing with service performance according to specification and the other is providing with degraded service performance. This model has considered the software reliability growth process and the upward tendency of difficulty in debugging. The time-dependent behavior of the system has been described by a Markov process. Several closed form expressions of stochastic quantities for software service availability measurement have been derived from our model. In particular, we have proposed the new measure referred to as the instantaneous software service availability which is defined as the expected value of service processing quantity per unit time; this is given as the function of time and the number of debugging activities. Numerical examples of the proposed measure have also been illustrated to investigate the relationship between the inherent software reliability growth characteristics and the system service performance evaluation. Most of previous works such as [8], [9], [10], [11], [12], and [16] have conducted the performance evaluation of the software system only in steady states; this means that they have not considered the reliability growth process although there is originally a possibility of dynamic quality/reliability growth of software systems. This paper has overcome the above issue by extending the existing software availability model and enables us to evaluate the service-oriented availability as well; this knowledge is very meaningful.

Expansion to the model considering the multiple level of service performance degradation remains as one of future studies. Furthermore, one of interesting issues is to consider the service availability assessment which is conscious of the mission time interval of the users [30,31,32].

Acknowledgments

This work was supported in part by Grants-in-Aid for Scientific Research (C) of the Ministry of Education, Culture, Sports, Science and Technology of Japan under Grant No. 18510124.

References

1. Gray, J., Siewiorek, D.P.: High-availability computer system. Computer 24, 39–48 (1991)
2. Tortorella, M.: Service reliability theory and engineering, I: Foundations. Quality Technology and Quantitative Management 2, 1–16 (2005)
3. Tortorella, M.: Service reliability theory and engineering, II: Models and examples. Quality Technology and Quantitative Management 2, 17–37 (2005)
4. Beaudry, M.D.: Performance-related reliability measures for computing systems. IEEE Transactions on Computers C-27, 540–547 (1978)
5. Meyer, J.F.: On evaluating the performability of degradable computing systems. IEEE Transactions on Computers C-29, 720–731 (1980)
6. Nakamura, M., Osaki, S.: Performance/reliability evaluation of a multi-processor system with computational demands. International Journal of Systems Sciences 15, 95–105 (1984)
7. Sols, A.: System degraded availability. Reliability Engineering & System Safety 56, 91–94 (1997)
8. Pfening, A., Garg, S., Puliafito, A., Telek, M., Trivedi, S.K.: Optimal software rejuvenation for tolerating soft failures. Performance Evaluation, 27–28, 491–506 (1996)
9. Garg, S., Puliafito, A., Telek, M., Trivedi, S.K.: Analysis of preventive maintenance in transactions based software systems. IEEE Transactions on Computers 47, 96–107 (1998)
10. Eto, H., Dohi, T.: Analysis of a service degradation model with preventive rejuvenation. In: Penkler, D., Reitenspiess, M., Tam, F. (eds.) ISAS 2006. LNCS, vol. 4328, pp. 17–29. Springer, Heidelberg (2006)
11. Kimura, M., Yamada, S.: Performance evaluation modeling for redundant real-time software systems (in Japanese). Transactions of IEICE J78-D-I, 708–715 (1995)
12. Kimura, M., Yamamoto, M., Yamada, S.: Performance evaluation modeling for fault-tolerant software systems with processing time limit (in Japanese). Journal of Reliability Engineering Association of Japan 20, 422–432 (1998)
13. Avižienis, A.: The N-version approach to fault-tolerant software. IEEE Transactions on Software Engineering SE-11, 1491–1501 (1985)

14. Randell, B.: System structure for software fault-tolerance. IEEE Transactions on Software Engineering SE-1, 220–232 (1975)
15. Malek, M.: A consensus-based model for responsive computing. IEICE Transactions on Information and Systems E76-D, 1319–1324 (1993)
16. Rinsaka, K., Dohi, T.: Behavioral analysis of a fault-tolerant software system with rejuvenation. IEICE Transactions on Information and Systems E88-D, 2681–2690 (2005)
17. Huang, Y., Kintala, C., Kolettis, N., Fulton, N.D.: Software rejuvenation: Analysis, module and applications. In: Proceedings of the 25th International Symposium on Fault Tolerant Computing, pp. 381–390. IEEE Computer Society Press, Los Alamitos (1995)
18. Musa, J.D.: Software Reliability Engineering. McGraw-Hill, New York (1999)
19. Tokuno, K., Yamada, S.: Stochastic performance evaluation for multi-task processing system with software availability model. Journal of Quality in Maintenance Engineering 12, 412–424 (2006)
20. Ross, S.M.: Introduction to Probability Models, 9th edn. Academic Press, New York (2007)
21. Tokuno, K., Fukuda, M., Yamada, S.: Stochastic performance evaluation for software system considering NHPP task arrival. International Journal of Performability Engineering 4, 57–70 (2008)
22. Muppala, J.K., Woolet, S.P., Trivedi, K.S.: Real-time-systems performance in the presence of failures. Computer 24, 37–47 (1991)
23. Tokuno, K., Yamada, S.: Markovian software availability measurement based on the number of restoration actions. IEICE Transactions on Fundamentals E83-A, 835–841 (2000)
24. Shooman, M.L., Trivedi, A.K.: A many-state Markov model for computer software performance parameters. IEEE Transactions on Reliability R-25, 66–68 (1976)
25. Okumoto, K., Goel, A.L.: Availability and other performance measures for system under imperfect maintenance. In: Proceedings of COMPSAC 1978, pp. 66–71 (1978)
26. Kim, J.H., Kim, Y.H., Park, C.J.: A modified Markov model for the estimation of computer software performance. Operations Research Letters 1, 253–257 (1982)
27. Osaki, S.: Applied Stochastic System Modeling. Springer, Heidelberg (1992)
28. Moranda, P.B.: Event-altered rate models for general reliability analysis. IEEE Transactions on Reliability R-28, 376–381 (1979)
29. Goel, A.L., Okumoto, K.: Time-dependent error-detection rate model for software reliability and other performance measures. IEEE Transactions on Reliability R-28, 206–211 (1979)
30. Rubino, G., Sericola, B.: Interval availability analysis using operational periods. Performance Evaluation 14, 257–272 (1992)
31. Platis, A.: A generalized formulation for performability indicator. Computers and Mathematics with Applications 51, 239–246 (2006)
32. Carrasco, J.A.: Two methods for computing bounds for the distribution of cumulative reward for large Markov models. Performance Evaluation 63, 1165–1195 (2006)

Execution Path Profiling for OS Device Drivers: Viability and Methodology*

Constantin Sârbu[1], Andréas Johansson[2], and Neeraj Suri[1]

[1] Department of Computer Science – Technische Universität Darmstadt,
Hochschulstr. 10, D–64289 Darmstadt, Germany
{cs,suri}@cs.tu-darmstadt.de
[2] Department of Mechatronics and Software – Volvo Technology Corporation,
Sven Hultins gata 9C, SE–41288 Göteborg, Sweden
andreas.olof.johansson@volvo.com

Abstract. Operating Systems (OSs) mediate across the hardware and software applications, leading to overall system service provision, but often sacrifice service robustness while favoring increasing feature richness and peripheral support. The OS interface to peripherals is implemented by components termed as *Device Drivers* (DDs). Unfortunately, despite extensive testing, DDs continue to constitute the prominent cause of system service failures.

To find DD's weakness areas, this paper proposes a novel technique for profiling kernel mode DDs execution paths. Such profiles highlight the frequently used parts of a driver for a workload, helping identify redundant tests. The communication interfaces between the OS and DDs are simultaneously monitored, revealing the kernel functions invoked at runtime and the followed code paths. To highlight execution hotspots, a cluster analysis scheme using string similarity metrics is proposed to distribute the code paths into equivalence classes, reflecting the occurrence weights of both kernel functions and code paths.

Keywords: Operating System, Device Driver, Code Path Profiling, Cluster Analysis, Black-box Testing.

1 Introduction

COTS OSs are invariably required to balance the tradeoff between service dependability and service performance. Often performance aspects are favored in order to offer extensive support for a wide spectrum of applications and peripherals. The OS interface to peripherals, namely device drivers (DDs), are typically produced by third-party developers, often lacking the necessary skill and knowledge required to develop high quality and robust DDs. Moreover, under the pressure to fulfill market demands, resources allocated to DD testing are often limited. Thus, while OS kernels have reached a certain maturity, the DDs are

---

* This research has been supported, in part, by Microsoft Research, EU FP6 NoE ReSIST and DFG TUD GK-MM.

T. Nanya et al. (Eds.): ISAS 2008, LNCS 5017, pp. 90–109, 2008.

prematurely released and therefore are more likely prone to failures, affecting the overall provisioning of OS' service robustness.

With hundreds of devices attached to each ordinary computing system (about 250 in a Windows XP or Vista installation [1]) the drivers' code represents a significant share of the total OS code. In Linux, for instance, about 70% of the total lines of code belongs to DDs [2]. Given the immaturity of their code, this trend suggests that driver code is responsible for many OS service outages. This observation is confirmed by the OS reliability research community's results from several independent [3], academic [4,5,6,2,7] and industry [8] sources.

As DDs coexist in privileged space with critical OS kernel structures, an error in a defective DD can propagate to the kernel, eventually leading to degraded OS service level or even generalized system failure. Recent studies [9,10] have shown that OS kernels are permeable to error propagation, mostly due to the fact that in kernel space various components communicate under a "gentleman's agreement". This means that, for the sake of performance, kernel components perform only minimal (if any!) parameter validation, assuming that their communication parties are error-free and non-malicious. DDs should also follow this policy, hence passing the responsibility of producing error-free code to driver developers. This means that, beside programming experience, driver developers have to possess a deep understanding of OS kernel intricacies and be fully aware of the DD's runtime context.

It is reasonable that system integrators themselves test the DDs installed in their systems to verify that the specified level of service and reliability is provided. Typically, *black-box* testing is the only viable approach. Therefore, working continually under deadline pressure, system integrators limit DD testing to simpler acceptance and integration tests.

Execution profiling information is an important prerequisite for helping rigorous DD validation. It is an abstract model describing how a DD behaves under the influence of external stimuli. As such it can help DD testers identify which part of the DD code is most exercised for a representative workload. This can be used to guide selection of test cases, by focusing on the *most frequently used parts in an operational setting*, which may substantially differ from statically selected test cases.

Regardless, the ability to identify DD execution profiles increasingly represents a serious technical challenge as: (a) the access to the OS kernel space is limited (debugging is non-trivial); (b) the access to source code is limited (usually, testers cannot access the source code of the tested object); and (c) envisioning the runtime environment for COTS DDs is difficult (virtually each individual computing system has its own unique set of HW and SW components).

1.1 Paper Emphasis and Contributions

With the overall aim to enhance OS robustness, in this paper we develop a profiling methodology for kernel-mode DD execution paths by considering an additional communication interface alongside with the I/O requests considered in our prior work [11,12]. In this communication paradigm, at runtime, a DD acts as a consumer of the services (i.e., functions) provided by various kernel libraries. Therefore, a DD's runtime activity can be defined by the sequences of calls made to external functions. As DDs act on kernel calls, the call sequences are delimited by the I/O requests generated by the OS, and thus infer the execution path taken in the DD's code, helping to evaluate and to compare the effects of different workloads (i.e., test suites or individual test cases) by revealing execution hotspots. The presented process for caption and evaluation of the call traces does not require source code access to any of the involved components.

The presented results show a key phenomenon, the tendency of call traces to cluster with respect to the code being executed. We consequently present a cluster analysis method to ascertain the relative similarity of the code paths taken. The obtained trace clusters represent (together with their occurrence indexes) effective representations of a DD's execution hotspots. From a testing perspective, this strongly indicates the possibility to significantly reduce the testing effort needed to cover the exercised code paths by thoroughly testing only a single representative code path from each equivalence class.

Additionally, we show how the number of equivalence classes can be decided by varying the similarity threshold (the cutoff factor of the dendrogram - a tree-like structure describing the clustering). This represents a powerful tool for directing the efforts that a subsequent testing campaign needs undergo.

Overall, this paper outlines a methodology to obtain execution profiles for kernel DDs, and ascertain its viability against a set of actual Windows DDs. By using tracing information from two driver communication interfaces, our technique provides insights that help understand a DD's runtime behavior in terms of execution paths. The main contributions of this paper are:

- A novel method to accurately profile a driver's runtime behavior in terms of the called kernel services.
- An occurrence-weighted list of kernel functions accessed by a driver indicating possible error propagation paths among kernel libraries and drivers.
- A novel application of clustering algorithms to identify and tune equivalence classes of test cases.
- A tendency of call traces to cluster is demonstrated in a real-world scenario, outlining execution hotspots for an actual DD (the floppy disk driver).

1.2   Paper Organization

The paper is organized as follows. Section 2 introduces the related work, followed in Sects. 3, 4 and 5 by the presentation of the terminology and main work concepts used throughout the paper. After a discussion on clustering aspects in Sect. 6, Sects. 7 and 8 present and then discuss the experimental validation of the method. Finally, Sect. 9 concludes and briefly presents our ongoing research activities.

2   Related Work

Weyuker recommends to focus testing of general SW onto the functionalities with high occurrence rates in the field [13, 14] in order to find faults with high likelihood to perturb service provision early on. Intuitively, such an option is enabled only under the assumption that a runtime profile of the program targeted by testing is available. Our methodology create such profiles for kernel DDs by revealing the taken code paths and the set of driver-external functionalities required at runtime. Defect localization studies for general [15] and OS-specific SW [6] support Weyuker's recommendation by showing that defects tend to cluster into certain areas of code. By profiling a DD's activity, the work presented in this paper guides a rigorous partitioning of the code by indicating runtime execution hotspots. Moreover, Weyuker warns about the necessity to validate COTS components in their new environments, even though they successfully passed their producers's testing campaigns. As our methodology is completely disconnected from the need to access any OS part's source code, it can be used for black-box level DD profiling, thus easing the testing efforts of a DD's user.

Johansson et al. proposed in [16] a selection method for SWIFI injection triggers which is based on call blocks of driver-external functions. The methodology presented in this paper for profile construction is similar in terms of the used monitoring strategy, but in contrast we consider the effects of the kernel's I/O requests on the DD's behavior. Mendonca and Neves [1] used a SWIFI technique to evaluate the robustness of the kernel libraries. The target functions were selected statically, by inspecting the import tables of the DDs (see 5.1) of several Windows installations and choosing the ones that are used by most of the DDs. In accordance with Weyuker's recommendations, our results suggest that the target functions should be selected on a dynamic basis (using profiling) by building occurrence indexes to guide the selection process.

Ball and Larus [17] acknowledged the application of path profiling for test coverage assessment, *"by profiling a program and reporting unexecuted statements or control flow"*. They used binary instrumentation to obtain instruction traces that reveal a program's control-flow to identify paths and their execution frequencies. The paths ended at loop and procedure boundaries. An extension is represented by the *"whole program paths"* described in [18], which cross both boundaries to reveal a better picture of a program's execution pattern. Though, these approaches are not directly applicable to DD as the they are implemented as function libraries rather than programs in the classical sense. Moreover, instrumentation induces a high execution overhead and produces large amounts of data, two characteristics which penalize the use of this approach inside the OS kernel space.

Leon and Podgursky [19] used profiles generated by individual test cases and a clustering technique for evaluating test suite minimization by selecting one test case per cluster. The profiles used were generated by third-party tools, so the cluster analysis had to rely on their accuracy. While test cost reduction is out of the scope of this paper, we focus on building viable and accurate DD profiles, as a prerequisite mean to reducing test efforts.

3   System Model: The Entailed OS Kernel Components

In this paper we consider a model of a computing system as depicted in Fig. 1.
It represents a computer equipped with Windows XP, the chosen OS for the case
studies presented in Sect. 7. Nevertheless, the system in Fig. 1 is general enough
to represent the architecture of most of contemporary COTS OSs. Here, the OS
defines the layer between the hardware and user-mode applications. It provides
to the applications an abstract view of the hardware peripherals and a set of
services for accessing and managing them. In Fig. 1, the entities relevant for the
approach are located inside the OS kernel space.

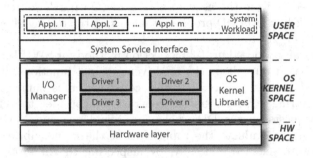

Fig. 1. A HW-SW system featuring a COTS OS with n DDs (*Windows XP*)

The *System Service Interface* provides a uniform service interface to the applications. That is, applications issue access requests to different services offered
by the OS and this abstraction layer translates them into specific calls to various
OS structures, hiding the diversity of the peripheral access interfaces from the
applications.

The *device drivers* (DDs) can be considered device-specialized toolboxes to
access each particular hardware peripheral. The DDs are loaded by the OS at
initialization time or on demand, when it needs to communicate with a certain
hardware device. In Windows XP, the structure of the DDs is specified by the
Windows Driver Model (WDM) [20]. WDM defines the format of the kernel
structures associated with DDs, the programming interface they need to follow
and the communication paradigm with the I/O Manager, described below. To
support the concepts described by the WDM, a Driver Developer Kit (DDK)
containing tools and documentation is available for DD development.

The *I/O Manager* is a combination of various OS kernel structures with role
in naming, registering and managing the DD objects. The I/O Manager is concerned with preparing and sending commands to the DDs, for OS administrative
purposes or on behalf of the applications. Also, the I/O Manager prepares the
results of the I/O invocations of the peripherals (received from the corresponding
DDs) and forwards them to the calling applications. Section 4 contains a more
detailed discussion on DD's interaction with the I/O Manager.

The *OS Kernel Libraries* are dynamic-linked libraries implementing general functionality and mechanisms that ensure core OS service provision (i.e., process and thread management, synchronization primitives, scheduling). In the Windows-family OSs the kernel libraries are built as portable executables, following the PE/Coff standard [21]. The DDs and other kernel components use the services offered by the kernel libraries by calling their exported functions. Section 5 discusses in detail how DDs use the functionalities stored in kernel libraries.

4 Developing the Basis for Code Tracing: The I/O Request Packet (IRP) Interface

I/O Request Packets (IRP) are kernel structures built by the I/O Manager when a request needs to be sent to a DD. The IRP structure contains the request type and the parameters needed by the recipient DD to start executing the request-associated activity. When a result of the operation is available, the DD uses the same IRP structure to piggyback it back to the I/O Manager.

Currently, WDM specifies 28 types of IRP requests (for instance READ for reading data from the device and CLEANUP for preparing the device for unload etc.). A DD must implement dispatch functions for every IRP type it supports and register its list of supported IRPs with the I/O Manager. This request type-based code separation of WDM-compliand DDs is relevant for our approach, as one can infer the functionality executed at any instant, based only on the type of the issued IRP.

4.1 The Processing of I/O Requests

To illustrate how an I/O request is processed, consider a simple example of an application that issues a read request to a hardware device. Figure 2 depicts this procedure where the main stages are: (1) the application calls ReadFile function of the WinAPI; (2) the WinAPI traps the OS kernel into the I/O Manager which selects the DD managing the target HW device; (3) the I/O Manager encodes the I/O request in an IRP structure and forwards it to the DD; (4) the DD contacts the HW device, instructs it to retrieve the data and completes the IRP; (5) the I/O Manager reads the completion information from the IRP and (6) returns the result to the WinAPI, in terms of a pointer to data; (7) the WinAPI copies the data to a buffer accessible to the calling application (in user space) and (8) informs the application about the result of the operation and the location of the requested data. In this paper, we capture the IRP flow between the I/O Manager and a DD. At this communication interface, two relevant events are recorded: *incoming IRPs* (from I/O Manager to DD, step (3)) and *outgoing IRPs* (from DD to the I/O Manager, step (5)). Onwards, we call this communication level the *"IRP interface"*.

According to the WDM specification, each HW device has at least two drivers servicing it, the *function driver* and *the bus driver*. The function driver is handling the receipt and completion of IRPs, whereas the bus driver is responsible

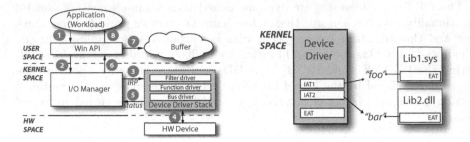

Fig. 2. Processing of I/O requests

Fig. 3. A DD importing functions from two libraries

for connecting the device with the host computer, being usually the driver located closest to the HW peripheral. On top of the function driver, a driver stack can contain one or several *filter drivers*, which act as wrappers for the underlying drivers. Filter drivers are usually responsible for the preparation of the the IRP structure or initialization of other kernel structures needed by the drivers located below in the stack.

In order to capture the IRP flow we have built a filter driver and installed it on the top of the driver stack. Its location enables it to be the first to receive the incoming IRPs and the last to see the outgoing ones. Our filter driver logs the incoming and outgoing IRPs and forwards them, unchanged, to their original recipients while keeping the induced computational overhead to minimum. As each incoming IRP triggers the execution of a dispatch function and each outgoing IRP signals the termination of the associated computation, we use the captured IRP flow logs to specify a DD's activity at any certain instant. The filter driver is written with portability in mind, so that it can be installed on top of any WDM-compliant DD, without requiring modifications.

4.2   Mode, Transition and Operational Profile of a Device Driver

As we do not assume access to the DD's source code, we consider that DD state changes are caused by the I/O request flow having the DD as recipient. In our previous work [11] we introduced an abstracted DD state definition called *mode* that allows for expressing DD activity at runtime. The *mode of a driver* is defined as follows:

Definition 1 (Driver Mode). *The mode of a driver D is the tuple of binary predicates, each assigned to one of the n distinct IRP types supported by the driver:*

$$M^D : \; < P_{IRP_1} \; P_{IRP_2} \; P_{IRP_3} \; .. \; P_{IRP_n} >, \quad where \, P_{IRP_i} \; is$$

$$P_{IRP_i} = \begin{cases} 1, & \textit{if \textbf{performing} the functionality triggered by receival of } IRP_i \\ 0, & \textit{otherwise} \end{cases}$$

A *transition* between modes is triggered by the receival of a new IRP or completing an executed IRP. As the I/O Manager serializes the IRP flow, our model assumes that only one bit of the tuple describing the mode of the DD is flipped at a time. Therefore, the DD can switch only to modes whose binary tuples are within Hamming distance of 1 from the current mode. Because of this behavior, the number of possible transitions in the model is $n \cdot 2^n$ (each mode can be left on n exit transitions).

We call the set of the modes (N_{op}) visited under a certain workload relevant for the DD, together with the traversed transitions (T_{op}) the *operational profile* of the DD. In [11] we have demonstrated that irrespective of the chosen workload, the operational profile is a small subset of the total, theoretically-possible state space of the DD ($N_{op} \ll 2^n$ and $T_{op} \ll n \cdot 2^n$).

5 Developing the Basis for Code Tracing: The Functional Interface

The communication between OS kernel and DDs is not limited to the IRP scheme. A DD also communicates with the OS kernel using a second interface, which we onwards call the *"functional interface"*. Enabled by the concept of dynamic linking, at this communication level the parties involved are kernel libraries and DDs, as image files. In fact, this scheme forms the basis of OS modularity, and is the most commonly used data communication paradigm between binaries. The OS provides a set of kernel libraries containing functions required by the different kernel components. Each library publishes a list of the available functions. On the other side, the DDs (as consumers of the services provided by the libraries) contain a list of necessary libraries and for each of them a list of the used functions from the respective library. For both kernel libraries and DDs the lists mentioned above are stored in the headers of the binary files.

5.1 The PE/COFF Executable Format and DLL-Proxying

In Windows, the PE/COFF format [21] specifies the file headers that permit a Windows executable file to publish the contained functions and variables (*exports*) and to use functions defined externally by another library (*imports*). The example in Fig. 3 depicts a DD that imports functions implemented in two external libraries, `Lib1.sys` and `Lib2.dll`. Each contains an Export Address Table (EAT) that publishes a list of functions exported by the respective library. At runtime, the DD links to the kernel libraries on demand, when the result of the functions `foo` and, respectively, `bar` are needed. Therefore, the header of the DD file contains an Import Address Table (IAT) for each of the needed libraries. The IAT contains only the function names which are used in the DD's code.

At DD load time, the OS automatically checks if all the required libraries are present in the system by inspecting the DD's IATs. If they cannot be found, an error message is issued and the DD loading is aborted. At load time, no verification is done to check if the libraries found actually contain the necessary functions for the DD to execute correctly. Only at runtime, when a portion of DD code containing calls to external functions is reached, the DD accesses the associated library to utilize its services.

The work presented in this paper relies on the ability to capture the calls to external functions at DD runtime. While various methods for capturing calls to externally located functions exist (eg., Detours [22], Spike [23]), they are specific to user-space software and are therefore not directly applicable to kernel-mode programs. In contrast, we need a kernel space mechanism to monitor the function calls. Therefore, we have chosen to implement a *DLL-proxying* technique. Briefly, DLL-proxying consists of building a DLL library which act as a wrapper of the original library. In order to leave the functionality of the DD unaffected, the wrapper library has to implement all the functions required by the DD, or to forward its calls to the original library. By modifying the IAT tables of the target DD to point to the wrapper library instead of the original one, the wrapper library (also called *DLL-proxy*) is interposed between the two parties. Section 7 details our implementation of DLL-proxies inside the Windows kernel.

Our kernel-mode library wrappers are used exclusively for capturing the sequences of functions called by a DD at runtime, when exercised by a selected workload. Consequently, we only need to log the function names but not modify any parameters or behavior of the wrapped kernel APIs. Therefore, the overhead induced by the DLL-proxy is kept to minimum.

5.2   Call Strings as Code Path Abstractions

As external function calls correspond to DD code being executed as a result of IRP requests (or other OS kernel maintenance requests), grouping them using IRPs as boundaries is intuitive. Therefore, we introduce the notion of *call string* as follows:

Definition 2 (Call String). *A call string (CS) is a sequence of DD-external function calls issued at runtime by a DD, delimited by incoming and outgoing IRP requests.*

In this paper we consider each CS an abstraction representing the code path taken by the DD at execution time. As we use the incoming and outgoing IRP requests as CS delimiters, each CS can be associated with a DD mode and, subsequently, with an IRP dispatch function.

Illustrating the CS capturing method, the left part of Fig. 4 shows an abstract representation of the WDM-compliant DD's code with dispatch functions for handling READ and WRITE requests. Assuming that the DD can handle only those two IRP requests, the visited modes are defined by bit strings with length two; the first bit is associated with READ and the second with WRITE operation. Note that both dispatch subroutines call functions implemented externally by other kernel libraries. Assuming that at a certain instant the DD receives the READ request followed by an WRITE request, the log file that combines the events recorded by monitoring the two communication interfaces is depicted on the

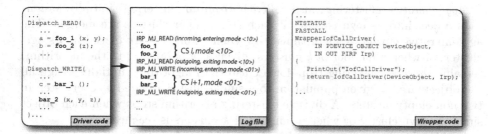

Fig. 4. The code path taken in a DD when READ and WRITE requests are called

```
...
NTSTATUS
FASTCALL
WrapperIofCallDriver(
        IN PDEVICE_OBJECT DeviceObject,
        IN OUT PIRP Irp)
{
    PrintOut("IofCallDriver");
    return IofCallDriver(DeviceObject, Irp);
}
...
```
Wrapper code

Fig. 5. A wrapper for the `NTOSKRNL::IofCallDriver` API

right side of Fig. 4. Hence, the call strings CS_i and CS_{i+1} can be constructed and associated with the modes $< 10 >$ and, respectively, $< 01 >$.

Consequently, the call CSs can be studied from two perspectives: (a) *per mode basis*, i.e., CSs belonging to the same DD mode are compared to reveal possible differences in the code paths taken each time the DD performs the activity associated with the respective mode, and (b) *per CS basis*, i.e., all CSs are compared among themselves to identify similarities and to group them accordingly in equivalence classes. Hence, we define the term *execution hotspot* as follows:

Definition 3 (Execution Hotspot). *A group of similar CSs belonging to the same equivalence class represents an* execution hotspot*. The magnitude of each hotspot is given by the sum of occurrences of the CSs contained within the equivalence class.*

The methodology for building kernel DD profiles presented in this paper reveals the execution hotspots together with their magnitudes. The construction of the equivalence classes is achieved by employing a cluster analysis algorithm, as described in the following section.

6 Identifying Execution Hotspots: Call String Clustering Aspects

Given the size of the pool of data collected in the monitoring phase, a data clustering method greatly facilitates organizing and interpreting the data trends. *Cluster analysis* is a multivariate technique that helps partitioning a population of objects into equivalence classes. The partitioning decision is taken on object similarity, i.e., similar objects are grouped together in the same *cluster*. The most common clustering approaches are hierarchical and partitional. Usually slower than hierarchical algorithms, the *partitional clustering* initially divides object population in k clusters (randomly), improving the clusters at each step by redistributing the objects. *Hierarchical clustering* approaches fall in two classes, agglomerative and divisive.

Agglomerative clustering (also called bottom-up clustering) initially assigns each object into its own cluster, at each step similar clusters are merged. The agglomerative clustering algorithms stop when all objects are placed in a single cluster, or when a number of k clusters (given as a parameter to the algorithm) remain. *Divisive* clustering (top-down clustering) algorithms initially assign all the objects from a given population to a single cluster, divided at every step in two non-empty clusters. A divisive clustering algorithm stops when each object sits in an own cluster or when a number of k clusters is reached.

In this paper we use automated agglomerative analysis to divide the CS population into similar clusters. We use `AgNes`, an agglomerative algorithm provided by the R statistical programming environment [24]. `AgNes` requires as input a matrix containing the distances between every pair of objects, in our case CSs. It outputs a dendrogram, which is a tree-like representation of the clustering. The Figs. 10 and 11 represent examples of such dendrograms. The CSs are represented as leaves, and branches intersect at a height equal to the dissimilarity among the children. Cutting the dendrogram at a given height reveals the clusters and the contained call sequences at the respective distance. That is, a *cutoff* of the dendrogram indicates the equivalence classes that partition the CS population for the respective distance. For a cutoff set at 0, the equivalence classes contain only the CSs which are identical. Therefore, the cutoff value acts as a tunable mask for CS diversity.

6.1   Metrics to Express Call String Similarity

To obtain relevant dendrograms of the CS clusters, an appropriate similarity metric has to be first selected. In the areas of bio-informatics and record linkage (duplicate detection) researchers have developed a series of metrics to quantify the relation between two strings. Depending on their application area, some metrics express the similarity while other measure the difference (dissimilarity) of the compared strings.

The *Levenshtein* distance (d_L) is based on the edit distance between the compared strings. Given two strings s_1 and s_2 whose distance needs to be computed, Levenshtein distance express the minimum number of operations needed to transform s_1 in s_2 or viceversa. The considered operations are character insert, delete or substitution and they all have the cost of 1. Used in bio-informatics to decide global or local alignments for protein sequences, *Needleman-Wunsch* and *Smith-Waterman* distances are versions of the Levenshtein metric, additionally considering gap penalties (gap = subsequence that do not match).

Jaro distance is not based on the edit distance, but instead on the number and order of the common characters. The Jaro distance is expressed by the following formula:

$$d_J = \frac{1}{3}\left(\frac{m}{|s_1|} + \frac{m}{|s_2|} + \frac{m-t}{m}\right) \tag{1}$$

where m is the number of matching characters and t is the number of necessary transpositions. Two characters are considered matching if they are not farther than $\left\lfloor \frac{max(|s_1|,|s_2|)}{2} \right\rfloor - 1$ from each other. An extension of the Jaro distance was proposed by Winkler, in order to reward with higher scores the strings that match from the beginning (they share a common prefix).

Therefore, the *Jaro-Winkler* distance is defined by the formula

$$d_{JW} = d_J + [0.1 \cdot l(1 - d_J)] \tag{2}$$

where l is the length of the common prefix and d_J is the Jaro distance between the strings.

Many other distance metrics exists and were evaluated for various applications [25]. We have also investigated several of them and subsequently chosen the Levenshtein and Jaro-Winkler metrics, as we believe they express best the distance among the CSs. Levenshtein was selected as it captures neutrally the variability of the CSs. As we expect the CSs to contain short, repetitive subsequences (generated by loops in the code path) and common sequences (generated by shared helper functions), we have also selected the Jaro-Winkler metric as it favors similarities between CSs showing this behavior.

To balance their effects and to minimize the impact of the metric choice on the final cluster structures, we combined them in a compound measure, a simple weighted average:

$$d_C = \frac{norm(d_L) + norm(d_{JW})}{2} \tag{3}$$

Our compound metric uses normalized values for both Levenshtein and Jaro-Winkler functions, therefore $0 \leq d_C \leq 1$. Being a dissimilarity function, small values of d_C indicate high similarity between the compared CSs. The distance matrix required by AgNes was computed using d_C for expressing the distance among every CS pairs.

6.2   Cluster Linkage Methods and Agglomeration Coefficient

Besides the distance matrix, AgNes requires that a clustering method is specified. *Simple linkage* merges at every step two clusters whose merger has the smallest diameter. This method has as disadvantage a tendency to form long cluster chains (i.e., at every step a single element is added to an existing cluster). *Complete linkage* merges clusters whose closest member objects have the smallest distance. This linkage method creates tighter clusters but is sensitive to outliers. To alleviate the disadvantages of simple and complete clusterings, *average linkage* groups clusters whose average distance between all pairs of objects is minimal.

AgNes provides a standard measure to express the strength of the clustering found in the population of CSs. A strong clustering tendency means larger inter-cluster dissimilarities and lower intra-cluster dissimilarities. If $d(i)$ is the dissimilarity of object i to the first cluster it is merged with divided by the dissimilarity of the last merger, the *agglomeration coefficient (AC)* is expressed by

AgNes as the average of all $1 - d(i)$. With $0 \leq AC \leq 1$, larger AC values indicate a good cluster structure of the object population.

For our clustering analysis experiments presented in Sect. 7 we have used the average linkage method as we believe this choice factors out best the impact of CS distance variance among the object population.

7   Evaluating the Viability of the Execution Profiling Methodology

For a comprehensive evaluation of the dual-interface DD profiling method presented in this paper, we have used it against the flpydisk.sys (v5.1.2600.2180), the floppy disk driver provided by Windows XP SP2.

Figure 6 depicts our experimental setup. To capture the requests occurring on the IRP interface of the target DD we have built a filter driver and installed it between the monitored DD and the I/O Manager. The filter driver receives the incoming and outgoing IRP requests, logs them to a file and forwards them to the original recipient. As the filter driver does not rely on the implementation details of the underlying DD, it can be used to monitor virtually any WDM-compliant DD, as shown in practice by the experimental work in [12].

The monitoring of the functional interface is more complex, as it requires building a wrapper library for each of the kernel libraries imported by the floppy driver (Fig. 6). flpydisk.sys imports functions from two kernel libraries: NTOSKRNL.EXE (61 functions) and HAL.DLL (4 functions). After building the library wrappers, the IAT tables of the target DDs were modified in order to look for the wrappers instead of the original libraries. Each API wrapper was built using exclusively the function prototypes provided in the header files available publicly from Windows DDK package. Each time the DD called a function, the API wrapper is called instead of the original function. The API wrappers are designed as extremely simple C constructs in order to minimize the computational overhead. When a wrapper is called, the call is logged and the call parameters are forwarded, unchanged, to the original function from the original library,

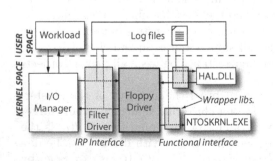

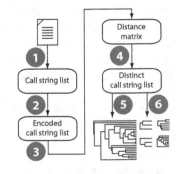

Fig. 6. Our DD monitoring strategy   **Fig. 7.** Our cluster analysis process

as depicted by the code snippet in Fig. 5. In this figure, IofCallDriver is the original function implemented by NTOSKRNL.EXE and WrapperIofCallDriver is our wrapper.

After the floppy driver is exercised by a relevant workload, the resulted log files are analyzed offline by a software application that extracts the CSs and constructs distance matrix files. These files are fed to the AgNes algorithm which builds clusterings of the CSs. More precisely, the procedure followed to build the clusterings that evaluate the CS relative similarity is depicted in Fig. 7: (1) collect the CSs by using the monitoring logs; (2) encode each function call to an Unicode character to be able to apply the string metrics; (3) calculate a distance matrix containing the distances between all pairs of CSs; (4) select the distinct CSs and count for each one the occurrence rate; (5) construct a clustering from all distinct CSs to evaluate inter-CS similarities; (6) for each mode, construct a clustering of CSs to reveal intra-mode paths.

Table 1. The workloads utilized to exercise the floppy driver and the overall experimental outcomes

| Benchmarks for flpydisk.sys | #Called Imports | | | #Modes | #CSs | | AC | Benchmark Description |
	Total	NT[1]	HAL[2]		Total	Distinct		
Sandra	27	25	2	3	9545	51	.859	Performance benchmark
DiskTestPro	28	26	2	5	588	13	.735	Surface scan, format
BurnInTest	21	19	2	5	1438	24	.823	Reliability benchmark
Enable_Disable	42	38	4	3	136	10	.388	DD load and unload
DC2	21	19	2	4	5102	9	.644	Robustness benchmark

To exercise the DD properly, we have used commercial performance and stability benchmark applications which are designed for testing the floppy disk drive. We have also used a robustness testing tool, DC2 (Device Path Exerciser). DC2 is part of the DDK package and evaluates if a DD submitted for certification with Windows is reliable enough for mass distribution. It sends the targeted DD a variety of valid and invalid (not supported, malformed etc.) I/O requests to reveal implementation vulnerabilities. The Table 1 lists the outcomes and provides a comparative evaluation of the clustering strength (see Sect. 6.2).

Sandra was the workload that issued the highest number of distinct CSs (51 out of 9545), showing the highest cluster strength in the distinct CS population, with $AC = 0.859$. Also, the DD visited only three modes, intuitively indicating that this workload might have the strongest tendency to reveal execution hotspots. At the other extreme, Enable_Disable only revealed 10 distinct CSs (out of 136), but instead the calls to the external functions were the most diverse, 38 from NTOSKRNL.EXE and 4 from HAL.DLL. As the agglomerative coefficient of this workload is relatively small, we expect that Enable_Disable has the weakest clustering tendency.

---

[1] The number of functions called from NTOSKRNL.EXE.
[2] The number of functions called from HAL.DLL.

7.1 Revealing the Execution Hotspots: MDS Plots of the CSs

To visualize the clustering tendency of the CSs generated by the used workloads and, implicitly, the execution hotspots in floppy driver's code, we used a multidimensional scaling (MDS) plot. MDS is a statistical technique designed to graphically express the degree of similarity or dissimilarity between objects. The points representing similar objects are clustered together in different regions of the 2D-space depicted by the MDS plot, while the points representing dissimilar objects are placed to be far apart from each other. The MDS plot in Fig. 8 is computed using the already available distance matrices.

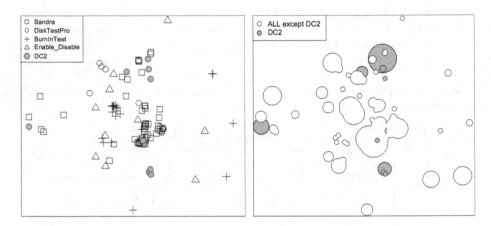

Fig. 8. MDS plot of the CSs for each workload

Fig. 9. MDS plot of the execution hotspots
with their magnitudes

With a high AC, `Sandra` forms the biggest clusters mostly in the center of the figure, while the areas exercised by the `Enable_Disable` are located farther apart from each other. This visual representation of the CSs also helped reveal another tight cluster close to the center of the Fig. 8, generated by the `BurnInTest` workload. Also, `DiskTestPro`'s executions form a hotspot, located in the second quadrant of Fig. 8. Overall, the grouping of the CSs in the middle of the MDS plot indicates that most of them share a certain degree of similarity.

Interestingly, the CSs generated by `DC2` are located quite differently from the rest of other CSs. This is explained by the fact that `DC2` is a robustness testing tool, therefore accessing areas of code seldomly visited under common executions. To better substantiate this tendency, Fig. 9 represents the same MDS plot, where each CS was enhanced with the magnitude of the associated CS. That is, a bigger circle represents a high rate of occurrence of the respective CS. The circles are scaled using a logarithmic function ($size = \log(magnitude_{CS})$) in order to create a visual balance between CSs having very different occurrence rates. Additionally, the execution hotspots generated by the first four workloads from Table 1 were merged, while the hotspots generated by the robustness testing tool DC2 were represented in gray. As DC2's hotspots are off-centered, it becomes apparent that the DC2 covers very few of the execution hotspots generated by all other studied workloads.

Nevertheless, the Figs. 8 and 9 validate our methodology and graphically motivate the usage of execution profiles as a prerequisite step for testing. We believe that a significant amount of testing can be saved by redistributing the effort to covering the execution hotspots. Doing so significantly reduces the test effort, while the test adequacy remains unaffected. While test case filtering is not the scope of this paper, we hypothesize that an iterative method based on comparisons of test suites against an existing execution hotspot map can be devised in order to guide this process.

7.2   Similarity Cutoffs: Testing Overhead Versus Diversity Masking

The dendrograms obtained at steps 5 and 6 in Fig. 7 represent useful support for deciding which code paths to test. To ensure high accuracy for the subsequent testing campaigns with respect to the execution hotspots, one should develop test cases that exercise the DD in the same manner as the workload does, or, alternatively, use the test cases themselves as workload for exercising the DD in the profiling phase.

We believe that the testing effort can be significantly reduced by testing only the distinct CSs. A prioritization scheme for this procedure should consider (and therefore be indexed by) the number of occurrences associated with each CS ($magnitude_{CS}$). Intuitively, a subsequent test campaign can reduce its overhead by testing only one CS per cluster. Figure 10 illustrates this concept: by setting a similarity cutoff $T = 0.2$, the dendrogram is split into four clusters and five alones (CS0, 1, 15, 22 and 23). This indicates nine code paths that must be tested: the alones and any one CS from each of the four clusters, since all the CSs that are contained in the cluster are considered similar. With $T = 0$, 24 CSs should be tested in order to achieve complete hotspot coverage. Therefore, setting the $T = 0.2$ gives an overall reduction of 62.5% of the testing cost (assuming that the cost of testing is equally distributed among the 24 distinct CSs). In practice, the similarity cutoff T has to be chosen as close to zero as possible, because large values of T have a tendency to mask CS diversity. Actually, dendrograms support the similarity threshold decision by their structure. If the CSs cluster at very low heights, a small cutoff value will group many CSs together, significantly reducing the test efforts without having to pay a high cost to diversity masking.

In contrast, Fig. 11 depicts the dendrograms of the CSs for each mode. In this representation it is apparent that in the visited modes the DD was taking at least three different paths into the code. The heights at which they cluster indicate that the CSs are quite dissimilar, even though they are basically associated with the same DD functionality. This reveals that the IRP dispatch subroutines are quite complex, possibly containing multiple decision branches in the code. In the case of the per-mode dendrograms (Fig. 11), a similarity cutoff T smaller than the shortest cluster will reveal all the code paths taken inside the mode. Though, to balance the testing efforts, T should be chosen anywhere between the height

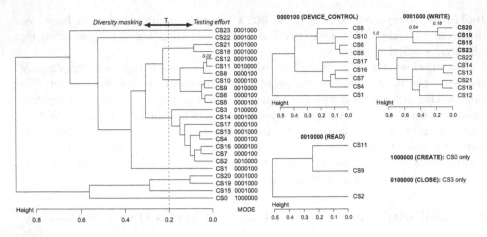

Fig. 10. BurnInTest: A threshold set to 0.2 reveals a clustering with 4 clusters and 5 alones (62.5% test cost reduction)

Fig. 11. BurnInTest: The distinct CSs called by every mode

of the smallest cluster and 1. With $T = 1$ the granularity of testing is the same as in our previous approach [11].

This represents one of the key contributions of this paper in contrast to our previous work, where the smallest DD behavior granularity unit was the notion of *mode*. Using the dual-interface approach presented in this paper, a subsequent testing technique can take advantage of the smaller granularity offered by the new concept of *CS*.

8   Discussion and Results Interpretation

Identification of Repeating Functions: Table 3 displays five distinct CSs, as generated by the BurnInTest workload. The respective CSs are highlighted also in Fig. 11. CS15 is formed by a call IofCompleteRequest function, followed by ExInterlockedRemoveHeadList and KeWaitForSingleObject, repeating twice. The distance from CS15 to CS19 is 0.54 and to CS23 is 1.0; the distance from CS19 to CS20 is 0.18 (also depicted in Fig. 11). The low similarity values shared by the CS15, CS19 and CS20 are mainly given by the fact that the sequences share a common prefix and the group of two functions that repeat themselves. These repetitions indicate the presence of short loops in the DD's code. In particular, according to the DDK documentation, ExInterlockedRemoveHeadList routine *"removes an entry from the head of a doubly linked list"* and KeWaitForSingleObject *"puts the current thread into a wait state"*. CS23 is heavily penalized when related to CS15 because the position of the only common character is not the same in the two CSs. In contrast, the distance from CS23 to CS0 is (only) 0.83 because both CSs are very short.

Figure 10 show cases when two CSs are very similar, even though they belong to different modes (i.e., CS11 and CS12, at a distance of 0.02). We believe that

Table 2. Five functions and their encodings (used in Table 3)

Function Name	Encoding Char
IofCompleteRequest	a
ExInterlockedRemoveHeadList	b
KeWaitForSingleObject	c
ExAcquireFastmutex	d
ExReleaseFastMutex	e

Table 3. Four distinct CSs issued by the BurnInTest

CS Name	Encoding	#Occurences
CS0	a	144
CS15	abcbc	2
CS19	abcbcbcbcbc	2
CS20	abcbcbcbc	1
CS23	dea	13

they share the same or large portions of a dispatch function. It is also possible that they share a large amount of helper functions, inside the DD's code. We are currently investigating in more depth the reasons behind this observed behavior on publicly available driver source code (the serial port driver).

Frequently Used Kernel Services: Our profiling approach reveals that the set of functions frequently used by a DD at runtime is very small. Table 4 lists the 20 function calls that make 99.97% of all the imports called by the flpydisk.sys at runtime in our experiments. In [1] Mendonca and Neves have chosen a set of 20 DDK functions for fault injection experiments by inspecting the IAT tables of all the DDs belonging to several Windows installations. Our results show that their static approach to select kernel APIs is irrelevant in such dynamic environments, as the set of functions called at runtime is radically different. Therefore, we recommend that subsequent fault injection campaigns should primarily target functions having higher runtime occurrence index.

Table 4. The function calls accounting for 99.97% of all recorded calls, for all workloads, sorted descending on occurrence. ExAcquireFastMutex and ExReleaseFastMutex belong to HAL.DLL, the rest to NTOSKRNL.EXE library.

Function Name	#Occ.	[%]	Function Name	#Occ.	[%]
ExAcquireFastMutex	60414	18.40	MmMapLockedPagesSpecifyCache	8178	2.49
ExReleaseFastMutex	60414	18.40	MmPageEntireDriver	24	0.01
IofCallDriver	45976	14.00	MmResetDriverPaging	23	0.01
KeInitializeEvent	40777	12.42	KeGetCurrentThread	10	0.00
IoBuildDeviceIoControlRequest	40771	12.41	KeSetPriortyThread	10	0.00
ExInterlockedRemoveHeadList	22007	6.70	ObfDereferenceObject	10	0.00
ExInterlockedInsertTailList	16123	4.91	ObReferenceObjectByHandle	10	0.00
IofCompleteRequest	11562	3.52	PsCreateSystemThread	10	0.00
KeWaitForSingleObject	11032	3.36	PsTerminateSystemThread	10	0.00
KeReleaseSemaphore	11003	3.35	ZwClose	10	0.00

9   Conclusions and Future Research Directions

In this paper we have presented a driver profiling technique that monitors the activity of a kernel driver at runtime onto two communication interfaces. Our technique disconnects execution profiling from the source code access requirement, for every of the involved OS kernel components. We consider that the driver is receiving requests on the *IRP interface* and start executing the IRP-associated activity. We revealed the effect of this computation as a sequence of calls to external functions, by monitoring the driver's *functional interface*. The CSs obtained were encoded as character strings and cross-compared for similarity. The distinct CSs were found to represent a very small number of the total number of CSs recorded during our experiments, indicating that the number of code paths taken by a driver at runtime is very small. Moreover, we employed an agglomerative cluster analysis technique in order to group together similar CSs and therefore suggest areas of code where the test effort of subsequent testing campaigns should concentrate. Using the same technique, the CSs belonging to the same mode were investigated and showed that the code paths taken by the driver differs even when executing the same IRP dispatch subroutine, a tendency that reveal code branches. Moreover, the MDS plots visually disclose the tendency of the CSs to cluster by revealing the execution hotspots. At the same time, the Figs. 8 and 9 show that DC2, a robustness testing tool for drivers from Microsoft, does not cover the execution hotspots generated by the other realistic workloads. This result intuitively supports the idea to re-balance the testing effort to the revealed execution hotspots, thus enhancing the odds to find early the faults having a high occurrence likelihood in the field.

Current research directions include the design and implementation of a fault injection method for testing the robustness of OS kernel drivers, based on the concepts introduced in this paper. The selection of test cases will consider the execution hotspots generated by a prior driver execution profiling phase, in order to reduce overall testing overhead. Test prioritization schemes will also be employed by applying the techniques described in our previous work [11, 12]. We also intend to investigate the possibility to implement state-aware robustness wrappers for kernel drivers, once we will establish a method for detecting deviations from "correct behavior".

References

1. Mendonca, M., Neves, N.: Robustness testing of the Windows DDK. In: Dependable Systems and Networks (DSN), June 2007, pp. 554–564 (2007)
2. Swift, M.M., Bershad, B.N., Levy, H.M.: Improving the reliability of commodity operating systems. ACM Transactions on Computer Systems 23(1), 77–110 (2005)
3. Ganapathi, A., Ganapathi, V., Patterson, D.: Windows XP kernel crash analysis. In: Large Installation System Administration Conference (LISA), pp. 12–22 (2006)
4. Albinet, A., Arlat, J., Fabre, J.C.: Characterization of the impact of faulty drivers on the robustness of the Linux kernel. In: Dependable Systems and Networks (DSN), pp. 867–876 (2004)
5. Arlat, J., Fabre, J.C., Rodriguez, M.: Dependability of COTS microkernel-based systems. IEEE Transactions on Computers 51(2), 138–163 (2002)
6. Chou, A., Yang, J., Chelf, B., Hallem, S., Engler, D.R.: An empirical study of operating system errors. In: Symposium on Operating Systems Principles (SOSP), pp. 73–88 (2001)
7. Duraes, J., Madeira, H.: Multidimensional characterization of the impact of faulty drivers on the operating systems behavior. IEICE Transactions on Information and Systems 86(12), 2563–2570 (2003)

8. Murphy, B., Garzia, M., Suri, N.: Closing the gap in failure analysis. In: Dependable Systems and Networks (DSN), pp. 59–61 (2006)

9. Johansson, A., Sârbu, A., Jhumka, A., Suri, N.: On enhancing the robustness of commercial operating systems. In: Malek, M., Reitenspiess, M., Kaiser, J. (eds.) ISAS 2004. LNCS, vol. 3335, pp. 148–159. Springer, Heidelberg (2005)

10. Johansson, A., Suri, N.: Error propagation profiling of operating systems. In: International Conference on Dependable Systems and Networks (DSN), pp. 86–95 (2005)

11. Sârbu, C., Johansson, A., Fraikin, F., Suri, N.: Improving robustness testing of COTS OS extensions. In: Penkler, D., Reitenspiess, M., Tam, F. (eds.) ISAS 2006. LNCS, vol. 4328, pp. 120–139. Springer, Heidelberg (2006)

12. Sârbu, C., Suri, N.: Runtime behavior-based profiling of OS drivers. Technical report, TR-TUD-DEEDS-05-02-2007 (2007), http://www.deeds.informatik.tu-darmstadt.de/research/TR/ TR-TUD-DEEDS-05-02-2007-Sarbu.pdf

13. Weyuker, E.J., Jeng, B.: Analyzing partition testing strategies. IEEE Transactions on Software Engineering 17(7), 703–711 (1991)

14. Weyuker, E.J.: Using operational distributions to judge testing progress. In: ACM Symposium on Applied Computing, pp. 1118–1122. ACM Press, New York (2003)

15. Möller, K.H., Paulish, D.: An empirical investigation of software fault distribution. In: First International Software Metrics Symposium (METRIC), May 1993, pp. 82–90 (1993)

16. Johansson, A., Suri, N., Murphy, B.: On the impact of injection triggers for os robustness evaluation. In: International Symposium on Software Reliability Engineering (ISSTA), pp. 127–136 (2007)

17. Ball, T., Larus, J.R.: Efficient path profiling. In: MICRO-29, pp. 46–57 (1996)

18. Larus, J.R.: Whole program paths. ACM SIGPLAN 34, 259–269 (1999)

19. Leon, D., Podgurski, A.: A comparison of coverage-based and distribution-based techniques for filtering and prioritizing test cases. In: 14th International Symposium on Software Reliability Engineering (ISSRE), pp. 442–453 (2003)

20. Oney, W.: Programming the MS Windows Driver Model. Microsoft Press, Redmond (2003)

21. Microsoft Corporation, Visual Studio, Microsoft portable executable and common object file format specification. Technical report (May 2006), http://www.microsoft.com/whdc/system/platform/firmware/PECOFF.mspx

22. Hunt, G., Brubacher, D.: Detours: Binary interception of Win32 functions. In: Proceedings of the 3rd USENIX Windows NT Symposium, July 1999, pp. 135–144 (1999)

23. Vasudevan, A., Yerraballi, R.: Spike: Engineering malware analysis tools using unobtrusive binary-instrumentation. In: Australasian Computer Science Conference (ACSC), pp. 311–320 (2006)

24. Ihaka, R., Gentleman, R.: R: A language for data analysis and graphics. Journal of Computational and Graphical Statistics 5(3), 299–314 (1996)

25. Cohen, W.W., Ravikumar, P., Fienberg, S.E.: A comparison of string distance metrics for name-matching tasks. In: International Joint Conference on Artificial Intelligence (IJCAI), pp. 73–78 (2003)

Analysis of a Software System with Rejuvenation, Restoration and Checkpointing

Hiroyuki Okamura and Tadashi Dohi

Department of Information Engineering, Graduate School of Engineering
Hiroshima University, Higashi-Hiroshima, 739–8527, Japan
{okamu,dohi}@rel.hiroshima-u.ac.jp

Abstract. In this paper we consider operational software system with two failure modes and develop a stochastic model to quantify steady-state system availability. Three kinds of preventive/corrective maintenance policies; rejuvenation, restoration and checkpointing, are incorporated in our unified availability model. We propose a dynamic programming algorithm to determine the joint optimal maintenance schedule maximizing the steady-state system availability and calculate the optimal aperiodic checkpoint sequence and preventive rejuvenation time simultaneously. In numerical examples, the sensitivity of model parameters to characterize failure modes are examined, and effects of the preventive/corrective maintenance policies are studied in details.

Keywords: software availability, rejuvenation, restoration, checkpoint, optimization, dynamic programing algorithm.

1 Introduction

Checkpointing is one of the most important techniques in dependable computing. This is a quite simple technique to place checkpoints for reducing downtime caused by a system failure in operational phase, and is effective with as a cost data/environment diversity technique. Each checkpoint preserves status of a process running on memory at a secondary storage devices such as a hard disk. Even if a system failure occurs, the process can be restarted from the latest checkpoint by referring to the status in the secondary storage device. Then the downtime caused by the system failure may become shorter by controlling placement of the checkpoints appropriately. Therefore, an appropriate checkpoint placement leads to the improvement of system availability for operational software systems. On the other hand, placing a checkpoint wasts a time overhead, called a checkpoint overhead, so that the system availability may not be improved if checkpoints are unnecessarily and excessively placed. Of course, since the lack of checkpoints may increase the recovery overhead that is a time overhead to refer to the preserved status on contrary, there is a trade-off relationship on the frequency of checkpoints. In fact, a huge number of checkpoint creation problems have been considered during the last four decades.

First Young [58] obtained the optimal checkpoint interval approximately for restarting a computation process after a system failure. Chandy *et al.* [10,11,53,57]

T. Nanya et al. (Eds.): ISAS 2008, LNCS 5017, pp. 110–128, 2008.

proposed some performance models for database recovery and calculated the optimal checkpoint intervals which maximize system availability or minimize an average overhead during normal operation. Since these early contributions, many authors developed checkpoint models to determine the optimal checkpointing schedules with respect to various dependability measures [3, 12, 14, 25, 26, 27, 28, 29, 30, 31, 32, 34, 39]. For the good survey of this topic, see Nicola [35]. Most of the above works focused on periodic checkpoint policies, *i.e.*, the case where checkpoint intervals are constant over time. Theoretically this type of policies may be applicable only when system failure time is described as an exponential distributed random variable. However, the periodic policy has been applied in the case where system failures occur according to non-exponential distributions.

Toueg and Babaõglu [50] considered a non-exponential failure case and developed a dynamic programming (DP) algorithm to determine aperiodic checkpoints. Variational calculus approaches in [18, 19, 33] are regarded as efficient approximation methods to treat aperiodic checkpoint placement problems. Recently, Dohi *et al.* [16] and Ozaki *et al.* [43] reconsidered a sequential checkpoint placement algorithm and dealt with non-constant checkpointing schedules. Okamura *et al.* [42] also developed a DP-based optimal checkpointing algorithm for real-time applications and refined Toueg and Babaõglu's [50] discrete DP algorithm in the context of continuous time domain. In this way, many checkpoint schemes have been extensively studied under general operational circumstances described by non-exponential failure times.

Apart from the checkpointing, the software systems running continuously for long time empirically causes system failures due to the aging. The aging in software system is defined as cumulative error conditions like leaking memories and zombie processes. Such aging-related bugs, which lead to resource exhaustion, may exist in operating systems, middleware and application software. For instance, typical operating system resources, swap space and free memory available are progressively depleted due to defects in software such as memory leaks and incomplete cleanup of resources after use. It is well known that *software aging* will affect the performance of applications and eventually cause failures [1, 2, 9]. Software aging has been observed in widely-used communication software like Internet Explorer, Netscape and xrn as well as commercial operating systems and middleware. In such a situation, the failures caused by the software aging cannot be distinguished from the common failures due to faults embedded in the software. In addition, the assumption that system failure times follow non-exponential distributions is more acceptable on the aging phenomenon rather than the checkpointing environment.

A complementary approach to handle software aging and its related transient failures, called *software rejuvenation*, has already become popular as a typical and low cost environment diversity technique of operational software. Software rejuvenation is a preventive and proactive solution that is particularly useful for counteracting the phenomenon of software aging. It involves stopping the running software occasionally, cleaning its internal state and restarting it. Cleaning the internal state of a software might involve garbage collection, flushing operating system kernel tables, reinitializing internal data structures and hardware reboot. In general, there is also a trade-off relationship between a rejuvenation overhead and downtime due to a system failure. For instance, Huang et al. [24] reported the aging phenomenon in telecommunication billing applications where over time the application experiences a crash or a hang failure. Subsequently, many authors considered the similar problems as [24], i.e., how to determine the optimal software rejuvenation schedules [7,8,13,15,17,20, 22,36,37,38,40,44,46,47,48,49,51,52,54,55,56]. This motivates us to handle the optimal rejuvenation schedule as well as checkpointing schedule.

Although these two software fault tolerant techniques are used for different purposes, it should be noted that they are implemented in a real software operational phase to complement each other. In other words, a unified model to incorporate the checkpointing and rejuvenation is useful to quantify both effects on system availability improvement. In the past literature, very a few papers challenged to this interesting modeling. Gare et al. [21] took account of both checkpointing and rejuvenation for a software system and evaluated its expected completion time. Since their model assumes that the system executes a software rejuvenation at a given checkpoint unless the system fails, the minimization of the expected completion time was solved under a specific maintenance schedule which consists of periodic checkpoint interval and the number to trigger the rejuvenation. Bobbio et al. [6] focused on a modeling technique for software system with rejuvenation, restoration and checkpointing. As an extension of usual stochastic Petri nets [20], they applied so-called fluid stochastic Petri nets to model behavior of the software system and assessed quantitative system dependability. Unfortunately, there are only two papers to treat both the fault tolerant techniques in a unified framework.

This paper challenges developing a stochastic model to quantify steady-state system availability under three kinds of preventive/corrective maintenance policies; rejuvenation, restoration and checkpointing in a unified availability model. In addition, we consider two failure modes; active and passive failures. These are different points from our previous work [41, 42]. Especially, active and passive failure modes concern failure detection in a distributed transmission system. Active failures can immediately be detected when the failures occur. On contrary, passive failures cannot detected unless the system performs a somewhat diagnosis action. The Internet service based on a distributed system using SOAP (simple object access protocol) may have a similar failure mechanism, namely, it faces a latency fault that cannot be detected immediately like passive failure mode. We propose a DP algorithm to determine a joint optimal maintenance schedule maximizing steady-state system availability and calculate the optimal aperiodic checkpoint sequence and preventive rejuvenation time simultaneously. The basic idea behind our DP algorithm comes from our research results in the different (simpler) contexts [41, 42] and is further different from the classical discrete DP algorithm in [50].

The remaining part of this paper is organized as follows. Section 2 describes a software availability model with two failure modes incorporating the actions;

rejuvenation, restoration and checkpointing. After describing model assumptions, we formulate steady-state system availability. In Section 3, we develop a DP-based optimization algorithm which maximize the steady-state system availability. Section 4 presents numerical examples with respect to two different failure distributions. Here sensitivity of the optimal checkpointing schedule on model parameters are examined, and we investigate an effect of the preventive/corrective maintenance policies in details. Finally the paper is concluded with some remarks in Section 5.

2   Software Availability Modeling

2.1   Model Description

We consider an operational software system with two failure modes. Suppose that the software system, *e.g.* a distributed storage system through the Internet via SOAP, starts its operation at $t = 0$ and may deteriorate with time due to the phenomenon of software aging. Let $F(t)$ be the system failure time distribution which is absolutely continuous and non-decreasing in time, where the probability density function and the mean are given by $f(t)$ and μ_f (> 0), respectively. Without any loss of generality, we suppose that $F(t)$ is IFR (Increasing Failure Rate) and that the failure rate $r(t) = f(t)/\overline{F}(t)$ is increasing in t, where in general $\overline{\psi}(\cdot) = 1 - \psi(\cdot)$, though this assumption does not affect the latter theoretical results. It is also assumed that the system failure can occur at one of two failure modes; *active* failure mode and *passive* failure mode. Letting $p \in [0,1]$ ($q = 1-p$) denote the probability that an active (passive) failure mode occurs, the corresponding system failure time distribution in each failure mode is given by $pF(t)$ ($qF(t)$).

For the software system, checkpoints are placed aperiodically at time $\pi = \{t_1, t_2, \ldots, t_N\}$, where N (> 0) is the number of checkpoints and is decided in advance, so that a bounded number of checkpoints are placed, where each checkpoint overhead to save the processes operated during two successive checkpoints unless the system failure occurs is given by μ_c (> 0). If an active failure occurs with probability p, then it can be detected immediately and a rollforward recovery takes place from the latest checkpoint. More specifically, when the active failure occurs at time $x \in (t_i, t_{i+1}]$ ($i = 0, 1, \ldots, N$), the rollforward procedure starts with the saved process information at t_i and completes within a finite time period. The restoration (recovery) overhead is $\rho(x) = \alpha x + \beta$, where αx denotes the time needed to re-execute the lost processes in the interval $[t_i, t_i + x)$ since the last checkpoint t_i and the second term is a fixed part. Even after the completion of restoration, the lost processes are recovered, it is evident that the software system still ages. To restart the system, it is rejuvenated with the rejuvenation overhead μ_m (≥ 0) and can become as good as new, where the failure rate $r(t)$ is initialized.

On the other hand, if a passive failure occurs with probability q, then it is regarded as a latent fault and cannot be detected immediately at the failure time point. However, since the latency of a fault leads to a deterioration of

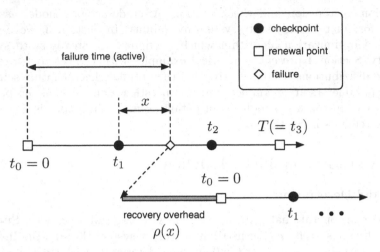

Fig. 1. Possible realization of software system in an active failure mode

performance, it can be detected at the next checkpoint after the failure with a somewhat diagnosis action of the system, so that upon a passive failure at time $x \in (t_i, t_{i+1}]$ $(i = 0, 1, \ldots, N)$ the rollforward procedure takes place from the checkpoint t_i to the fault detection point t_{i+1}, where the associated restoration overhead is given by $\rho(t_{i+1} - t_i) = \alpha(t_{i+1} - t_i) + \beta$. In that sense, the probability q (p) can be considered as an *imperfect detection* (*perfect detection*) probability. After the lost processes are recovered, the software system is rejuvenated with the same rejuvenation overhead μ_m and can become as good as new.

Let T (> 0) be a preventive maintenance time. If the software system does not fail until the time T fortunately, the preventive maintenance for the unfailed system is performed and the software system is rejuvenated with the overhead μ_m. We define time length from $t = 0$ to the time when the software system can become as good as new, as one cycle. The same cycle repeats again and again over an infinite time horizon. Of course, during the rejuvenation, restoration and checkpointing, the processes are not operated. The stochastic model under consideration generalizes some existing checkpointing and/or rejuvenation models. For example, when $T \to \infty$, $p = 1$ $(q = 0)$ and $\mu_m = 0$, it reduces the basic checkpoint model with aperiodic checkpoint intervals [43]. If we apply the exponential distribution as the failure distribution, the corresponding model is the Vaidya's model [53] with periodic checkpoint interval. As the simplest case, if $N = 0$, $p = 1$ $(q = 0)$ and $\rho(x) = \beta$, our model represents the well-known age replacement model [4].

The typical example for a software system with two failure modes would be a distributed transmission system. In this system, the receiver can immediately detect a transmission error by means of any coding technique such as Hamming code, but it is difficult to identify whether the sender is alive or not, *i.e.* the error of sender. In such a transmission system, two kinds of failures; active and passive failures, are possibly considered. Figures 1 and 2 depict possible behavior

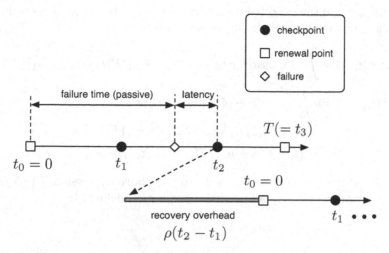

Fig. 2. Possible realization of software system in a passive failure mode

of the software system with two failure modes under three maintenance activities; rejuvenation, restoration and checkpointing.

2.2 Formulation of System Availability

Of our concern here is the formulation of steady-state system availability which is defined as the probability that the software system is operative in the steady state. For the purpose, we define the renewal points at which the system failure time distribution is initialized. Since all the completion times of the preventive/corrective maintenance actions are the renewal points, we focus on the probabilistic behavior between two successive renewal points, *i.e.* during the one cycle. From the familiar renewal reward argument [4], the steady-state system availability with the checkpoint schedule π and the preventive maintenance T is represented by

$$
\begin{aligned}
Ass(\pi, T) &= \lim_{t \to \infty} \frac{E[\text{system operation time during } [0, t)]}{t} \\
&= \frac{E[\text{system operation time during one cycle}]}{E[\text{time length of one cycle}]},
\end{aligned}
\tag{1}
$$

where E denotes the mathematical expectation operator. Then, the problem is to find the optimal maintenance schedule (π^*, T^*) maximizing the steady-state system availability $Ass(\pi, T)$.

For the sake of simplicity, we rewrite the optimal maintenance schedule as $\tilde{\pi} = \{t_1, \ldots, t_N, t_{N+1}\}$, where $t_{N+1} = T$. During the interval between two successive checkpoints $[t_{i-1}, t_i)$, we derive the expected up time (expected operative time) $A(t_i|t_{i-1})$ and the expected total time $S(t_i|t_{i-1})$ during $[t_{i-1}, t_i)$ including rejuvenation, restoration and checkpoint overheads by

$$A(t_i|t_{i-1}) = \int_0^{t_i-t_{i-1}} x dF(x|t_{i-1}) + (t_i - t_{i-1})\overline{F}(t_i - t_{i-1}|t_{i-1}), \qquad (2)$$

$$\begin{aligned} S(t_i|t_{i-1}) =&p \int_0^{t_i-t_{i-1}} \{x + \rho(x) + \mu_m\} dF(x|t_{i-1}) \\ &+ q\{t_i - t_{i-1} + \rho(t_i - t_{i-1}) + \mu_m\}F(t_i - t_{i-1}|t_{i-1}) \\ &+ \{t_i - t_{i-1} + \mu_c\}\overline{F}(t_i - t_{i-1}|t_{i-1}), \end{aligned} \qquad (3)$$

respectively, where $t_0 = 0$ and $t_{N+1} = T$. In the above expression, $F(\cdot|\cdot)$ represents the conditional system failure time distribution defined by

$$F(s|t) = 1 - \overline{F}(t+s)/\overline{F}(t). \qquad (4)$$

In the last time period $[t_N, t_{N+1})$, it is noted that the preventive rejuvenation is carried out unless the system failure occurs and that it can be regarded as a boundary time period. Then, the expected up time and the expected total time are given by

$$A(t_{N+1}|t_N) = \int_0^{t_{N+1}-t_N} x dF(x|t_N) + (t_{N+1} - t_N)\overline{F}(t_{N+1} - t_N|t_N), \qquad (5)$$

$$\begin{aligned} S(t_{N+1}|t_N) =&p \int_0^{t_{N+1}-t_N} \{x + \rho(x) + \mu_m\} dF(x|t_N) \\ &+ q\{t_{N+1} - t_N + \rho(t_{N+1} - t_N) + \mu_m\}F(t_{N+1} - t_N|t_N) \\ &+ (t_{N+1} - t_N + \mu_m)\overline{F}(t_{N+1} - t_N|t_N), \end{aligned} \qquad (6)$$

respectively. Based on the above results, the steady-state system availability is formulated as a fraction of time when the software system is up during one cycle, and is straightforwardly given by

$$Ass(\tilde{\pi}) = \frac{\sum_{i=1}^N \overline{F}(t_{i-1})A(t_i|t_{i-1})}{\sum_{i=1}^N \overline{F}(t_{i-1})S(t_i|t_{i-1})}. \qquad (7)$$

3   Optimization Algorithm

Since the steady-state system availability is given as a function of $\tilde{\pi}$, the problem is reduced to a non-linear maximization problem $\max_{\tilde{\pi}} Ass(\tilde{\pi})$, provided that the number of checkpoints N is given. It is worth noting that there is no effective algorithm to find the optimal pair $(\tilde{\pi}^*, N^*)$ simultaneously, so that the number of checkpoints must be carefully adjusted in a heuristic manner. For a fixed N, the most popular method to find the optimal $\tilde{\pi}^*$ would be the Newton's method or its iterative variant. However, since the Newton's method is a general-purpose non-linear optimization algorithm, it may not often function better to solve the maximization problem with many parameter constraints. In our maximization problem, the decision variables $\tilde{\pi}$ are restricted. For such a sequential optimization problem, it is well known that the dynamic programming (DP) can be used effectively.

The essential idea of the DP algorithm is to solve recursively the optimality equations which are typical functional equations. Hence, it seems to be straightforward to give the optimality equations which the optimal maintenance schedule $\tilde{\pi}^*$ must satisfy. Suppose that there exists the unique maximum steady-state system availability ξ. From the principle of optimality [5], we obtain the following optimality equations for the maximization problem of the steady-state system availability:

$$h_i = \max_{t_i} W(t_i|t^*_{i-1}, h_1, h_{i+1}), \qquad i = 1, \ldots, N, \tag{8}$$

$$h_{N+1} = \max_{t_{n+1}} W(t_{N+1}|t^*_N, h_1, h_1), \tag{9}$$

where the function $W(t_i|t_{i-1}, h_1, h_{i+1})$ is given by

$$W(t_i|t_{i-1}, h_1, h_{i+1}) = A(t_i|t_{i-1}) - \xi S(t_i|t_{i-1})$$
$$+ h_1 F(t_i - t_{i-1}|t_{i-1}) + h_{i+1}\overline{F}(t_i - t_{i-1}|t_{i-1}) \tag{10}$$

and the function h_i, $i = 1, \ldots, N + 1$, are called the *relative value functions*.

Since Eqs. (8) and (9) are necessary and sufficient conditions of the optimal maintenance schedule, the next step is to solve the above optimality equations. In the long history of the DP research, there are a couple of algorithms to solve the optimality equations. In this paper we apply the *policy iteration* scheme [45] to develop the maintenance scheduling algorithm. The optimization algorithm consists of two steps; the optimization of the maintenance schedule under a given relative value function and the computation of the relative value function based on the updated maintenance schedule. These steps are repeatedly executed until the resulting the maintenance schedule converges to the optimal value.

In the optimization phase, it should be noted that the functions

$$W(t_i|t_{i-1}, h_1, h_{i+1}), \quad i = 1, \ldots, N, \tag{11}$$

are not always concave with respect to the decision variables t_i. Our problem is the case. This fact leads to the difficulty for maximizing the steady-state system availability. In order to overcome this problem, we define the following composite function:

$$W(t_i|t_{i-1}, h_1, W(t_{i+1}|t_i, h_1, h_{i+2})), \quad i = 1, \ldots, N \tag{12}$$

and propose to use it instead of $W(t_i|t_{i-1}, h_1, h_{i+1})$. Because the above composite function is a concave function, it is possible to find the optimal maintenance schedule in each iteration phase by maximizing the composite function for $i = 1, \ldots, N$.

In the computation phase of the relative value function, on the other hand, we solve the following linear system:

$$Mx = b, \tag{13}$$

where for a given maintenance schedule, the relative value functions h_i and the maximum steady-state system availability ξ must satisfy where

$$[M]_{i,j} = \begin{cases} -\overline{F}(t_i - t_{i-1}|t_{i-1}) & \text{if } i = j \text{ and } j \neq N+1, \\ 1 & \text{if } i = j+1, \\ S(t_i|t_{i-1}) & \text{if } j = N+1, \\ 0 & \text{otherwise,} \end{cases} \tag{14}$$

$$x = (h_2, \ldots, h_N, h_{N+1}, \xi)', \tag{15}$$

$$b = (A(t_1|t_0), \ldots, A(t_N|t_{N-1}), A(t_{N+1}|t_N))', \tag{16}$$

$[\cdot]_{i,j}$ denotes the (i, j)-element of matrix, and the prime ($\prime$) represents transpose of vector. The above results come from the direct application of the optimality equations (8) and (9). Note that $h_1 = 0$, since we are here interested in the relative value function h_i and ξ.

Finally, we given the DP-based maintenance optimization algorithm as follows.

DP-Based Optimization Algorithm

- **Step 1:** Give initial values

$$k := 0,$$

$$t_0 := 0,$$

$$\tilde{\pi}^{(0)} := \{t_1^{(0)}, \ldots, t_N^{(0)}, t_{N+1}^{(0)}\}.$$

- **Step 2:** Compute $h_1^{(k)}, \ldots, h_{N+1}^{(k)}, \xi^{(k)}$ for the linear system (13) with the optimal maintenance schedule $\tilde{\pi}^{(k)}$.
- **Step 3:** Solve the following optimization problems:

$$t_i^{(k+1)} := \underset{t_{i-1}^{(k)} \leq t \leq t_{i+1}^{(k)}}{\operatorname{argmax}} \; W(t|t_{i-1}^{(k)}, 0, W(t_{i+1}^{(k)}|t_i, 0, h_{i+2}^{(k)})),$$

$$\text{for } i = 0, 1, \ldots, N-1,$$

$$t_N^{(k+1)} := \underset{t_{N-1}^{(k)} \leq t \leq t_{N+1}^{(k)}}{\operatorname{argmax}} \; W(t|t_{N-1}^{(k)}, 0, W(t_{N+1}^{(k)}|t, 0, 0)),$$

$$t_{N+1}^{(k+1)} := \underset{t_N^{(k)} \leq t < \infty}{\operatorname{argmax}} \; W(t|t_N^{(k)}, 0, 0).$$

- **Step 4:** For all $i = 1, \ldots, N+1$, if $|t_i^{(k+1)} - t_i^{(k)}| < \delta$, stop the algorithm, where δ is an error tolerance level. Otherwise, let $k := k+1$ and go to Step 2.

In Step 3, an arbitrary optimization technique has to be applied. Since the composite function is concave in the range $[t_{i-1}, t_{i+1})$, it is relatively easy to calculate the optimal checkpoint sequence and the optimal preventive maintenance time. In fact, the golden section method [23] would be effective to find the solution. In the following section, we give some numerical examples to calculate the optimal maintenance schedule based on the proposed DP algorithm.

4   Numerical Examples

4.1   Exponential System Failure Time

Suppose that the system failure time obeys the exponential distribution; $F(t) = 1 - \exp(-t/\mu_f)$, where μ_f represents the mean time to failure (MTTF) and the failure rate is given by $r(t) = 1/\mu_f$. To simplify the analysis, we assume $\alpha = 1$ and $\beta = 0$, so that the restoration overheads in respective modes are given by $\rho(x) = x$ and $\rho(t_{i+1} - t_i) = t_{i+1} - t_i$. This means that the restoration operations require the exactly same time amount as the processing time since the last checkpoint. Also, we set the other model parameters, $\mu_f = 1.0$, $\mu_c = 0.0$ and $\mu_m = 0.01$, *i.e.* no checkpoint overhead is needed, to clarify the parameter sensitivity. For the purpose to calculate the optimal maintenance schedule, we developed a computation program written by C language with GSL (GNU Scientific Library)[1]. This is available even in the case where the system failure time is given by the non-exponential distributions.

Figure 3 illustrates the optimal maintenance schedule (checkpoints and preventive maintenance time) in the case where all the failures can occur in the active mode. In the figure, the horizontal lines correspond to respective cases where the numbers of checkpoints placed by the preventive maintenance time are $N = 0, 1, \ldots, 10$. Since the horizontal line indicates the elapsed time, each point (dot) represents the time at which a checkpoint is placed, and the last one is the preventive maintenance time. From this result, it is seen that the resulting checkpoint interval becomes almost constant in all the cases. This is because the system failure time is exponentially distributed and that the effect of 'truncation' by the preventive maintenance does not appear in this example (see [43]). Also it is observed that the checkpoint interval tends to be shorter as the number of checkpoints over the time horizon $[0, T)$ increases. Since in this example the effect on checkpoint overhead is ignored, the system availability can be improved without checkpointing cost.

Figure 4 shows the result in the case where all the system failures occur in the passive mode. Though the behavior of the resulting checkpoint sequence is almost same as the active failure case, the scale on the sequence is rather different and the optimal checkpoint intervals are much shorter. This is because the checkpointing may acts as a failure detector in the passive failure case. In Fig. 5, we compare the maximum values of the associated steady-state system availability in terms of the number of checkpoints. For both active and passive failure modes, it can be seen that only a few checkpoints in early phase can improve the steady-state system availability drastically, but the remaining (8 or more) checkpoints make the system availability increasing slowly.

Next, we examine the dependence of checkpoint overhead on the optimal maintenance schedule, where $\mu_c = 0.005$ is assumed. Figures 6 and 7 present the respective optimal maintenance schedules in active and passive failure cases. In a

---

[1] The program can be downloaded at
http://www.rel.hiroshima-u.ac.jp/okamu/chkpcomp/

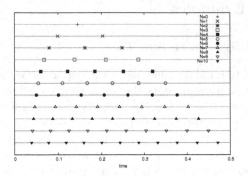

Fig. 3. Optimal maintenance schedule in exponential failure case ($p = 0.0$, $\mu_c = 0.0$)

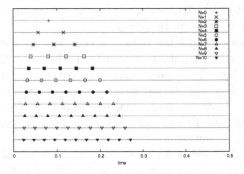

Fig. 4. Optimal maintenance schedule in exponential failure case ($p = 1.0$, $\mu_c = 0.0$)

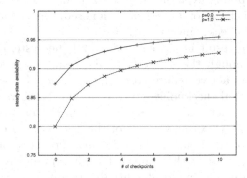

Fig. 5. Comparison of steady-state system availabilities with the optimal maintenance schedules in exponential failure case ($\mu_c = 0.0$)

fashion similar to the previous examples with $\mu_c = 0.0$, it is seen that the optimal checkpoint intervals become constant. Figure 8 plots the maximized values of the steady-state system availability with respect to the number of checkpoints.

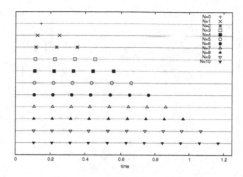

Fig. 6. Optimal maintenance schedule in exponential failure case ($p = 0.0$, $\mu_c = 0.005$)

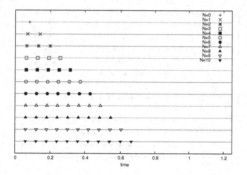

Fig. 7. Optimal maintenance schedule in exponential failure case ($p = 1.0$, $\mu_c = 0.005$)

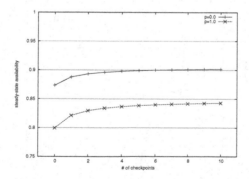

Fig. 8. Comparison of steady-state system availabilities with the optimal maintenance schedules in exponential failure case ($\mu_c = 0.005$)

The result indicates the flat movement in accordance with the frequency of checkpoint placement. In other words, the maximized system availability with checkpoint overhead is less sensitive than no overhead case. Therefore as the checkpoint

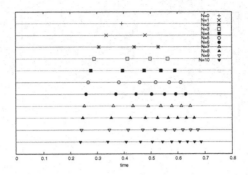

Fig. 9. Optimal maintenance schedule in Weibull failure case ($p = 0.0$, $\mu_c = 0.0$)

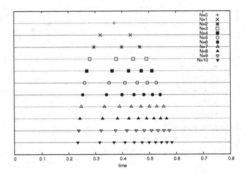

Fig. 10. Optimal maintenance schedule in Weibull failure case ($p = 1.0$, $\mu_c = 0.0$)

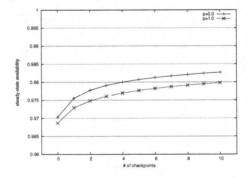

Fig. 11. Comparison of steady-state system availabilities with the optimal maintenance schedules in exponential failure case ($\mu_c = 0.0$)

overhead gets close to the preventive maintenance overhead, the checkpoint becomes unnecessary in the case of exponential failure, so that the accumulation of checkpoint overheads penalizes the increase of system availability.

4.2   Weibull System Failure Time

It is more appropriate to consider the non-exponential case if the software system may deteriorate by the aging. Suppose that the system failure time distribution is given by the Weibull failure distribution:

$$F(t) = 1 - \exp\left\{-\left(\frac{t}{\eta}\right)^{\phi}\right\}, \tag{17}$$

where η (> 0) and ϕ (> 0) are scale and shape parameters. If ϕ $>$ ($<$) 1, then the system failure time distribution is IFR (DFR). The case with $\phi = 1$ corresponds to the exponential distribution. The MTTF and the failure rate for the Weibull distribution are given by $\mu_f = \eta\Gamma(1 + 1/\psi)$ and $r(t) = \phi t^{\phi-1}/\eta^{\phi}$, respectively, where $\Gamma(\cdot)$ is the standard gamma function. In this example, we set $\phi = 5.0$ and adjust the scale parameter so as to satisfy that MTTF just equals 1.0. The other model parameters are same as those used in the exponential case.

Figures 9 through 11 show the optimal maintenance schedules and their associated maximum steady-state system availabilities in the Weibull failure case. Unlike the exponential failure case, the optimal checkpoint intervals are not constant and can be characterized as a decreasing sequence in the IFR case. Moreover, in the Weibull case, the checkpoints are placed in the later phase than the exponential failure case. This is caused by the characteristics of the Weibull distribution. Since $\phi = 5$ is assumed in this example, the variance of system failure time, $\eta^2\{\Gamma(1 + 2/\psi) - [\Gamma(1 + 1/\psi)]^2\}$, takes a small value, say, 0.0525. That is, the system failure may frequently occur around the MTTF ($= 1.0$) but not in the early phase. Therefore, as the result, the checkpoint tends to be placed in the later phase.

In the passive failure mode (see Fig. 10), it is found that the resulting checkpoints are shifted to the early operational phase compared to those in the active failure mode. This is because the checkpointing behaves like a failure detector for passive failures, and then the small variance of system failure time affects to the checkpoint placement more than the active failure case. Figure 11 explores the dependence of the steady-state system availability with the optimal maintenance schedule. From this figure, we observe that the system availability in the case of the Weibull failure distribution can be improved much more than the exponential failure case, by controlling the number of checkpoints. This phenomenon is also caused by the small variance in the Weibull system failure case.

Figures 12 and 13 show the results on the optimal maintenance schedule in $\mu_c = 0.001$. Since this is just 10% of the preventive rejuvenation overhead, the optimal checkpoint intervals do not change in comparison with the case of $\mu_c = 0$. However, a remarkable change does appear in the determination of the number of checkpoints. Figure 14 presents the maximized system availability for varying the number of checkpoints, $N = 0, \ldots, 10$. Dissimilar to the other cases, the system availability becomes a unimodal function of the number of checkpoints, and there is an optimal number of checkpoints. Concretely speaking, it is optimal to place two checkpoints over the whole operation period, $N^* = 2$, in both active

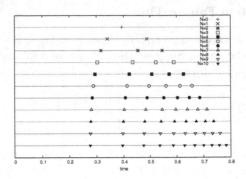

Fig. 12. Optimal checkpointing and maintenance times in Weibull failure case ($p = 0.0$, $\mu_c = 0.001$)

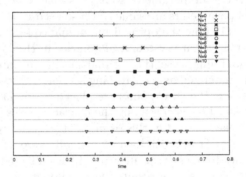

Fig. 13. Optimal checkpointing and maintenance times in Weibull failure case ($p = 1.0$, $\mu_c = 0.001$)

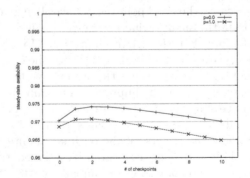

Fig. 14. Maximum steady-state availability in Weibull failure case ($\mu_c = 0.001$)

and passive failure modes. This phenomenon can be explained as follows. In the case of exponential failure with constant failure rate, the preventive rejuvenation does not improve the system availability. This implies that the preventive rejuvenation time T should be infinity if an infinite number of checkpoints are allowed. On the other hand, in the Weibull failure case with IFR property, the software rejuvenation as a preventive maintenance is definitely necessary to improve the system availability. In other words, even if an unbounded number of checkpoints are placed, the optimal preventive maintenance time should be finite. This implies that the checkpoint placement problem with a finite time horizon is significant for the maintenance optimization with rejuvenation, restoration and checkpointing.

5 Conclusions

In this paper, we have considered an operational software system with two failure modes; active and passive failures, and developed a stochastic model with three preventive/corrective maintenance actions; rejuvenation, restoration and checkpointing. We have proposed a dynamic programming algorithm to determine a joint optimal maintenance schedule maximizing steady-state system availability. In numerical examples, dependence of the optimal maintenance schedule which involves checkpoint sequence and preventive rejuvenation time, on some model parameters characterizing system failure tendency, has been examined in details.

Lessons learned from the numerical examples are that (i) the optimal checkpoint interval for exponential failure distribution is always constant, (ii) the optimal checkpoint interval in the case of IFR forms a deceasing sequence, (iii) checkpoints should be dense in the case where the ratio of passive failure modes is large, (iv) an optimal design of the number of checkpoints is needed in the IFR case with checkpoint overhead. The observations (i) and (ii) are analogue to the existing results from the checkpoint placement without preventive maintenance [43]. But the remaining observations have not been known yet in the past literature. These experimental insights would also be useful to design the software system which provides the Internet services, such as a Web-based application.

In future, we will refine the proposed DP-based algorithm by using a discretization technique with respect to computational speed, and develop an on-line maintenance algorithm to control rejuvenation, restoration and checkpointing simultaneously. Furthermore we will explore possibility of an on-line control scheme based on Bayesian learning.

References

1. Adams, E.: Optimizing preventive service of the software products. IBM Journal of Research & Development 28, 2–14 (1984)
2. Avritzer, A., Weyuker, E.J.: Monitoring smoothly degrading systems for increased dependability. Empirical Software Engineering 2, 59–77 (1997)
3. Baccelli, F.: Analysis of s service facility with periodic checkpointing. Acta Informatica 15, 67–81 (1981)
4. Barlow, R., Proschan, F.: Mathematical Theory of Reliability. John Wiley & Sons, Chichester (1965)

5. Bellman, R.E.: Dynamic Programming. Princeton University Press, Princeton (1957)
6. Bobbio, A., Garg, S., Gribaudo, M., Horvath, A., Sereno, M., Telek, M.: Modeling software systems with rejuvenation, restoration and checkpointing through fluid stochastic Petri nets. In: Proceedings of International Workshop on Petri Nets and Performance Models (PNPM 1999), pp. 82–91. IEEE CS Press, Los Alamitos (1999)
7. Bobbio, A., Sereno, M., Anglano, C.: Fine grained software degradation models for optimal rejuvenation policies. Performance Evaluation 46, 45–62 (2001)
8. Bao, Y., Sun, X., Trivedi, K.S.: A workload-based analysis of software aging, and rejuvenation. IEEE Transactions on Reliability 54(3), 541–548 (2005)
9. Castelli, V., Harper, R.E., Heidelberger, P., Hunter, S.W., Trivedi, K.S., Vaidyanathan, K., Zeggert, W.P.: Proactive management of software aging. IBM J. Research & Development 45, 311–332 (2001)
10. Chandy, K.M.: A survey of analytic models of roll-back and recovery strategies. Computer 8(5), 40–47 (1975)
11. Chandy, K.M., Browne, J.C., Dissly, C.W., Uhrig, W.R.: Analytic models for roll-back and recovery strategies in database systems. IEEE Transactions on Software Engineering SE-1(1), 100–110 (1975)
12. Dohi, T., Kaio, N., Osaki, S.: The optimal age-dependent checkpoint strategy for a stochastic system subject to general failure mode. Journal of Mathematical Analysis and Applications 249, 80–94 (2000)
13. Dohi, T., Goseva-Popstojanova, K., Trivedi, K.S.: Estimating software rejuvenation schedule in high assurance systems. The Computer Journal 44(6), 473–485 (2001)
14. Dohi, T., Kaio, N., Trivedi, K.S.: Availability models with age dependent-checkpointing. In: Proceedings of 21st Symposium on Reliable Distributed Systems (SRDS 2002), pp. 130–139. IEEE CS Press, Los Alamitos (2002)
15. Dohi, T., Suzuki, H., Trivedi, K.S.: Comparing software rejuvenation policies under different dependability measures. IEICE Transactions on Information and Systems (D) E87-D(8), 2078–2085 (2004)
16. Dohi, T., Ozaki, T., Kaio, N.: Optimal sequential checkpoint placement with equality constraints. In: Proceedings of The 2nd IEEE International Symposium on Dependable Autonomic and Secure Computing (DASC 2006), pp. 77–84. IEEE CS Press, Los Alamitos (2006)
17. Eto, H., Dohi, T.: Analysis of a service degradation model with preventive rejuvenation. In: Penkler, D., Reitenspiess, M., Tam, F. (eds.) ISAS 2006. LNCS, vol. 4328, pp. 17–29. Springer, Heidelberg (2006)
18. Fukumoto, S., Kaio, N., Osaki, S.: A study of checkpoint generations for a database recovery mechanism. Computers Math. Applic. 24, 63–70 (1992)
19. Fukumoto, S., Kaio, N., Osaki, S.: Optimal checkpointing strategies using the checkpointing density. Journal of Information Processing 15, 87–92 (1992)
20. Garg, S., Telek, M., Puliafito, A., Trivedi, K.S.: Analysis of software rejuvenation using Markov regenerative stochastic Petri net. In: Proceedings of 6th International Symposium on Software Reliability Engineering (ISSRE 1995), pp. 24–27. IEEE CS Press, Los Alamitos (1995)
21. Garg, S., Huang, Y., Kintala, C., Trivedi, K.S.: Minimizing completion time of a program by checkpointing and rejuvenation. In: Proceedings of 1996 ACM SIGMETRICS Conference, pp. 252–261. ACM Press, New York (1996)
22. Garg, S., Pfening, S., Puliafito, A., Telek, M., Trivedi, K.S.: Analysis of preventive maintenance in transactions based software systems. IEEE Transactions on Computers 47, 96–107 (1998)

23. Gottfried, B.S.: A stopping criterion for the golden-ratio search. Operations Research 23, 553–555 (1975)
24. Huang, Y., Kintala, C., Kolettin, N., Funton, N.D.: Software rejuvenation: analysis, module and applications. In: Proceedings 25th International Symposium on Fault Tolerant Computing (FTC 1995), pp. 381–390. IEEE CS Press, Los Alamitos (1995)
25. Gelenbe, E., Derochette, D.: Performance of rollback recovery systems under intermittent failures. Communications of the ACM 21(6), 493–499 (1978)
26. Gelenbe, E.: On the optimum checkpoint interval. Journal of the ACM 26(2), 259–270 (1979)
27. Gelenbe, E.E., Hernandez, M.: Optimum checkpoints with age dependent failures. Acta Informatica 27, 519–531 (1990)
28. Goes, P.B., Sumita, U.: Stochastic models for performance analysis of database recovery control. IEEE Transactions on Computers C-44(4), 561–576 (1995)
29. Goes, P.B.: A stochastic model for performance evaluation of main memory resident database systems. ORSA Journal of Computing 7(3), 269–282 (1997)
30. Grassi, V., Donatiello, L., Tucci, S.: On the optimal checkpointing of critical tasks and transaction-oriented systems. IEEE Transactions on Software Engineering SE-18(1), 72–77 (1992)
31. Kulkarni, V.G., Nicola, V.F., Trivedi, K.S.: Effects of checkpointing and queueing on program performance. Stochastic Models 6(4), 615–648 (1990)
32. L'Ecuyer, P., Malenfant, J.: Computing optimal checkpointing strategies for rollback and recovery systems. IEEE Transactions on Computers C-37(4), 491–496 (1988)
33. Ling, Y., Mi, J., Lin, X.: A variational calculus approach to optimal checkpoint placement. IEEE Transactions on Computers 50(7), 699–707 (2001)
34. Nicola, V.F., Van Spanje, J.M.: Comparative analysis of different models of checkpointing and recovery. IEEE Transactions on Software Engineering SE-16(8), 807–821 (1990)
35. Nicola, V.F.: Checkpointing and modeling of program execution time. In: Lyu, M.R. (ed.) Software Fault Tolerance, pp. 167–188. John Wiley & Sons, Chichester (1995)
36. Okamura, H., Miyahara, S., Dohi, T.: Dependability analysis of a client/server software systems with rejuvenation. In: Proceedings of 13th International Symposium on Software Reliability Engineering (ISSRE 2002), pp. 171–180. IEEE CS Press, Los Alamitos (2002)
37. Okamura, H., Miyahara, S., Dohi, T.: Dependability analysis of a transaction-based multi server system with rejuvenation. IEICE Transactions on Fundamentals of Electronics, Communications and Computer Sciences (A) E86-A(8), 2081–2090 (2003)
38. Okamura, H., Fujio, H., Dohi, T.: Fine-grained shock models to rejuvenate software systems. IEICE Transactions on Information and Systems (D) E86-D(10), 2165–2171 (2003)
39. Okamura, H., Nishimura, Y., Dohi, T.: A dynamic checkpointing scheme based on reinforcement learning. In: Proceedings of The 10th International Symposium on Pacific Rim Dependable Computing (PRDC 2004), pp. 151–158. IEEE CS Press, Los Alamitos (2004)
40. Okamura, H., Miyahara, S., Dohi, T.: Rejuvenating communication network system with burst arrival. IEICE Transactions on Communications (B) E88-B(12), 4498–4506 (2005)

41. Okamura, H., Iwamoto, K., Dohi, T.: A dynamic programming algorithm for software rejuvenation scheduling under distributed computation circumstance. In: Proceedings of IEEE 11th International Conference on Parallel and Distributed Systems (ICPDS 2005), vol. II, pp. 493–497. IEEE CS Press, Los Alamitos (2005)
42. Okamura, H., Iwamoto, K., Dohi, T.: A DP-based optimal checkpointing algorithm for real-time appications. International Journal of Reliability, Quality and Safety Engineering 13(4), 323–340 (2006)
43. Ozaki, T., Dohi, T., Okamura, H., Kaio, N.: Distribution-free checkpoint placement algorithms based on min-max principle. IEEE Transactions on Dependable and Secure Computing 3(2), 130–140 (2006)
44. Pfening, S., Garg, S., Puliafito, A., Telek, M., Trivedi, K.S.: Optimal rejuvenation for tolerating soft failure. Performance Evaluation 27/28(4), 491–506 (1996)
45. Puterman, M.: Markov Decision Processes. John Wiley & Sons, New York (1994)
46. Reinecke, P., van Moorsel, A.P., Wolter, K.: A measurement study of the interplay between application level restart and transport protocol. In: Malek, M., Reitenspiess, M., Kaiser, J. (eds.) ISAS 2004. LNCS, vol. 3335, pp. 86–100. Springer, Heidelberg (2005)
47. Rinsaka, K., Dohi, T.: Behavioral analysis of fault-torellant software systems with rejuvenation. IEICE Transactions on Information and Systems (D) E88-D(12), 2681–2690 (2005)
48. Rinsaka, K., Dohi, T.: A faster estimation algorithm for periodic preventive rejuvenation schedule maximizing system availability. In: Malek, M., Reitenspieß, M., van Moorsel, A. (eds.) ISAS 2007. LNCS, vol. 4526, pp. 94–104. Springer, Heidelberg (2007)
49. Tai, A.T., Alkalai, L., Chau, S.N.: On-board preventive maintenance: a design-oriented analytic study for long-life applications. Performance Evaluation 35(3/4), 215–232 (1999)
50. Toueg, S., Babaoğlu, Ö.: On the optimum checkpoint selection problem. SIAM Journal of Computing 13(3), 630–649 (1984)
51. Vaidyanathan, K.V., Harper, R.E., Hunter, S.W., Trivedi, K.S.: Analysis of software rejuvenation in cluster systems. In: Proceedings of ACM SIGMETRICS 2001/Performance 2001, pp. 62–71. ACM Press, New York (2001)
52. Vaidyanathan, K.V., Trivedi, K.S.: A comprehensive model for software rejuvenation. IEEE Transactions on Dependable and Secure Computing 2(2), 124–137 (2005)
53. Vaidya, N.H.: Impact of checkpoint latency on overhead ratio of a checkpointing scheme. IEEE Transactions on Computers C-46(8), 942–947 (1997)
54. van Moorsel, A.P., Wolter, K.: Optimal restart times for moments of completion time. IEE Proceedings of Software 151(5), 219–223 (2004)
55. van Moorsel, A.P., Wolter, K.: Analysis of restart mechanisms in software systems. IEEE Transactions on Software Engineering 32(8), 547–558 (2006)
56. Wang, D., Xie, W., Trivedi, K.S.: Performability analysis of clustered systems with rejuvenation under varying workload. Performance Evaluation (in press)
57. Ziv, A., Bruck, J.: An on-line algorithm for checkpoint placement. IEEE Transactions on Computers C-46(9), 976–985 (1997)
58. Young, J.W.: A first order approximation to the optimum checkpoint interval. Communications of the ACM 17(9), 530–531 (1974)

A Platform for Cooperative Server Backups
Based on Virtual Machines

Akiyoshi Sugiki[1], Kei Yamatozaki[2], Richard Potter[1], and Kazuhiko Kato[2,1]

[1] CREST, Japan Science and Technology Agency
[2] Department of Computer Science, University of Tsukuba
1-1-1 Tennodai, Tsukuba, Ibaraki, 305-8573 Japan
{sugiki,k-yamatozaki,potter}@osss.cs.tsukuba.ac.jp,
kato@cs.tsukuba.ac.jp

Abstract. We present a virtual machine-based peer-to-peer platform
that allows many Internet services to back up their services cooperatively. The goal of our platform is to provide a highly-available and
service-independent solution that is cost-effective for smaller, independent service providers. Use of virtual machines makes it possible to encapsulate the complete service state and to share physical hosts. A multicast
protocol guarantees that service state is replicated reliably on multiple
physical hosts so that in case of failures, recent state can be recovered. We
implemented a prototype and evaluated it by experiments to show that
our design can adapt to dynamic host changes and evaluate the runtime
and failure recovery performance possible with Xen and SBUML virtual
machines.

Keywords: middleware, virtual machines, Internet services, passive
replication, peer-to-peer.

1 Introduction

Service availability is a crucial requirement for the growing number of Internet services. A traditional fault-tolerance or disaster-recovery solution for high
availability is to replicate service state on multiple physical hosts in different
locations. This technique is reliable and widely deployed. However, existing implementations are too expensive for small Internet services that are typically
hosted on a single physical computer. These small services are prevalent because
of the long-tail of the Internet and the large number of small startup companies,
non profit organizations and schools have their own web sites and mail servers.
In universities or companies, they also have many individual servers in their de-
partments. They can not afford to purchase the multiple servers for necessary
for traditional service availability techniques, so their availability is very limited.
Even if they do use multiple physical hosts, most of the computing resources are
unused resulting in costly inefficiency.

In this paper, we present a virtual machine-based peer-to-peer platform that
allows many Internet services to back up their services cooperatively. By constructing a cooperative platform on top of individual physical hosts, we provide

T. Nanya et al. (Eds.): ISAS 2008, LNCS 5017, pp. 129–141, 2008.

a highly-available and cost-effective solution especially for small, independent service providers.

Virtual machines help the platform be reliable by allowing the service state to be checkpointed and migrated to another host. The service state can be complete, including everything from the operating system (OS) to the service software. Virtual machines make this possible without requiring any special modifications to the service code. In addition, virtual machines provide isolation, so that when multiple services share the same physical host, problems in one service will not cause failures in other services.

Our approach is based on passive replication of the virtual machine state to backup hosts in order to provide a service-independent solution. A reliable delivery protocol guarantees that the virtual machine checkpointed service state is replicated reliably on multiple hosts. In case of failures, a consistent virtual machine image can be resumed on a backup, which takes over providing the service. Dynamic backup host additions and departures are managed by a membership protocol in a decentralized manner.

The main contribution of this paper is that we show the use of virtualization for a such cooperative platform is one promising way to achieve highly-available Internet services cost-effectively. We implemented a prototype and evaluated it by the experiments. We currently support two hypervisors: Xen [1] and Scrap Book for User-Mode Linux (SBUML) [2,3]. Experimental results show that our mechanism can adapt to dynamic host configurations and successfully recover from failures.

The rest of this paper is organized as follows. Section 2 describes the overview of our platform. Section 3 explains the basic system architecture. Section 4 shows our implementation and the results of the experiments. Section 5 presents related work. Finally, we conclude the paper in Section 6.

2   Cooperative Platform for Service Backups

Figure 1 shows the overview of our platform. The platform runs on the top of separate physical hosts which are used to host their own services independently. Because our ultimate goal is to provide disaster-recovery by cooperation in WAN environments, we cannot assume shared disks exist as is required by HA clusters like VMware HA [4] and Bressoud and Schneider's research [5] on HP PA-RISC. We also assume fault-tolerance in LAN environments by sharing department servers in companies or universities. The overall architecture is designed and implemented to be modular so that it can work with various virtual machines.

Service providers do not have to prepare multiple physical hosts for high availability or modify their service. They only have to install their service inside a virtual machine. By using replication, the platform provides highly available Internet services. Services are replicated on multiple hosts and the clients interact with a single instance of them. If a failure occurs, one of the other hosts continues to provide that service. By sharing the individual machines of many service providers, the platform can achieve it cost-effectively. When a backup server is

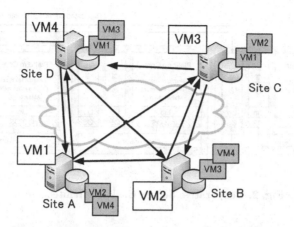

Fig. 1. Virtual machine-based cooperative platform

required, virtualization allows multiple servers to run on the same host without interference.

Virtual machines increase reliability on such platform by the following advantages:

- **Service transparency:** Virtual machines can transparently capture service state by checkpointing and replicate it to different locations. No delicate or tailored modification of service software is required.
- **Completeness:** Virtual machines encapsulate the complete service state, including service software, libraries, and OS. In contrast, traditional fault-tolerant systems are implemented as libraries and limit encapsulated state to only the service software.
- **Isolation:** Virtual machines provide the similar level of security to physical hosts. Even if one virtual machine is down, the other virtual machines on the same host can continue their processes. Some virtual machines like Xen also provide performance-isolation mechanism.
- **Resource efficiency:** Multiple virtual machines can run simultaneously on the same host. Because recent PC servers have ample disk space, a large number of virtual machine checkpoints from another physical hosts can be saved.
- **Recovery from hot-state:** In most traditional fault-tolerant systems, a service must read the disk state from storage and reboot the service software to recover from failures. In contrast, virtual machines encapsulate the running state.

The use of virtual machines is attractive, especially for the many new Internet services that are developed with extreme time and cost constraints. Thus, we propose virtual machine-based platform to provide a service-transparent and reliable solution.

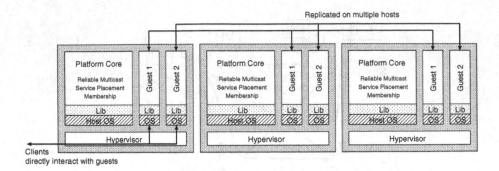

Fig. 2. Cooperative Server Backup Architecture

3   System Architecture

Although virtual machines simplify many problems, coordination between the cooperating hosts raises many issues. In this paper, we especially deal with the core architecture for the cooperative platform. This paper addresses physical host management, reliable replication of virtual machines, and virtual machine placement problems. Other problems like guest address resolutions are beyond the scope of this paper and remain for future work.

Figure 2 shows the basic system architecture. We assume a hypervisor is running inside each host. A service is encapsulated by a virtual machine, which has the service software, libraries, and OS required for the service. The clients directly interact with the server programs inside the virtual machines so that they do not have to be aware that the service is running inside the virtual machine and on the top of our platform.

In the current design, we simply trust all hosts. The core software runs inside host OS. Alternatively, we can run it in a separated and dedicated guest OS. The core software of the platform consists of several components. The main ones are:

- **Reliable multicast:** The reliable multicast component provides reliable replication of the virtual machine states. It guarantees the replicated virtual machine states to be consistent.
- **Service placement:** This component determines the actual placement and number of primary and backup virtual machines.
- **Membership:** This component manages all physical hosts. Every time a host joins or departs, this component reacts. It also provides failure detection mechanism.

The following sections describe each of the components in more detail: Section 3.1 describes the reliable multicast component, Section 3.2 explains the virtual machine placement component, and the membership component is shown in Section 3.3.

Table 1. Comparison of active and passive standby

	Replication method	Service assumption	CPU cost	Network cost	Incremental recovery trails
Active standby	Request replication	Deterministic	×	√	×
Passive standby	Checkpoint replication	—	√	×	√

3.1 Reliable Replication of Virtual Machines

Design choices. *State replication* approach is commonly used for highly available services. In this approach, a service is replicated on multiple hosts and their hosts continuously transition to the same state in same order. Two major classes of techniques ensure the consistency (Table 1) :

- **Active Standby:** In this approach, every host processes the requests from the clients and transitions independently. This technique is useful since replicating requests incurs a smaller network cost than replicating the checkpoints. However, it has two important drawbacks: (1) this approach implies high computational resource usage, and more importantly (2) the requests have to be processed in a deterministic manner. Generally, a service may result in different states by reorder of interrupts, timer, scheduling and others.
- **Passive Standby:** With the passive standby, one of the hosts called the *primary* plays a special role: it receives the requests from the clients and replies responses. The *backup* hosts periodically receive state update messages from the primary. This technique is attractive since it requires less computational resource usage than active standby and makes no assumption on determinism for processing requests.

Our virtual machine-based state replication is based on passive standby, because our goal is a service-independent solution, which cannot expect the service to run deterministically. Also, most hypervisors support checkpoint mechanisms that can easily encapsulate the complete service state. Although their virtual machine checkpoints are large, coarse grained, and must be handled as a black-box, they are widely available. Furthermore, if one of the backup hosts cannot recover from the recent checkpoint, it can retry the recovery process from an accumulated history of checkpoints. This cannot implemented by active standby approach.

Approach. A Paxos [6,7]-based reliable multicast protocol is used to reliably achieve passive standby. Paxos guarantees the safety properties and can run asynchronously avoiding performance degradation caused by slow down or temporal unavailability of backup hosts.

Our protocol is based on Mazières' hand out [8], which we slightly optimized for virtual machine replication. We collapsed the three roles in the protocol into two roles: primary host and backup hosts, and use the following sequence for replication: (1) the primary takes an incremental checkpoint and propagates it

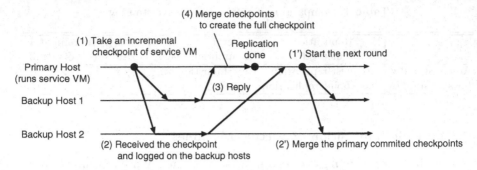

Fig. 3. Virtual machine replication process

to the backup hosts. Because the base virtual machine is assumed to have been already transferred, only smaller checkpoints are transmitted in this step. Next, (2) the backup hosts receive the checkpoint and immediately write it to their logs. Then, (3) the backup hosts reply acknowledgments to the primary. (4) Once the primary receives acknowledgments from the majority, the primary commits the incremental checkpoint by merging it into the full checkpoint to save disk space. In the next round, the primary piggybacks the recent committed position of checkpoints on the first message and the backup hosts do the same merge operation. By this overlap, the checkpoints are replicated efficiently. Failures in the intermediate steps force the reconfiguration protocol described in [8] to run for recovery. Even if some backup hosts slow down or are temporarily unavailable in the normal operations, they can catch up to the recent state safely by using the reconfiguration protocol. Only a single configuration is selected even if multiple hosts request reconfiguration simultaneously. If a hypervisor does not support incremental checkpoints like Xen, we use full checkpoints instead.

The current design is constructed based on several assumptions. First, we assume an asynchronous system with failure detectors. We also assume only fail-stop failures of host OSes and hardware and assume network channels are reliable. But, this model can be extended by variants of state replication approaches like [9] because this limitation comes from the use of the basic Paxos algorithm. In contrast, a guest OS is not limited to fail-stop failures if it can be detected by a failure detector. Second, to survive F host failures, the replication mechanism requires $2F + 1$ hosts. This assumption can be loosen by the Paxos variants like [10]. Even in the current system, service providers can dynamically change the number of replicated hosts by running a reconfiguration protocol. Finally, we assume general Internet connections instead of leased lines and our protocol design was made based on this assumption. From the clients' perspective our protocol replicate services state without lock-step and all the replicated state is either up-to-date or still unchanged from the previous state. Because there is an obvious trade-off between the service performance and the up-to-dateness of the replicated state, we give a priority to replicated virtual machine

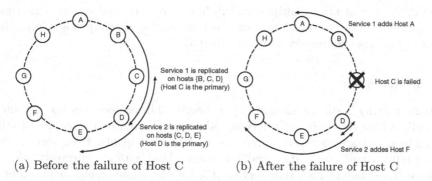

(a) Before the failure of Host C   (b) After the failure of Host C

Fig. 4. Example of dynamic host configuration

state to be consistent rather than up-to-date. We have a plan to throttle the checkpoint interval based on observations of the service performance.

3.2 Service Placement

Currently, the platform supports a Chord [11]-like service placement policy (Figure 4). We use SHA-1 hash to generate a 160-bit identifier which is used to determine which hosts are responsible for that service. We call the key for a host a *host key* and that for a service a *service key*. All hosts know the keys because they are piggybacked on membership messages. All participating hosts are mapped onto the single ring according to the keys and closest host to the service key becomes the primary host for that service. The backup hosts are selected from the neighbors at both sides. The number of backup hosts can be changed by specifying in the service configuration file. In the event of host departure, closest host takes over the responsibility.

Figure 4 depicts an example of dynamic configuration change. Initially, Service 1 is provided by hosts {B, C, D} and Service 2 is hosted by hosts {C, D, E}. Hosts C and D are the primary hosts respectively. Once the host C has failed, the configuration for Service 1 is changed to {A, B, D} and that for Service 2 is changed to {D, E, F}. At this time, closest host for each service is selected.

Each service provider wishes to provide its service at the initial host if possible until the failure occurs. Therefore, we use the host key of the initial host as the service key in the current implementation. By this technique, the initial hosts can provide their own services until the failures occur. If an initial host recovers from the failure, it can become the primary again.

Because our platform operates cooperatively, there is no centralized management of service placement. Service placement must be calculated by the individual hosts. But, if multiple hosts calculate simultaneously the placement for the same service, results may be inconsistent. Therefore, we adopt the strategy that the primary host for each service is responsible for the placement. When a host becomes the primary, the service placement component is activated and it calculates the placement of the service. Those of the other hosts are deactivated.

If the primary host fails, multiple backup hosts are activated at the same time and compete in an election. Once one of the previous backup hosts wins the election, the other components are deactivated.

3.3 Membership

All participating hosts are managed by a membership protocol. Hosts are automatically added to the *candidate view* and removed from it in the case of failures. The candidate view can be seen by all the participants. Each service can choose replica hosts from the candidate view. The platform currently adopts a gossip-based failure detection service [12] for the membership management, which provides scalable and robust management by each participant periodically propagating the list of known hosts to another randomly selected host. We also combines TCP connection monitoring for faster failure detection.

When a host joins and leaves, the membership protocol automatically notifies the event to the server placement component, and the service placement reacts accordingly.

4 Experiments

We implemented a prototype as a part of Sustainable Service Framework [13] that we have been developing. To optimize the productivity, it was implemented in Java and consists of 19,260 lines of code. Although it was implemented in Java, we did many optimizations to maximize the performance. The internal structure is split into multiple stages similar to the SEDA architecture [14] and requests are processed by an event-driven design. While ordinary messages are passed by Java's serialization mechanism, large file transfers like virtual machine checkpoints are sent by the Java nio's `sendfile` mechanism. Although they are mixed, FIFO order is preserved.

The type of virtual machines used can integrated into the system with small code additions. We currently support two virtual machines: Xen and ScrapBook for User-Mode Linux [2,3]. Xen is a well known open-source hypervisor and SBUML is a descendant of User-Mode Linux which supports checkpoint mechanism the original does not support. The performance of Xen is relatively good but it requires a Xen supported host and guest kernels. In contrast, SBUML can run with many Linux distributions with no host kernel modification but the performance is limited due to the user-level implementation. Furthermore, SBUML supports incremental checkpoint mechanism while Xen only supports full checkpoints.

In this paper, we conducted three types of experiments to verify our method applicability: measuring the overhead of Java-implemented replication mechanism, the virtual machine bare checkpointing time, and observing the behavior of dynamic host changes. Although we plan to use our mechanism in WAN environments, we conducted all experiments using a LAN to understand the bare replication overheads and performance.

Table 2. Service performance overheads incurred by virtual machines

Benchmark	Native [MB/s]	SBUML [MB/s]	Xen [MB/s]
dbench	421.48	14.85 (3.5%)	257.71 (61.1%)
tbench	83.42	8.69 (10.4%)	67.03 (80.3%)

() shows the ratio to the native performance.

Table 3. Checkpointing overheads

		SBUML	Xen
Checkpoint size	[MB]	126.1	268.7
Checkpoint time	[sec]	4.37	8.45
Recovery time	[sec]	3.70	8.08

4.1 Experimental Setup

All experiments were conducted on 5 identical PC servers. Each was equipped with Dual Xeon 3.60GHz CPUs, 2GB memory, and a single 36GB SCSI disk. Each was connected to a single switch via 1000Base-T network adapter. Fedora 8 (Linux 2.6.21-xen or 2.6.23) was used for host OS and guest OS of Xen. Guest OS of SBUML was CentOS 3.9 (Linux 2.4.24-1um-1sb). Sun JDK 1.6.0 was used for Java and guest domains were assigned 256MB memory during all experiments.

4.2 Replication Overheads

To understand the overhead of our Java-implemented reliable multicast, we measured the replication performance without virtual machines. We first show the elapsed time for replicating null requests on three physical hosts. Although the messages were replicated, replicated hosts did not involve any request processing. We conducted 10,000 measurements and each replication only took 2.78 ms on an average. This results was similar to a simple key/value service results (2.98 ms) that was implemented in C [15], so the overhead of implementing in Java was sufficiently small. In contrast, the average time of constructing the first view was 69.79 ms. This time was slightly longer than that of Paxos normal operations due to more complex message exchanges.

4.3 Virtual Machine Overheads

In the next experiment, we measured service performance overhead incurred by virtual machines. Table 2 shows the results in both SBUML and Xen. We used the dbench and tbench commands included by dbench [16] suite for this benchmark. dbench generates disk I/O part of an emulated samba workload and tbench generates only TCP connection part of that workload.

From Table 2, the throughput of SBUML was much lower than the native performance. The throughputs of dbench and tbench were 3.5% and 10.4% of the

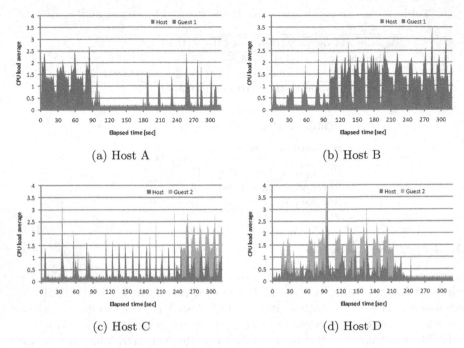

(a) Host A   (b) Host B

(c) Host C   (d) Host D

Fig. 5. Handling dynamic changes

native performance respectively. This was due to the poor I/O implementation of User-mode Linux and the original User-mode Linux has the same problem. The performance of Xen was relatively good it is a more tolerable degradation. These throughputs were 61.1% and 80.3% of the native throughput. The performance comparison of Xen and User-mode Linux was also shown in Xen's paper [1].

Next, we measured the overhead of virtual machine checkpointing. Table 3 shows checkpoint overheads for dbench workload. Table 3 shows the average checkpoint size, average time for taking checkpoints, and average time to recover from the checkpoints for each virtual machine. SBUML was relatively fast and its checkpoint size was smaller than that of Xen. The size and time were 46.9% and 51.7% of those of Xen respectively.

4.4   Handling Changes

This subsection studies how our platform recovers from system failures. In this benchmark, we used Xen as a hypervisor. We started four hosts and ran two services, Service 1 and 2, which consume much CPU time. During the benchmark, we artificially injected failures by killing processes.

Figure 5 shows the CPU load average transitions of all hosts. We observed the transitions for 320 seconds. Initially, Service 1 and 2 were running on Host A and D respectively. These services were replicated on the hosts {A, B, C} and {B, C, D} and replication was periodically done at 30 seconds interval. During

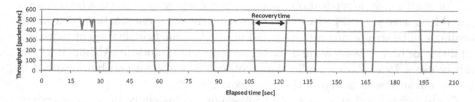

Fig. 6. Handling failures (client perspective)

checkpointing, the load average of guest OSes are degraded because Xen must suspend the guest OSes during checkpointing. The load average of host OSes in Host A and D increased immediately after the finish of checkpointing due to the replication process.

After 100 seconds, Host A was caused to failed. Our platform immediately detected the failure and it caused a reconfiguration protocol to run. Host B took over for Host A. Host A rejoined to the platform at 180 seconds. After 240 seconds, a failure was introduced to Host D. This caused a reconfiguration protocol to run again and Host C was used for take-over.

Figure 6 shows the configuration changes from a client's view in another experiment. We ran four hosts with a single service and the client continuously sends UDP ping messages to the server inside the Xen virtual machine. Figure 6 shows these throughput of the messages over time. The throughput was periodically degraded for about 8 seconds due to checkpointing. A failure was artificially introduced at 108 seconds, and our reconfiguration was immediately ran. After 123 seconds, the throughput recovered. From clients' perspective, it can be seen as a single server were continuously providing service.

5   Related Work

Several recent research projects have been investigating virtual machine-based fault-tolerant or disaster-recovery systems, but our goal is different from these efforts. Our goal is to construct a general cooperative platform for fault-tolerance rather that can be used with various virtual machine implementations. These other projects develop techniques aimed at specific virtual machine implementations.

Second Site [17,18] aims for the disaster protection of the common server. Although their goal is ambitious, only a single position paper and talk slides have been revealed at this time. They are based on the modification of Xen's live migration and frequently replicate the event level checkpoints of virtual machines. But, the details of replication protocol is unknown and their goal is different from our goal of constructing a cooperative platform. VM-FIT [19] uses active standby of virtual machines for fault tolerant systems. Stodden [20] studies semi-active standby of Xen for fault-tolerance. All these researches are studying techniques specific to particular virtual machines rather than constructing the cooperative platform.

The state machine replication approach is not a new idea and has been investigated for many years [21]. However, only recently has virtualization been widely available. The strong encapsulation and migration functionality opens more possibilities for highly-available and service-independent solutions. Although we currently use a Paxos-based replication protocol, our system can be improved by recent advancement in replication protocols like [22].

Cooperative platforms have been investigated especially in storage systems [23], proxies [24], and the other peer-to-peer systems. Our approach is a first step toward a virtual machine based cooperative platform to achieve highly available Internet services cost-effectively.

6   Conclusions and Future Work

We presented a platform that allows Internet service providers to cooperatively replicating service state among their host servers. It provides highly-available and cost-effective solution especially for small Internet services. Our approach is based on virtual machines to capture the complete service state and make it possible to safely share physical hosts. A Paxos-based reliable multicast guarantees that service state is reliably replicated on multiple hosts, which allows automatic recovery from recently committed state in the case of failures. We implemented a prototype and evaluated it by the experiments. Our results show that our prototype can adapt to dynamic host changes and successfully recover from failures.

In future work, we will further investigate to make our platform more reliable and practical. First, we will address a quantitative study in WAN environments. To this goal, a guest address hand-over mechanism in WAN is required. Second, we will implement a faster checkpoint mechanism for the virtual machines. Third, by incorporating a request logging mechanism between a server and the clients, we will achieve zero-loss recovery. Finally, we will investigate dynamic reconfiguration based on host resource usage.

Acknowledgements. This research was partially supported by Core Research for Evolutional Science and Technology (CREST) program of Japan Science and Technology Agency.

References

1. Barham, P., Dragovic, B., Fraser, K., Hand, S., Harris, T., Ho, A., Neugebauer, R., Pratt, I., Warfield, A.: Xen and the art of virtualization. In: ACM SOSP 2003, pp. 164–177 (2003)
2. Potter, R.: Scrap book for user-mode linux, http://sbuml.sourceforge.net/
3. Potter, R.: One-click distribution of preconfigured Linux runtime state. In: USENIX VM 2004 WiPs (2004)
4. VMware Inc.: VMware High Availability, http://www.vmware.com/products/vi/vc/ha.html

5. Bressoud, T.C., Schneider, F.B.: Hypervisor-based fault tolerance. ACM TOCS 14(1), 80–107 (1996)
6. Lamport, L.: The part-time parliament. ACM TOCS 16(2), 133–169 (1998)
7. Lamport, L.: Paxos made simple. ACM SIGACT News 32(4), 51–58 (2001)
8. Mazières, D.: Paxos made practical (2007),
   http://www.scs.stanford.edu/07wi-cs244b/sched/readings/paxos.pdf
9. Castro, M., Liskov, B.: Practical byzantine fault tolerance. In: USENIX OSDI 1999, pp. 173–186 (1999)
10. Lamport, L., Massa, M.: Cheap Paxos. In: IEEE/IFIP DSN 2004, pp. 307–314 (2004)
11. Stoica, I., Morris, R., Karger, D., Kaashoek, M.F., Balakrishnan, H.: Chord: A scalable peer-to-peer lookup service for Internet applications. In: ACM SIGCOMM 2001, pp. 149–160 (2001)
12. van Renesse, R., Minsky, Y., Hayden, M.: A gossip-style failure detection service. In: IFIP Middleware 1998, pp. 55–70 (1998)
13. Koiso, T., Abe, H., Ikejima, S., Ishikawa, M., Potter, R., Kato, K.: Design of an infrastructure toolkit for sustainable service. IPSJ Trans. on Advanced Computing System 48(SIG3 (ACS 17)) , 13–26 (2007) (in Japanese)
14. Welsh, M., Culler, D., Brewer, E.: SEDA: an architecture for well-conditioned, scalable Internet services. In: ACM SOSP 2001, pp. 230–243 (2001)
15. Lorch, J.R., Adya, A., Bolosky, W.J., Chaiken, R., Douceur, J.R., Howell, J.: The SMART way to migrate replicated stateful services. In: ACM EuroSys 2006, pp. 103–115 (2006)
16. Tridgell, A.: dbench, http://samba.org/ftp/triage/dbench/
17. Cully, B., Warfield, A.: Secondsite: Disaster protection for the common server. In: USENIX HotDep 2006 (2006)
18. Cully, B.: High-speed checkpointing for high availability. In: Xen Summit 5 (2007)
19. Reiser, H.P., Kapitza, R.: Hypervisor-based efficient proactive recovery. In: IEEE SRDS 2007, pp. 83–92 (2007)
20. Stodden, D.: Semi-active workload replication and live migration with paravirtual machines. In: Xen Summit, Spring 2007 (2007)
21. Defago, X., Schiper, A., Sergent, N.: Semi-passive replication. In: IEEE SRDS 1998, pp. 43–50 (1998)
22. Marchetti, C., Baldoni, R., Tucci-Piergiovanni, S., Virgillito, A.: Fully distributed three-tier active software replication. IEEE TPDS 17(7)(1), 633–645
23. Haeberlen, A., Mislove, A., Druschel, P.: Glacier: highly durable, decentralized storage despite massive correlated failures. In: USENIX NSDI 2005, pp. 143–158 (2005)
24. Wolman, A., Voelker, M., Sharma, N., Cardwell, N., Karlin, A., Levy, H.M.: On the scale and performance of cooperative Web proxy caching. In: ACM SOSP 1999, pp. 16–31 (1999)

Platform Management with SA Forum and Its Role to Achieve High Availability

Ulrich Kleber[1], Frédéric Herrmann[2], and Ulrich Horstmann[1]

[1] Nokia Siemens Networks, St.Martin-Str.76, 81541 Munich, Germany
[2] Sun Microsystems, Viale Fulvio Testi, 327, 20162 Milano, Italia
Ulrich.Kleber@nsn.com, Frederic.Herrmann@sun.com,
Ulrich.Horstmann@nsn.com

Abstract. With its next release, SA Forum will provide a new platform management service and so will close the gap between HPI and AIS services. This
new service will match the configured system to the actually present hardware
and will make hardware states easily accessible for software via the information
model. At the same time it extends the information model with objects that represent operating systems and virtualization layers. The new service provides a
state model for all these objects and APIs to inform its users about changes,
such as operator interactions with the equipment. Administrative commands can
be used for platform maintenance. The complete information model will allow
fault correlation over all platform layers up to the application. This is necessary
for proper fault analysis and to really achieve high availability.

1 Introduction

When talking about high availability of computer systems, we spend much time in
computing the probability of hardware failures; we provide redundancy by allowing a
failed unit to be substituted by another one, and we take large efforts to enable the
software to catch up with tasks started on the failed unit. SA Forum provides standards to access the hardware (with its Hardware Platform Interface HPI) and standards for the software to manage redundancy (the Application Interface Specification
AIS). However, currently there is no standardized way to correlate hardware events to
affected software entities. HPI provides a view of the system, based on discovery of
the present hardware, which is identified by its so-called entity path. Any software
having direct hardware dependency needs to perform sophisticated analysis of HPI
events to be able to take appropriate actions. On the other hand, AIS provides very
flexible means for location-transparent execution of software services. Applications
can run in different redundancy schemes on different hardware in a system. Health
monitoring is done independently from hardware events, which is important to cover
hardware and software errors. But when redundancy mechanisms recover the system
from an error - be it with or without service interruption - it is necessary to analyze
the error and isolate it. Faulty hardware should be switched off and replaced; software
errors must be analyzed and corrections provided.

With its next release, SA Forum will provide the first step to standardize platform
management. A new service will be provided to enable AIS middleware and application

T. Nanya et al. (Eds.): ISAS 2008, LNCS 5017, pp. 142–154, 2008.
© Springer-Verlag Berlin Heidelberg 2008

software to access hardware and low-level software (i.e. operating system and virtualization layers) in a more abstract way. The new service will use the same paradigms as other AIS services: it will provide an information model to represent hardware and low level software, states for its objects, and subscriber/callback interfaces in the usual way.

In the following chapters, we will outline the principles behind this new service, and thus provide an overview of the upcoming specification.

2 System Model

One of the main differences between an HPI view and an AIS view of a system is that HPI is based on hardware discovery, whereas AIS works on a pre-configured system model (called the information model in SA Forum terminology). The IMM service (information model management, part of AIS) provides access to the information model for all AIS services and for applications. In more detail this means:

- HPI discovers what is there. It reports to its users the present hardware, its types and capabilities, and also its health. However, it does not provide any assessment on whether this hardware is really what the system architecture needs to run the configured software.
- The AIS information model contains the desired system configuration - independent of the actual existing hardware. So the user can configure applications on non-existing nodes and do all the necessary maintenance operations like locking, deleting, or creating configured entities - independent of the hardware being present. This modeling allows the definition of maintenance procedures, like locking a faulty piece of hardware which had been powered down for fault isolation before it is replaced.

  The configuration element in the current information model that is closest to the hardware is a cluster node. A cluster node can be configured even when the hardware where it is meant to run does not exist. If the cluster node is administratively locked while its hardware is inserted, an operator can control its start-up and, if necessary, perform a complete hardware diagnosis before services are allowed to run.

So the system configuration as stored in the AIS information model must be matched to the existing hardware (its type and version) as found by HPI discovery. Software should only be started if the present hardware type is supported.

2.1 Information Model for Physical Resources

The new platform management service PLM provides objects in the information model that represent the configured hardware entities. These objects store the necessary data to allow hardware type checking and to indicate the relationship between hardware entities. As an example, a mezzanine module sitting on a computing blade or carrier board is represented by an object in a containment tree, the carrier board being its parent. When the carrier board is physically removed from the system, all contained entities are affected in the same way as when the mezzanine module is extracted.

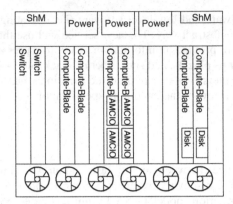

Fig. 1. Example System Configuration

We illustrate this with a small example system. Let's have one shelf, equipped with 6 computing blades plus two switches. Two of the computing blades have AMC disks (one each); two other blades have specialized AMC IO modules (two each).

This hardware configuration would be represented in the information model like this:

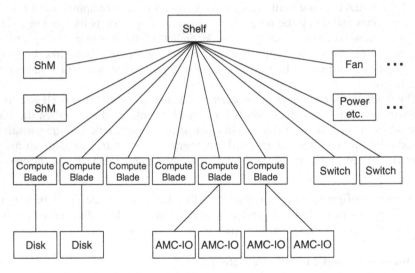

Fig. 2. Hardware Information Model of Example System Configuration

The shelf object is parent to all the blades (including switch blades) and also to the field replaceable units of the infrastructure, like shelf managers, fans, and power entry modules. Blades in the same way parent the sub-modules, in this case AMC-IO cards and disks.

This modeling allows PLM to also provide appropriate state management for these objects. State changes of a blade thus also affect its sub-modules: a disk in this configuration cannot be accessed if its carrier CPU-blade is faulty; all AMC cards get extracted if their carrier blade is extracted.

PLM provides its users with callbacks to inform them about important hardware events on the objects they are interested in. An application running on one of the disk-less blades may store its data on one of those AMC disks in the example configuration.

Assume that the operator wants to exchange the disk blade and opens the latches. In that case PLM will inform users that are subscribed for this entity that an extraction request is pending. The application can now safely close all files and do the necessary replication, before allowing the blade to be extracted. PLM will use HPI hot swap management to communicate with the hardware. The application could also directly subscribe for HPI hot swap events, but there may be multiple users of that AMC disk. So who is going to decide that it is now safe to extract the disk? Now PLM service will be the owner of the IMM object representing the disk and will also act as an HPI user that does all the steps in HPI that are necessary for proper hot swap management.

2.2 Information Model for Execution Environments

Additional to this representation of physical resources, PLM introduces objects to model virtualized architectures, where virtualization facilities (VF, sometimes also called hypervisor or Virtual Machine Monitor) are able to run multiple operating systems on virtual machines. For more details on virtualization, see chapter 5.

The PLM information model will represent the containment hierarchy of virtualization facilities and virtual machines with so-called execution environment objects. These objects allow the information model to reflect the dependencies when cluster nodes run on virtual machines on the same hardware.

Let's assume we run a virtualized architecture on the blades that do not have AMC cards. So we have a Virtual Machine Monitor and a number of virtual machines (for instance, 16 virtual machines) managed by each monitor. This is reflected in the information model as follows:

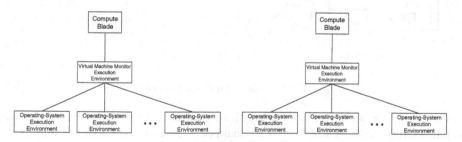

Fig. 3. Example Information Model of a Virtualized Architecture

This hierarchy shows directly which environments are affected in case of hardware events of the CPU blades.

Also the dependencies within this hierarchy need to be considered. Redundancy configuration in the Availability Management Framework (AMF) should make sure that active and stand-by roles always get assigned to components running on different hardware, if possible. Otherwise AMF could assign all services in a protection group to nodes running on virtual machines on the same blade and this protection group would completely fail in case the blade fails.

2.3 Dependencies

Not all dependencies between PLM objects are reflected in the containment tree.

As a simple example, an operating system often depends on a disk being accessible. Therefore PLM will introduce additional means to model dependencies between all types of entities in its information model. Also dependency on groups will be supported. For instance, a raid system will still be working if one disk fails, but it needs a minimum of physical disks being available.

2.4 PLM Objects within the Overall AIS Information Model

PLM objects fit into the overall AIS information model in the following way:

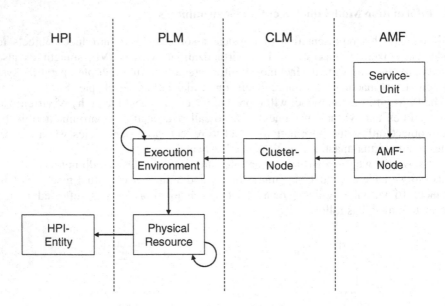

Fig. 4. PLM position in information model

The circled arrows show that there may be a hierarchy of physical resource objects. So CLM (cluster management) nodes are mapped to execution environment objects in the same way as today AMF maps its entities to CLM nodes.

With PLM objects, the information model can now easily show which AMF components are running on which blade. At the same time it allows high flexibility. There may be execution environments which do not run cluster nodes, but only software entities that are not aware of the SA Forum middleware. Configuration of services can be done without knowing whether there is a virtualized architecture on this hardware or not.

By mapping entities of higher level services to the hardware, PLM service closes the gap between AIS and HPI, and thus a complete view of the system is provided in the information model.

3 Operation Administration and Maintenance

PLM uses its objects in the infomation model to control operation and administration. It provides administrative commands for these objects and uses the objects to locate errors and inform users about physical actions of the operator, such as extraction and insertion of field replaceable units.

The information model directly reflects the physical structure of the hardware. Since PLM objects are used to control all actions an operator may take maintaining the system (for instance, extract a piece of hardware), all field replaceable units should be modeled as PLM objects. The system architect is free to model a finer granularity, i.e. create objects for hardware entities that are not separately replaceable. This allows him to separately manage sub-components, if HPI supports the operations. On the other hand, if the operational rules and procedures do not allow to exchange a certain entity, in that case no object is needed to represent that entity in the information model. PLM then will assume errors of the entity as errors of its parent.

PLM service will inform its users using callbacks if the operator starts physical actions. In the same way, it will inform users about administrative operations. This is done using a track interface as it is usual for AIS services.

Some events allow graceful termination of all affected services, but other events do not allow that. In case of a lock command and also if the latches of an entity are opened, services can be gracefully terminated. However, this graceful termination may not be possible in case of hardware faults.

Also if the operator does not wait for the blue LEDs, and extracts the board before all services are terminated, it is important to inform users about the situation.

4 State Model

Redundancy management in AIS is based on state management. State changes are reported using notifications and state changes trigger actions on dependent entities. PLM defines states for physical resources and for execution environments.

4.1 States for Physical Resources

For a configured physical resource, the states in the information model reflect whether the corresponding hardware is present and active. The HPI hot-swap state of the represented hardware entity is shown, and whether the entity is considered faulty. Additionally, administrative states are provided for hardware entities, so they can be locked, if the operator does not wish that they provide service. PLM also provides the locked-instantiation state, which is known by AMF, and which typically can be mapped to the power state of the hardware.

4.2 States for Execution Environments

States for execution environments represent the states of software, and thus they will be very similar to the states used by AMF for its service units and components and will reflect if the entity is loaded or not. PLM also provides administrative operations and states, which become very important in virtualized architectures.

4.3 Summary State

For all its objects, PLM will provide a summary state, indicating whether an entity is in service or not. As in AMF, this state is called the readiness state. So the PLM state model is nothing new for users being familiar with HPI and AMF states. At the same time it can be mapped to X.731 state management and so allows standardized management on this level.

The readiness state of an entity is also affected by state changes of entities it depends on. An entity can only be in-service when its parent is in-service.

Usually PLM users are interested in changes of the readiness state. That is, they need to be informed about a state change of an entity from being in-service to out-of-service or vice versa. PLM users for instance are not interested if an entity that is already powered off, later is physically extracted from the system. But the cause of a state-change is important information. Physical extraction may need different handling than administrative commands or faults.

5 Virtualization Support

In short, virtualization is a technique for hiding and abstracting the physical computer resources and to logically replicate a hardware platform (processors, co-processor, memory, devices …).

So since PLM is the intermediary between HPI and AIS, management of this abstraction of the physical resources is also the task of the PLM service.

Virtualization on a given hardware is performed by a control program which creates a simulated computer environment for its consumers or guests. The control program is called hypervisor, virtual machine monitor (VMM), or virtualization facility (VF), and it

- may run directly on the physical hardware (bare metal hypervisor) or
- requires an operating system to run on.

The consumers or guests of a virtualized computer environment are called virtual machines (VM) and often also include an operating system. Usually a couple of such VMs execute on one physical machine.

A typical example for virtualization is server consolidation, where virtual machines are used to consolidate several physical servers into fewer. The demand for these kinds of solutions increases with the increase of CPU performance.

Assuming that you have clustered HA-implementation and transform it to a virtualized environment availability aspects need to be considered again. Since nodes are not fixed on hardware, you have to ensure that in the case of a failure a failover to a different physical server takes place. This can be achieved by configuring services to be part of a specific cluster instance.

Virtualization support in PLM is provided with the introduction of the execution environment (EE) object.

If a hardware entity is running one single operating system, the operating system is modeled as a single child-EE of the respective physical resource object.

In environments with virtualization support, parent-EEs host child- or leaf-EEs.

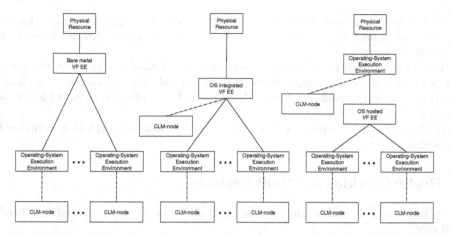

Fig. 5. Different virtualized architectures in PLM information model

In the bare metal case, the VF is modeled as an EE running directly on the physical resource, and (child-) EEs being the VMs or operating systems running under its control.

There could also be the case that an operating system also acts as a VF. We have a similar containment with an EE being the parent-EE for some child-EEs.

This way, the PLM information model will represent the containment hierarchy with virtualization facilities and virtual machines. The actual embedding of virtualization depends on the architecture of the implementation of virtualization facilities.

PLM will need to interact with the VF in a similar way as it does with HPI. However, the different VF implementations provide different interfaces, and there is no standard available. Nevertheless, PLM must interact with the VF to fulfill the following tasks:

- Start, stop, or reset virtual machines
- Get informed if a virtual machine starts up or terminates without being triggered by PLM.
- Get informed if an error on virtual machine level occurs
- Get informed if an error within the virtualization facilities occurs
- Get informed if virtual machine configuration is changed
- Optionally, also create or delete virtual machines or change their configuration
- Some implementations provide functionality to move virtual machines to a different hardware. In that case, PLM also needs to be informed.

VF implementations that do not provide the necessary interfaces cannot be used in HA systems.

An implementation of the PLM service that supports a VF implementation needs to hide the proprietary interfaces from AIS middleware and higher layers. PLM will reflect all changes in the virtual machines in its information model and will notify its users using the track callback interface. That way AIS middleware configuration can be kept independent from the VF implementation and still be aware of changes in the cluster architecture.

This is very important for high availability. Standby assignments or checkpoint replicas can protect applications from hardware failures only if they are located on different hardware.

This includes also other hardware dependencies. Virtual machines on the same hardware entity can share local resources. All dependencies of execution environments on physical resources can be modeled in the PLM information model and then are visible for other software.

PLM can provide its users with all necessary information to run in a virtualized architecture.

6   Health Checking and Fault Analysis

PLM provides a central service to analyze fault states of hardware and low level software.

In all cases PLM uses the information model to inform its users about fault situations. Users register on the objects they are interested in, and the PLM service notifies them in case of changes of the readiness state using callbacks.

PLM will also isolate the faulty entity or try automatic repair actions.

Hardware usually is isolated by powering off, if this is supported. In other cases, asserting a reset can be the appropriate means.

In case of execution environments usually a restart can be issued as a repair action. If the restart is not successful PLM can stop the execution environment by different means. In case of an operating system running on a virtual machine, the virtualization monitor can be called to stop that virtual machine. In other cases it can be stopped by hardware means.

6.1   Faults of Physical Resources

Hardware provides many sensors for an entity. HPI reports changes of the states of these sensors using events, but in many cases sensors must be read actively, and their values need to be analyzed and interpreted. This analysis is not trivial, and in many cases operators will like to tune the fault analysis to their specific needs. Depending on the availability requirements, it may be necessary to take hardware out-of-service in case of high temperature - to protect from greater damage, while with different requirements, it may be necessary to use the hardware as long as possible. So the sensitivity of such a hardware health monitoring must be very specifically configurable. For some operators, it may be natural to detect possible fault situations as early as possible and isolate the affected hardware, while other operators will try to use the hardware as long as possible - even while it may already be running in much too high temperature. So PLM will provide means to configure that.

When PLM detects a hardware fault situation, it will isolate the faulty hardware, if possible, and it will inform software applications about the outage. In case of predictive failure detection, it will be possible to smoothly terminate services. Also the actions to isolate faulty hardware need to be adapted to the operators' needs.

It is very important to centralize the analysis of hardware health states, because usually there are multiple users affected if a hardware entity becomes faulty. However, not every program should do its own analysis.

6.2 Faults of Execution Environments

PLM normally can do health checking and fault analysis for hardware completely by using HPI. However, PLM needs to implement specific mechanisms to manage an execution environment, depending on the supported operating systems and virtual machine monitors. Also on this level health monitoring and fault analysis is important.

In virtualized architectures, the virtual machine monitor can perform isolation of execution environments or issue repair actions. These actions need to be controlled by PLM as needed by the SA Forum middleware.

7 Correlation

Hardware faults and faults of the operating system layer usually cause a number of subsequent state changes in the system. For instance, components are terminated when an operator starts to remove replaceable units from the system; services are failed over or even terminate. In a live system, it is important to be able to identify the root causes of these events. Especially in case of service outage, it is very important to know whether the outage was caused by a hardware failure, a software programming error, or by an interaction of the operator. Only by knowing the cause, the appropriate repair procedure can be started.

Platform management can support this correlation by providing root causes in most of the frequent cases. Thus it enables other services to correlate their actions to these root causes.

Let us demonstrate this with an example.

We use again the AMC disk in a system like the example architecture above. Let us assume the disk contains the system partition of a UNIX-type operating system running on that blade. On top of this operating system, we have a cluster node, AIS services and applications. The disk may fail or run out of free space.

Let us first discuss what happens without special handling by platform management.

When the disk suddenly fails, an HPI event is generated. The operating system will continue running for a short time, but it will crash as soon as it accesses the disk. AMF health checking will detect that all components and service units on that cluster node have died and perform failover. Loss of data or communication sessions will be kept to a minimum by AIS mechanisms. However, it is not easy to correlate their failover to the disk outage.

When platform management is in place, it will transform the HPI event reporting the disk failure to a notification using AIS notification service (NTF). This notification provides a unique identification, the correlation id of the root-cause. By configuration, PLM is aware that the execution environment depends on the disk. So it can automatically decide that the OS must be terminated and issue notifications about this state change. NTF service allows sending information about the root cause with these subsequent notifications. This information is provided just by including the correlation id of the root cause in the subsequent notifications. PLM will also inform the cluster management service CLM about the OS termination and will provide the root cause correlation id. The cluster node leaves membership, and CLM service reports this event with a notification which includes the correlation id. CLM informs AMF and also passes to it the correlation id of the root cause. AMF performing the redundancy failovers again includes the root cause correlation id in all state change notifications and also in the interface to the applications. Thus, fault analysis can easily be done by providing root cause and intermediate notification ids. The user knows which application events are caused by the disk outage without further analysis. Of course, it may happen that fault handling of higher layers starts before the correlation id is provided. In that case, fault analysis still needs to find the correlation.

In the same way PLM provides correlation ids not only when the root cause is a fault situation. Common root causes are also physical extraction or insertion of hardware entities or administrative operations.

8   Upgrade Support

The system model with physical resources and execution environments as object instances in the information model is also the basis for upgrading these entities. It provides the necessary administrative commands to define operational procedures for hardware upgrade and allows defining software upgrade campaigns with the SA Forum software management framework (SMF). The UML definitions of the object classes for PLM objects include versioned types in the same way as versioned types are used for applications in the SA Forum SMF specification. Thus PLM prepares rolling operating system upgrade using SMF.

8.1   Operating System Upgrade

The upgrade campaign for an operating system will use PLM administrative operations to lock, restart, and unlock the respective execution environment as needed for the specific case. PLM service while executing the lock command takes care of the termination of affected services in a graceful way via callbacks to registered users like CLM or AMF. While the operating system is locked, SMF can run the necessary install scripts, for instance, to install OS patches, or even to install complete new software. SMF uses a PLM administrative operation to reboot the OS, and it unlocks the execution environment when the installation is completed. When PLM carries out the unlock operation, the middleware services and applications will be started as configured, and eventually everything will be in-service again.

Please note that upgrade campaigns for operating systems are done in the same way in virtualized architectures as without virtualization. PLM service knows, whether virtualization is present and the monitor can be used e.g. to issue a hard reset for an operating system.

8.2   Hardware Upgrade

Hardware upgrades usually include software upgrades. Hardware upgrade procedures will use SMF upgrade campaigns and PLM administrative operations on physical resource entities. In most cases, reconfiguration of the information model for the physical resource entities will be necessary. This reconfiguration can be included in SMF campaigns to allow for a better control of the whole procedure.

9 Achieving 5 Nines in Reality

SA Forum AIS services provide the necessary means to enable services to provide high availability, that is 99,999% of the time a system provides the service. With 24h per day and 7 days per week, this is about 5 minutes of allowed average service outage per year.

No technician is able to replace faulty hardware in 5 minutes after the fault was reported, and in a large system, usually more than one hardware outage happens per year, considering hardware fault probabilities and mean time between failures. Therefore, redundant systems are provided. As soon as a fault occurs, redundant entities are used. However, the occurrence of a second fault before the first failure is repaired can often cause an outage.

That means, there are always times in reality when redundancy is not there anymore - due to hardware faults. SA Forum AMF provides complex redundancy schemes and the possibility to provide spare units in addition to the most common active/standby model. As providing double redundancy may be very expensive, times without redundancy must be kept as short as possible. Several measures can be used to achieve this; and usually only a combination of those measures really helps.

9.1 Reduce the Time to Repair

The time to repair usually contains several things the operator or technician needs to do:

- Identify what needs to be done.
- Get the spare part from the store.
- Get to the location of the system.
- Perform the replacement.

Two of these points can only be improved by logistics, but in telecommunication, often traveling cannot be avoided. So we need to reduce the time to identify the right repair procedure, and the time the operator needs to carry it out.

The actual replacement time in case of hardware exchange depends mostly on hardware architecture and on logistics. Start-up time of the new hardware also needs to be considered.

Platform management service may help significantly in identifying the right repair procedure. Without the right information, even a "simple" case for hardware exchange can be mistaken. So it is very important to quickly identify hardware faults, and also to identify the root cause when a system is sending out high numbers of event notifications. SA Forum PLM service and its correlation support play an important role here.

9.2 Avoid Blaming Hardware as Faulty When It Is Not Faulty

Usually hardware replacement is costly. Not only the costs for the spare part need to be considered; the costs for doing the replacement are high, too. The faulty hardware normally is tested again in the factory, and will be sent back if it seems functional.

Centralizing hardware fault analysis in platform management allows improving the rate of correct fault categorization.

10 Summary and Outlook

Well designed platform management is essential to achieve high availability not only in theory but also in reality, when high numbers of systems need to be maintained in the field.

SA Forum will provide in its next release a specification for a new platform management service. This service will close the gap between AIS middleware and HPI specification. It completes the information model by representing hardware, operating system and virtualization layer, and it standardizes the interaction between those layers, middleware and application services. The PLM service is the basis to provide fault correlation to improve service maintenance.

References

1. Service Availability Forum, Service Availability Interface, Overview, SAI-Overview-B.03.01
2. Service Availability Forum Hardware Platform Interface, SAI-HPI-B.02.01
3. Service Availability Forum, Application Interface Specification, Information Model Management Service, SAI-AIS-IMM-A.02.01
4. Service Availability Forum, Application Interface Specification, Availability Management Framework, SAI-AIS-AMF-B.03.01
5. Service Availability Forum, Application Interface Specification, Cluster Membership Service, SAI-AIS-CLM-B.03.01
6. Service Availability Forum, Application Interface Specification, Software Management Framework, SAI-AIS-SMF-A.01.01
7. CCITT Recommendation X.731 I ISO/IEC 10164-2, State Management Function
8. Virtualization: State of the Art. Published by SCOPE Alliance, http://www.scope-alliance.org

Automatic Generation of AMF Compliant Configurations

Ali Kanso[1], Maria Toeroe[2], Ferhat Khendek[1], and Abdelwahab Hamou-Lhadj[1]

[1] Electrical and Computer Engineering Department
Concordia University, Montréal, Canada
{al_kan,khendek,abdelw}@ece.concordia.ca
[2] Ericsson Inc., Montréal, Canada
Maria.Toeroe@ericsson.com

Abstract. Service Availability Forum has defined a set of APIs to enable the building of off-the-shelf components for applications providing highly available services. A set of services has been defined and the Availability Management Framework is the service responsible of managing availability and therefore shifting this task from the applications to the middleware. Designing an AMF compliant configuration, for a given application, can be a tedious and error prone task because of the large number of attributes and parameters to be taken into account. In this paper, we propose an algorithm and the corresponding tool prototype for generating an AMF compliant configuration. We illustrate our approach with an example and discuss the main issues of the automatic generation.

Keywords: AIS, AMF, AMF Information Model, Entity Type File, Configurations Generation.

1 Introduction

Service Availability Forum (SAF) [1] aims at providing high availability of network elements, systems and services through the usage of commercial off-the-shelf building blocks. High availability requires first of all no single point of failure, which is achieved by clustering, by use of different redundancy models, and by coordination of the resources within a cluster. SAF is developing and maintaining an Application Interface Specification (AIS) [2] for high availability middleware that is independent from any hardware platform and any specific vendor implementation. The SAF AIS defines the Availability Management Framework (AMF) to enable the management of the availability of services of applications that comply with the AMF information model and API [2]. Based on this information model, AMF coordinates the different resources in a cluster using the API.

The AMF information model describes the system configuration to be managed by AMF in terms of different software entities. Some of these entities characterize the service providers and their organization while others are related to the provided services assigned dynamically by AMF to the service providers depending of their

T. Nanya et al. (Eds.): ISAS 2008, LNCS 5017, pp. 155–170, 2008.

health and eligibility. The AMF information model also describes the types of these entities, as well as the cluster and its nodes where the entities are deployed.

The information model is provided to AMF through the Information Management Model service (IMM) [3]. An AMF compliant configuration to be loaded into IMM is described in XML (eXtensible Markup Language) [4] and accessed by AMF through the IMM service. A more formal and complete discussion of an AMF compliant configuration is provided in Section 2.

Developing a configuration in order to provide and protect services may be a tedious and error prone task to be undertaken manually by system developers. In this paper, we describe our approach for generating automatically an AMF compliant configuration from a set of type descriptors provided by the software vendor and from the configuration designer requirements, which include the service to be provided, its protection level indicating the redundancy model and the system to be deployed on. Obviously from a given set of type descriptors and a set of requirements, several AMF compliant configurations may be generated for the same system, which can be compared according to different criteria. In the approach presented in this paper, we are aiming at generating one AMF compliant configuration by integrating directly into the generation algorithm a certain number of design/configuration decisions. We discuss these decisions and their impact as they are encountered. We have implemented our algorithm in an ECLIPSE environment.

In the rest of this paper, we first provide the background knowledge on AMF configurations and related concepts. In Section 3, we elaborate on our approach for automatic generation of AMF compliant configurations from a given set of requirements provided by the configuration designer and a set of types describing the software coming from the vendor. We present the prototype tool and its application in Section 4. In Section 5, we discuss issues that have arisen during this research and future work.

2   AMF Compliant Configurations: Background and Related Work

2.1   Background

AMF is part of AIS, it defines a set of APIs for availability management through coordination of redundant resources [2]. In order to provide high availability, AMF requires a certain organization of the resources, i.e. a configuration, which is described by the information model. This information model consists of the different software entities to be managed by AMF in the running system in order to provide service availability, the types of these software entities that describe common features of the entities belonging to them, and the cluster nodes on which the software entities are deployed.

2.1.1   Software Entities

According to the AMF information model [2], the basic building block of an AMF configuration is a component. An AMF component is a set of software and/or hardware resources. Components are grouped into a service unit (SU) that combines their functionality to provide some services. In order to provide and protect services, SUs are grouped into service groups (SGs). An SG protects a set of services, which are represented as service instances (SIs). SIs are composed of component service instances (CSIs), when a particular SI is assigned to an SU, its composing CSIs are assigned to the components in this SU. The grouping of service groups forms an AMF application. Each SU is deployed on an AMF node, thus an SG is deployed on a node group. The set of all AMF nodes forms the AMF cluster.

AMF coordinates redundant entities (SUs and their components) according to a certain redundancy model that defines how many SUs (respectively components) are active, how many SUs (respectively components) are standby for protecting an SI (respectively CSI). For each SI AMF selects at runtime which SU shall perform in which role and makes the appropriate assignments via API callbacks to the components. Several redundancy models have been defined in the standard [2]. Each of them has its own characteristics. In the 2N model for instance, at most one SU can be active for all SIs, and at most one other SU can be standby for all SIs [2] the SG protects. A redundancy model may require specific component capabilities in order to protect the CSIs of the SIs. A component capability is defined as pair (x, y), where x represents the maximum number of active CSI assignments and y the maximum number of standby CSI assignments the component can have for a particular component service type. Therefore, depending on the redundancy model and the services to be provided, certain component types may be more suitable than others and some other component types may not be usable at all. For example, a component type that can have only active or only standby assignments at a time can be used in an SG that has a 2N redundancy model, but it is not valid for a SG that has an N-way redundancy model where each of the SUs may be active for some SIs and standby for others simultaneously.

Fig. 1 shows an example configuration of AMF entities. In this example, a cluster is composed of two nodes, A and B, with one SG protecting one SI in a 2N redundancy model. The SG has two SUs, SU1 and SU2, each composed of two components. The distribution of the active and standby assignments is decided by AMF at runtime.

2.1.2 Entity Types

There are two sorts of AMF entities: typed entities and non-typed entities. The typed entities are: the application (application type), the service group (SG type), the service unit (SU type), the component (component type), the service instance (service type), and the component service instance (CS type). The non-typed entities are: the cluster and the node. Although not shown in Fig. 1, each typed entity must refer to a type, since types are an integral part of the configuration.

Types are used in the AMF information model to define a set of common characteristics shared by all the entities referring to the same type. The entity types also determine the relation they have with other entity types. Thus, defining the relations their entities need to fulfill toward entities of other types. For example the SU type specifies the set of component types it contains, which defines components of what types must compose each of the SUs of the SU type. In the configuration generation algorithm in Section III, we pay particular attention to these types. The AMF entities and types and the relationships among them are described in the standard using a UML class diagram [5].

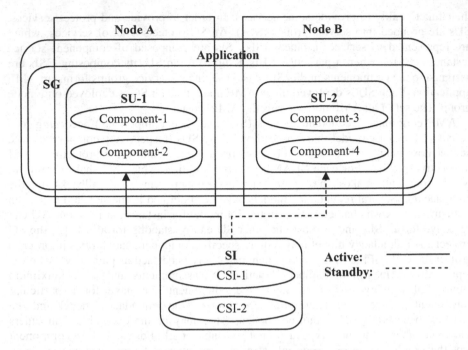

Fig. 1. Example of configuration of AMF entities

2.1.3 SMF View vs AMF View of Entity Types

The data required to configure these types, entities and their attributes, comes from two sources: The Entity Type File (ETF) [7] and the configuration designer. The SAF Software Management Framework (SMF) specification [6] standardizes the content and the format of ETF [7] to allow software vendors to describe their products by means of types they implement. In this SMF context, types are used to characterize the software for all its possible deployments and settings. Hence, they differ from the types used in the context of AMF, which focuses on the runtime management aspects. Types of the SMF view could be perceived as meta-types to the types of the AMF information model.

ETF is an XML file provided by the software vendor to describe the software from SAF SMF perspective. For an AMF application implementation, it describes at least the component types and component service types implemented, including the dependencies and compatibility among these types. If there are further constraints on how and which the above types can collaborate to provide services, these constraints are specified in SU types, SG types, service types, and application types as necessary. As a result, the ETF may not be complete with respect to types for an application implementation, whereas in an AMF configuration all the AMF types must be present and complete.

Due to their purpose, there exist correspondences and discrepancies between the types described in an ETF and the types described in an AMF model. For example, AMF describes only the attribute names of CS types whereas in ETF in addition to this, the attribute type and range can be specified by the software vendor, to be able to configure the CSIs as AMF requires specific values for all the attributes. Similarly, dependency between component types may be specified in an ETF, but this is not reflected by the AMF information model since AMF does not need to know these dependencies among types. However, dependencies between components are captured in a different way. The instantiation level of components within an SU informs AMF to instantiate an independent component before those depending on it.

2.1.4 The IMM View of the AMF Information Model

AMF entities and types are represented as objects in the SA Forum Information Model [8]. The IMM service is the SAF service that manages these classes and corresponding objects. The SAF information model, including the AMF configuration can be described using a standardized schema, called the IMM XML schema [3]. An IMM XML file of a given configuration is loaded into IMM at system start up and made available to the SAF services including AMF through an API.

2.1.5 The Challenge of Generating an AMF Configuration

The goal of the configuration generation is to identify the set of service provider entities that matches the requested set of services and can protect them according to the requested redundancy model on a particular cluster. Generating such an AMF configuration is not straightforward. First of all, there are just too many inter-related entity and type objects that a configuration designer needs to work with. Consistency checks must be performed at various levels of the configuration generation process. For example, one must ensure that the ETF type dependencies and constraints are respected when creating components, assigning components to service units, etc. There are also key decisions that need to be made taking into consideration various constraints such as the maximum number of components of a certain type in an SU, the capability of a component when providing a certain component service type, etc. In short, generating an AMF configuration could be a tedious and overwhelming task for a designer without tool assistance. Moreover, an automatic generation of the configuration will allow for the exploration of several potential configurations and compare and rank them according to predefined criteria.

2.2 Related Work

The standardization at SAF is ongoing, existing service specification are reviewed and updated as necessary, and more of the services are being defined. The B.03.01 version of the AMF specification on which the reported work is based differs significantly from earlier versions as it introduced the AMF types to be aligned with the first release of the Software Management Framework specification.

The work on implementing the APIs is ongoing in different places; OpenAIS [14]. OpenSAF [15] and OpenClovis [16] are open source projects aiming at developing a SAF compliant middleware for high availability. These provide limited if any support for automatic configuration design and none of them considers the AMF types yet.

The closest research work to the contents of this paper in the context of SAF has been reported in [10]. The authors in [10] apply the Model Driven Approach (MDA) to the design of AIS configurations. In this approach an initial AIS compliant configuration is devised using predefined design patterns, gathered from previous experiences. This initial configuration is referred to as the Platform Independent Model (PIM), which is then transformed and specialized automatically to a Platform Specific Model (PSM) to be used in a specific implementation of AIS. Meta-models are used for the transformation and for the validation of configurations. Our work is different from this approach, as we automatically generate this initial configuration or PIM.

More work on configuration generation has been done in the more general context of software configuration management, particularly using constraint satisfaction techniques and policies as reported in [11, 12]. Authors in [12], for instance, propose an approach for generating a configuration specification and the corresponding deployment workflow from a set of user requirements, operator and technical constraints, which are all modeled as policies. An example of constraints is, for instance, a given operating system can only run on certain processor architectures. Generating a configuration is formulated as a resource composition problem taking into account the constraints. Our approach is similar from this point of view; however, our focus is on the availability and AMF constraints instead of general utility computing environments. Challenging constraints, such as redundancy models to be provided, are not taken into account in [12].

3   Configuration Generation

In this section, we introduce and discuss the main steps of our configuration generation algorithm. In the current approach, we consider the generation of a configuration for only one AMF application consisting of SA-aware components only, i.e. those that implement the AMF API. Thus, there is only one application type, and all other types are considered as subordinates to this type.

As shown in Fig. 2, the algorithm takes as input the ETF provided by the software vendor and the configuration requirements provided by the configuration designer including the application services to be supported. The next step focuses on determining the AMF entity types that can support these required application services: namely the SU types and the SG types. Once these types are determined, we proceed with creating their entities: components, SUs, SGs, as well as assigning SIs to SGs. Finally, the remaining entity and type attributes are completed. The generated configuration is specified in IMM XML.

3.1 Input Data and Validation

The algorithm takes three sets of input data:

- A set of ETF types that describe the software to be used,
- A set of services to be provided by the application, and
- A set of nodes on which the configuration has to be deployed.

As discussed in the previous section, the ETF types describe the software application from the vendor's perspective. This ETF must contain at least component

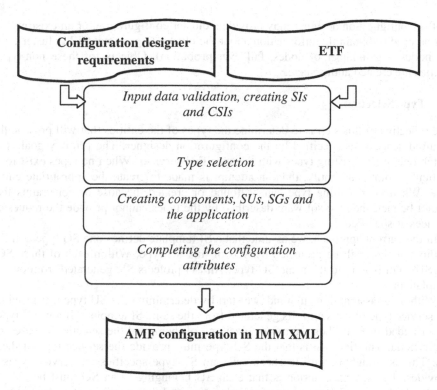

Fig. 2. Main steps for configuration generation

types and CS types. Other entity types such as SU types, SG types, and the application types may also be provided in order to capture limitations and constraints of the software. However, they are not necessarily provided in ETF.

The second set of input data is provided by the configuration designer and characterizes the services that the target configuration should support, i.e. what is the expected workload that needs to be handled. If any of the service types that needs to be provided by the target system is not specified by ETF, the designer must define them using existing CS types. The SIs and CSIs are specified for these service types. To facilitate this task the concept of templates has been introduced for specifying SIs. In an SI template, the configuration designer specifies for each necessary service type the total number of SIs to be created, within that the number of SIs to be assigned to the same SG, and the redundancy model of the SG that will protect these SIs.

Since SIs are collections of CSIs, each SI template is associated with a set of CSI templates based on the CS types defined for the service type. In each CSI template, the designer specifies the number of CSIs to be created for each required CS type within the SI. This must be in accordance with any constraints defined by service type, like the minimum/maximum number of CSI of a certain CS type that can be present in an SI.

Based on the SI and CSI templates the objects for the SIs and CSIs are generated and added to the configuration. The current solution does not cover the parameterization of CSIs. At this stage it is still a discussion topic.

The configuration designer may provide a cluster configuration, or an existing one can be used to obtain the information about the cluster (e.g. name, CLM cluster), and the nodes (e.g. number of nodes, fail over probation). Objects for these non-typed entities are created at this stage.

3.2 Type Selection

The objective of this step is to determine the types of the entities that will provide the required services as specified by the configuration designer. The primary goal is to match one of the existing types with the specified services. When no types exist for a particular compound entity, then an attempt is made to create the appropriate entity type. When no matching type can be found or created, because of constraints that cannot be met, then the software described by the types cannot provide the requested services as specified.

In the current approach, we assume that a SI template defines one SG type. All SIs of this template will be protected by SGs of this SG type. Within each of these SGs the SUs will belong to the same SU type. An SG protects SIs generated from one SI template only.

With these assumptions in mind, we start by determining the SU type that provides the service type of the set of SIs generated from the same SI template. If any SU types are provided in ETF, then we try to select one of them, and the selection is based on two criteria. The first one is that the SU type must provide the service type of these SIs. This is straightforward to check since an SU type specifies the service types it provides. The second criterion is that each SU belonging to an SG must be able to handle the load of SI assignments for both active and the standby states. An SU type may put restrictions with respect to the number of components the SU of this type can contain and each of the components has its active/standby capability according to the component type specification. As a result an SU of an SU type may have capacity limitations that must be respected during the selection. For illustrating the constraint of load to assign to an SU, let us consider an SG with 5 SUs in an N+M redundancy model (with for instance 3 active and 2 standby). If, for instance, 60 SIs are to be protected by this SG, then each SU should have the capability of being active for 20 SIs or standby for 30 SIs.

The load each SU is expected to handle is calculated for the active/standby roles according to each redundancy model. It takes into account the number of SIs the appropriate SG shall protect, the number of assignments for each of the roles within the SG and the number of SUs among which this task is distributed within the SG at any given time. This gives the minimum number of SIs an SU needs to be able to handle in active/standby role. The calculated values are compared with the respective capacity of each SU type that can provide the necessary service type. The maximum active and standby capacities are calculated by first calculating the maximum number of SIs that the SU type can handle with respect to each CS type the SIs contain. Subsequently the minimum of these numbers is taken as the maximum capacity for the SI.

Several SU types that provide the required service type with the required capacity may be described in the ETF. On the other hand, it may happen that no such SU type exits in the ETF. In this case, the configuration generation fails. When no SU types are provided in ETF, i.e. fewer constraints are provided in the ETF, we build an SU type that provides the required service type with the required capacity. For the construction of this SU type, it may happen that more than one component types can be used. In the current approach, the preference is given to component types that have higher capability. The configuration generation will also fail, if based on the component capability no component type matches the redundancy model specified for the SIs.

Once an SU type is found or created, the algorithm proceeds to select from ETF an SG type based on the redundancy model specified in the SI template and which refers to the selected SU type. Note that many of the SG type's parameters were already used in the SU type selection. The algorithm terminates if none of the SG types matches. If no SG type is given in ETF then – as in case of the SU type – a new SG type is created using the selected SU type and the requested redundancy model.

The selection of SG and SU types is repeated for each SI template until all of them have been satisfied.

Provided that only types from ETF were selected in the previous steps, the algorithm applies the selection process to the application types specified in ETF. It selects the application type that references all the SG types that were selected previously. Otherwise it constructs a new application type as a union of the selected SG types.

3.3 Generating the Remaining AMF Entities

Once all the types have been determined and the corresponding configuration objects have been added to the configuration, we proceed with the creation of the configuration objects for the AMF entities of these types. That is, the objects for SUs, components, SGs, and the application are created and configured.

In the SI template, the configuration designer specified – indirectly through the redundancy model – the number of SUs and SGs to be created, but not the number of components. To configure an SU, we need to determine this number. The number of components of each component type that must be created in an SU depends on the load, i.e. number of SIs assigned to the SU, the number of CSIs within those SIs, and the component capabilities. For an illustration, let us consider an SG that has 2 SUs protecting one SI composed of 5 CSIs of CST-A according to the 2N redundancy model. Let us assume the capability of the component that supports CST-A is 1 active and 10 standby. In this case, we need 5 components in our SU. While one component is enough to standby for all the CSIs, we need 5 components to be active for all the CSIs. .

The same calculation is repeated for every set of CSIs of the service type the SIs belong to. Thus, we populate the first SU of the first SG with all the necessary components. Subsequent SUs of the same SG are created by duplicating the first one and the SG is assigned a set of SIs that have been generated from the appropriate SI template at the beginning of the configuration generation algorithm as described in Section 3.1. Subsequent SGs for the same SI template are also created by duplicating the first one. The procedure is repeated for all SI templates until all SIs have been assigned to SGs.

3.4 Completing the Configuration Attributes

When the procedures described in Sections 3.1-3.3 have been completed, major part of the configuration attributes of the selected types and generated entities are determined based on the different selection and generation criteria described, however not all of them. To complete the configuration generation some additional attributes need to be assigned values. Here we briefly touch on a few that require further procedures.

If not specified explicitly in the configuration, an AMF implementation will decide on the assignment to nodes of the different SUs within the information model. The assignment procedure is not standardized, which means that different AMF implementations may do it differently. Our algorithm includes a procedure for distributing the generated SUs among the nodes of the AMF cluster and fill in the appropriate configuration attributes: The procedure assumes that the AMF nodes have equal capacities and therefore equally distribute the SUs among them.

In addition, we have developed a ranking procedure that enables equal assignment of SIs to SUs within an SG by completing the SU rank attribute for each SI. In other words, we ensure load balancing among SUs. Moreover, in the case of the N+M redundancy model, we rank SUs in a way that ensures that AMF would not replace an active SU that fails, with two standbys. The procedure for ranking SUs for SIs is dependent of the redundancy model attributes of the SG and the number of SIs.

4 The Configuration Generator Tool

The algorithm presented in the previous section has been implemented in a prototype tool developed in Java, using the Eclipse environment. It is anticipated to make this tool as an Eclipse plug-in to take full advantage of the capabilities of the Eclipse integrated environment.

4.1 Description of the Tool

Fig. 3 shows the overall flow of information. The user interacts with the tool through a Graphical User Interface (GUI).

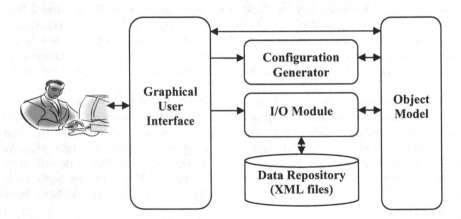

Fig. 3. The data flow diagram of the configuration generation tool

The Object Model is based on the AMF information model described in the AMF specifications [2]. Additional classes and associations have been created to map the entity types defined in ETF schema [7] to the ones defined in AMF.

The Configuration Generator module encompasses the configuration generation algorithm presented in the previous section. It populates the AMF information model within the Object Model. The I/O module is used to save the configuration in IMM XML.

The I/O module also contains methods to read ETF and extract information from it. For this purpose, an ETF parser has been created. The data repository stores all data necessary for generating configurations including IMM XML and ETF.

4.2 The Tool User Interface

A snapshot of the prototype tool GUI is shown in Fig. 4; it consists of four views: The Input view (the left pane), the Attribute view (the middle pane), the AMF Instance view (the upper-right pane), and the Description view (lower-right pane). They are used to present the content of the Object Model from different perspectives.

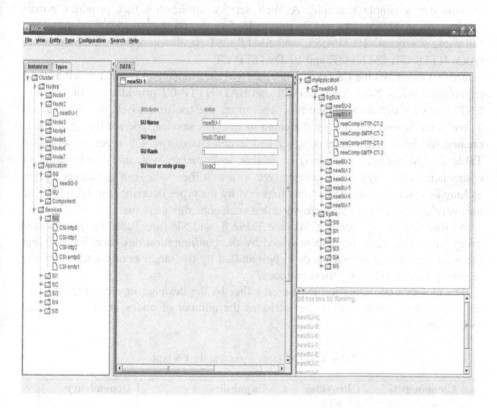

Fig. 4. Snapshot of the tool GUI

The primary role of the Input view is receiving the input data for the configuration generation. Under the Types tab the AMF entity types read from ETF are presented to the configuration designer. It also allows for adding additional types that are not present in ETF yet the designer would like to consider for the configuration. Under the Instances tab the SI and CSI templates can be entered together with the non-typed entities. After running the configuration generation, this view will be completed with the generated entities and possibly new types.

The AMF Instance view is so called because it follows the structure of the AMF Instance View defined in the specification [2]. It contains the AMF entities of the resulting configuration after it has been generated. The Attribute view is used to display the attributes for the different objects selected either from the Input view or the AMF Instance view. Finally, the Description view displays in a textual form any additional information about the configuration which may not be present in any of the other views, such as the per SI SU ranking.

4.3 Application Example

To demonstrate the generation of an AMF configuration using the prototype tool, let us consider a simple example: A Web service application that provides e-mail services using HTTP and SMTP protocols. Let us assume the ETF contains the following CS types: HTTP-CST, and SMTP-CST. It also contains the components types: HTTP-CT, SMTP-CT, and BAD-HTTP-CT.

Table 1 describes the CS types provided by these component types, as well as their capability models. Note that HTTP-CT and BAD-HTTP-CT provide the same HTTP-CST, but with different capabilities. Therefore, the tool has to choose from them. There is no dependency among the components. The service type for this example is created by the configuration designer and it consists of two CS types as shown in Table 2. The configuration designer is free to come up with any combination of component service types into service type to match the services of the target system as long as it satisfies the constraints imposed by the types described in the ETF. The tool verifies when the input is provided that such constraints are met.

As discussed in Section 3, CSIs (see Table 3) and SIs (see Table 4) are specified using templates. They are also provided by the configuration designer. They reflect the workload or traffic that needs to be handled by the target configuration and the desired protection level for these services.

The cluster's configuration is entered either by the designer or extracted from the current system configuration. This includes the number of nodes in the cluster, fail over probation, etc.

Table 1. Component types and the CS types

Component Type	Provides CSTs	Capability	Dependency
HTTP-CT	HTTP-CST	4 active and 3 stand by	None
BAD-HTTP-CT	HTTP-CST	1 active or 1 stand by	None
SMTP-CT	SMTP-CST	3 active or 2 stand by	None

Table 2. The service type

Service type	Member component service types
Email-services	HTTP-CST, SMTP-CST

Table 3. The content of the CSI templates

CSI template name	Number of CSIs	CST
HTTP-CSI-temp	3	HTTP-CST
SMTP-CSI-temp	2	SMTP-CST

Table 4. The content of the SI template

SI template name	Number of SIs	Service Type	Member CSI-templates	Redund. model	Number of SUs
SI-temp	6	Email-services	HTTP-CSI-temp SMTP-CSI-temp	5 plus 3	8

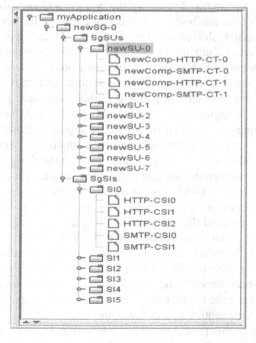

Fig. 5. A snapshot of the AMF Instance view for the example

The configuration generated is displayed in Fig. 5. It contains one application that has one SG (NewSG-0) with 8 SUs (newSU-0 – newSU-7) as requested for the redundancy model in Table 4 (5 plus 3) and each SU has 4 components (newComp-HTTP-CT-0, newComp-SMTP-CT-0, newComp-HTTP-CT-1, newComp-SMTP-CT-1). Since 6 SIs need to be provided by the SG, this load should be split among 5 SUs for the active assignments and 3 SUs for the standby assignments. As it is decided at runtime, which SU is in which role, all of them have to be able to provide either role, which means 2 SIs per SU in each role. This means 6 HTTP-CST and 4 SMTP-CST assignments per SU have to be compared with the component capabilities. The tool gives preference to HTTP-CT based on its capability, which means 2 of such components are needed. The SMTP-CST is matched up only with SMTP-CT and also 2 of them are needed.

The size of the IMM XML file for this simple configuration is 85KBs. The size of this file for real life applications may be very challenging to be handled manually by developers.

5   Conclusions

In the current approach, we consider the generation of only one AMF compliant configuration. This one configuration is created based on the strategy implemented in the generation algorithm during the selection or creation of different types, such as component types, SU types or SG types. However, using different strategies different configurations can be generated with a choice of alternative component types, SU types, or SG types. The criteria of selecting the types can change due to changing the preference for some of the attributes or in the future in case further description of the types are provided, such as the resources required by each entity of a specific type, of the mean time between failure for components, licensing cost, and many others as those taken into account in [13]. Having these attributes will allow us to generate multiple configurations according to different criteria and thus exploring a wider space of configurations and choosing the one that best suits the environment of deployment and the designer requirements. Moreover, we have considered the generation of a configuration for a single SA-aware application only.

It is important to mention again that there are situations where a configuration cannot be generated. This is the case, for instance, when the designer requirements do not match the system's hardware configuration. For example, this is the case when the designer requires hardware redundancy for an SG, but the number of SUs in the SG exceeds the number of nodes. While this may be easy to spot in some cases, in other cases it is not straightforward that the configuration designer requirements cannot be met with the given ETF and its constraints, that is, due to limitations of the software. For instance, one may find that there is no component type capable of supporting the required redundancy model; or the required load to provide the requested protection for the service instances exceeds the capacity of any service unit type provided in ETF due to limitations in the number of components or their capability; or none of the SG types in ETF uses the required redundancy model.

During the course of this project, we have encountered some challenges and came across some limitations of the AMF information model and ETF. The AMF information model will certainly benefit from some refinements and clarifications using inheritance, especially at the component and component type level. As for the limitations, one can mention that when more than one component can take a particular CS type in a given SU, there is no way to configure for AMF which component should be assigned. This becomes critical if there is a dependency between the component types and the CS types, which should be matched by the CSI assignments, but AMF has no information about it. The current form of ETF is not powerful enough to express all the dependencies/requirements a component type may have towards its environment (e.g. operating system, other applications). ETF allows for limited ways to define the valid combinations of component types. This is done through SU types and SG types. These combinations depend on the component types' interfaces toward each other, which is not captured in SAF.

This work is in progress and our approach is still evolving. This exercise helped us, the academic partners involved in the project, tremendously in understanding SAF specifications, the different aspects of AMF types (ETF versus AMF), the complex dependencies among the different types and their entities. We are working on improving our method in order to overcome its limitations, e.g. consider multiple applications and from different categories as described in the AMF specification. We also plan to use more formal settings, such as the technique of constraints satisfaction as described in [11, 12], in order to explore efficiently all the potential solutions and compare them according to predefined criteria.

Acknowledgements. This work has been partially supported by the Natural Sciences and Engineering Research Council of Canada (NSERC) and Ericsson Software Research.

References

1. Service Availability Forum at: http://www.saforum.org
2. Service Availability Forum, Application Interface Specification. Availability Management Framework SAI-AIS-AMF-B.03.01
3. Service Availability Forum, Application Interface Specification. Information Model Management Service SAI-AIS-IMM-A.02.01
4. eXtensible Markup Language (XML) at http://xml.org
5. Unified Modeling Language (UML), http://www.uml.org
6. Service Availability, Forum. Application Interface Specification. Software Management Framework SAI-AIS-SMF-A.01.01
7. SAI-AIS-SMF-ETF-A.01.01.xsd
8. SAI-XMI-A.02.00.09.18.xml.zip
9. SAI-AIS-IMM-XSD-A.01.01.xsd
10. Kövi, A., Varró, D.: An Eclipse-Based Framework for AIS Service Configurations. In: Malek, M., Reitenspieß, M., van Moorsel, A. (eds.) ISAS 2007. LNCS, vol. 4526, pp. 110–126. Springer, Heidelberg (2007)
11. Hinrich, T., Love, N., Petrie, C., Ramshaw, L., Sahai, A., Singhal, S.: Using Object-Oriented Constraint Satisfaction for automated Configuration Generation. In: Sahai, A., Wu, F. (eds.) DSOM 2004. LNCS, vol. 3278, pp. 159–170. Springer, Heidelberg (2004)

12. Sahai, A., Singhal, S., Joshi, R., Machiraju, V.: Automated Generation of Resource Configurations through Policies. In: Fifth IEEE International Workshop on Policies for Distributed Systems and Networks (POLICY 2004), June 7-9, 2004, Yorktown Heights, New York (2004)
13. Janakiraman, G., Santos, J.R., Turner, Y.: Automated Multi-Tier System Design for Service Availability. HP Laboratories Palo Alto, May 22 (2003)
14. http://www.openais.org/
15. http://www.opensaf.org/
16. http://www.openclovis.org/

Dependability Evaluation of a Replication Service for Mobile Applications in Dynamic Ad-Hoc Networks*

Erling V. Matthiesen[1], Ossama Hamouda[2,3],
Mohamed Kaâniche[2,3], and Hans-Peter Schwefel[1,4]

[1] CTIF, Aalborg University, Niels Jernes Vej 12/A5-212
9220 Aalborg-Øst, Denmark
{evm,hps}@es.aau.dk
[2] CNRS; LAAS ; 7, avenue du Colonel Roche, F-31077 Toulouse, France
[3] Université de Toulouse ; UPS, INSA, INP, ISAE ; LAAS-CNRS : Toulouse, France
{ossama.hamouda,mohamed.kaaniche}@laas.fr
[4] Forschungszentrum Telekommunikation Wien - FTW, Donau - City Straße 1,
1220 Vienna, Austria

Abstract. In order to increase availability and reliability of stateful applications, redundancy as provided by replication in cluster solutions is a well-known and frequently utilized approach. For mobile services in dynamic ad-hoc networks, such replication mechanisms have to be adapted to deal with the frequently higher communication delays and with the intermittent connectivity. Dynamic clustering strategies in which the replica set is adjusted to the current network state can help to handle the network dynamicity. The paper develops a stochastic Petri net model (and its corresponding Markov chain representation) to analyze the resulting availability and replica consistency in such dynamic clusters. The numerical results are interpreted in the context of a vehicular (c2c) communication use-case and can be used to determine optimized cluster configuration parameters.

1 Introduction

Many of the future networking scenarios consist both of wireless multi-hop parts and infrastructure based network components. For new application types and future service platforms, server-based applications access is not only offered by the infrastructure network part, but also by the potentially mobile nodes in the ad-hoc domain. An example for such service provisioning scenarios is the vehicular communication setting [2], in which cars will be able to communicate with each other. This communication will be used for safety critical applications that require high availability. For applications used in automotive traffic this is especially true since application failure could affect driver behavior or directly affect the state of the car, e.g., spurious application of brakes. Traditional solutions for high-availability rely on redundancy offered by cluster implementations, in which Middleware services [1] support the timely replication and fail-over in case of crash failures of individual

---

* This work was partially supported by the HIDENETs project (EU-IST-FP6-26979).

T. Nanya et al. (Eds.): ISAS 2008, LNCS 5017, pp. 171–186, 2008.

cluster nodes [7]. For stateful applications, such fail-over capability typically involves timely replication of application state, which could be implemented by a redundant distributed shared memory [5].

In mobile ad hoc networks (MANETs) the lifetime of a communication path may be short [2]. Communication delays in principle are unbounded due to the unpredictability of the Medium Access procedures on the link-layer and potential re-routing delays in dynamic multi-hop scenarios [9]. Replication strategies for dynamic data such as application state need to take these communication properties into account [8]: Larger communication delays can increase the probability of inconsistent replica state, so that dynamic cluster member selection can lead to substantial improvements in mobile scenarios [12]. The replication manager (RM) defined in [3] an example of such a middleware component that provides applications with a resilient shared memory area and performs management of such a dynamic cluster. Heuristic algorithms as investigated in [8], based on measured communication delays and geographic positioning and speed information, can be utilized to trigger membership reconfiguration in a mobile ad-hoc network setting.

In this paper, we evaluate the dependability of a replicated stateful application service based on dynamic cluster formation as provided by the Replication Manager. The metrics we evaluate are the number of participating nodes in the cluster, replica data consistency, and application availability. The former can be an important metric to improve client-access to the replicated service in delay-constrained scenarios, as client-nodes can potentially select the server instance with shortest communication delay to the clients [10]. Replica consistency is expressed as the number of nodes that store the correct data, where correctness here refers to the real-time ordering of write operations to the distributed memory area storing the changing application state.

Using numerical results from analytic Stochastic Petri Net models of this dynamic replication scenario, we experiment with different geographic mobility types, and different degrees of dynamicity of the application state [6].

The rest of the paper is organized as follows. Section 2 describes basic background about: a) typical applications and use scenarios that illustrate the context of the study, b) replication management and data consistency related problems and challenges, and c) the main concepts behind the design of the replication manager investigated in this paper. The dependability models of the replication manager allowing the assessment of the probabilities characterizing the number of replica in the network and their consistency are presented in Section 3. Numerical and sensitivity analysis results are discussed in Section 4. Finally, Section 5 summarizes the main conclusions and discusses future work.

2   Background

In this section we present necessary background information needed to understand the scenarios investigated in this paper, both with respect to replication and vehicular ad-hoc networks. First we describe the scenario and then we go into the problem of data consistency in a distributed shared memory area and also the problems involved with service replication in ad-hoc networks.

2.1 Scenario Description

Various applications in vehicular settings could benefit from the replication service investigated in this paper [11]. We can consider as an example, an ad-hoc network based road-traffic information service, whose information base is dynamically updated. Utilizing the Replication Manager middleware service, the application state (traffic information) is kept in a memory area which is shared among the participating servers in the replica set. In case the network topology (connectivity graph) changes significantly, e.g., when a server node is exiting the highway, the intra-cluster communication with that node will experience increasing delays as the geographic distance and eventually the multi-hop communication path length grows. As the communication with a node deteriorates, the probability of an inconsistent application state will increase.

The model presented in this paper and the sensitivity analysis results are intended to quantify and investigate the impact of different traffic situations and dynamic behaviors on the resulting application availability and the probability of state inconsistency of the participating servers in replica set.

In a replication manager use case, three different nodes and roles can be distinguished: user nodes, relay nodes and service nodes. The user nodes are the clients of the application service which is provided by the service nodes. Although different replica sets can co-exist and overlap, the subsequent discussions will without loss of generality focus on a single replicated service instance. In order to start using the replicated application service, the RM middleware will need to identify the corresponding replica node set, e.g., via a dynamic naming service. Upon crash failure of the service node or degraded/disconnected communication properties, the RM service in the user node can failover to other service nodes in the replica group. Relay nodes are network nodes that relay packets in the network in a multi-hop communication scenario. In principle, all service nodes within the reach of the multi-hop connectivity are eligible to act as application service replicas; however, in order to limit communication delays between replica nodes, the communication path-lengths may be bounded to a maximum hop-count H; in the extreme case H=1, only direct neighbors (within link-layer connectivity) would be eligible to act as replicas. Any replica node can modify the data in the shared memory area (e.g., in reaction to processing requests by users).

In the rest of the paper we will refer to the maximum number of eligible replica nodes in the network as n, and to the number of service nodes active in the replica group as k.

2.2 Background on Data Consistency

Dynamic application state (as in the traffic information example) requires timely update and replication of the stored data. The replication model used in the RM is a simple shared memory area. As a node is taken into the replica group, it becomes accessible as a server to the users. Consistent data replication implies that all updates must have been received from all other nodes in the group before a node can be considered consistent. A typical shared memory area involves locking mechanisms to ensure that the memory is consistent at the time of a write operation. Locking or other concurrency or consistency control mechanisms however require communication overhead and cause additional delays. Furthermore, in scenarios of unbounded communication delays and for short-lived connectivity relations, the design of such mechanisms is very challenging. Due to the unreliability of the communication channel in mobile ad-hoc networks we choose to design the RM with optimistic replication and no concurrency control mechanisms. The sensitivity analysis provided in this paper shows the feasibility of this approach and gives guidelines as to which scenarios the RM will be able to provide a dependable dynamic shared memory area to the application. Omitting concurrency control is a choice to reduce replication overhead. The models presented in this paper show that replication is possible without concurrency control under certain circumstances.

2.3 Replication Management Problems and Proposed Design Concepts

In a car-to-car ad-hoc network the topology may change so frequently that the amount of signaling needed to keep a group of replicas consistent is potentially large [13]. The smaller the number of active replicas, the higher the unavailability of the application service due to crash failures of the server (which is undistinguishable from the server leaving the connected network). On the other hand service replication by broadcasting state information to all nodes in the network will increase wireless bandwidth consumption and may lead to congestion. The number of replicas to select is hence a tradeoff between low overhead and availability. The design goal of the RM is to provide services to the user with a high perceived quality of service, while keeping replication and reconfiguration overhead as low as possible. Therefore we have chosen to favor the tradeoffs that give the best perceived service to the user node.

The metrics with the highest impact on user perceived quality of service are service response time, service availability, and the correctness of the service [4]. Correctness is influenced by the consistency of the replicated data. If a user is getting a service which is provided based on out-of-date data the service is not correct. Incorrect service influences the user's perception of the service dependability. The faults that affect the user perceived quality of service are closely related to the metrics already described. For example packet loss or excess delay affects the timeliness of the service and also the correctness. A lost update packet is extending the time where the replica server is in an inconsistent state until a successful retransmission or a new update message is received. The same is true for large delay. If a single server in the group is experiencing these types of faults, it can be excluded from the group and a new service node – if any eligible ones reachable in the network - can be included. The replicas are selected in order to achieve stable clusters as this is preferred to minimize reconfiguration overhead; see [1] for strategies to increase stability.

In summary the most important problems addressed by the RM are:

- Selection of replicas with stability criteria and best communication metrics.
- Reduction of reconfiguration overhead.
- Reduction of service response time.

Any node in the replica group can propose new group members; when a member is proposed all existing members must acknowledge the adoption of the new members.

If the majority of the existing members accept the new group member by sending a positive acknowledgement to the proposing node, the latter will send an updated membership list to all nodes in the group and to all user nodes using the service provided by the group. The user nodes need to get member updates in order to have an up to date list of failover candidates in case they loose their connection with the server they are already using. The state manager part of the replication manager is responsible for sending update messages in case of a state change caused by a write operation to the shared memory region, to store received state variables and to send an acknowledgement when a state update message has been received. In this way the write operation will be replicated to the other group members. The retrieval part is responsible for selecting a server to be used by the user nodes in case they loose the connection with the server they were already using. The retrieval part of the RM is storing the updated list of group members and selects the failover server based on communication metrics and geographic properties of the servers. Furthermore the retrieval part of the RM is responsible for retrieving the state of the shared memory area when a new service node joins the replica group.

3 Dependability Modeling for Replica Consistency

In this section, we present the methodology and the approach of our dependability modeling. Moreover, the objective discussed in this section is to develop a method and a model making it possible to evaluate quantitative measures characterizing the consistency of the dynamic application state in the replica group. Markov chains and generalized stochastic Petri nets (GSPNs) [15] are commonly used to perform dependability evaluation studies and sensitivity analyses aimed at identifying parameters having the most significant impact on the measures. When using analytical techniques e.g., GSPNs and Markov chains, the system must be described at a high level of abstraction. Simplified assumptions are generally needed to obtain tractable models. Although simulation can be used to describe the system at a more detailed level, it is more costly in terms of the processing time needed to obtain accurate and statistically significant quantitative results.

This section develops GSPN models considering exponential assumptions for the underlying stochastic processes. Although such assumptions may not faithfully reflect reality, the results obtained from the models and sensitivity analysis give preliminary indications and estimations about the expected behaviors and trends that can be observed. More accurate results can be obtained considering more general distributions, using for example Matrix-Exponential distributions [14] or non Markovian models.

In the following, we represent a generic GSPN model and the corresponding Markov chains [5]. Then, we present the quantitative measures evaluated from the models to assess the data consistency and application availability. Finally, we discuss the main parameters that are considered in the sensitivity analysis.

3.1 GSPN Model for the Replica Consistency Estimation

Fig.1 represents the proposed GSPN model describing the potential evolution of replication group size and inconsistency. The model has four input parameters. The

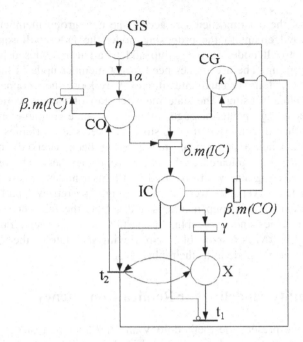

Fig. 1. GSPN model of network size *n* and replication group size *k*

first parameter denoted by α is the rate at which new eligible service nodes enter the (multi-hop) communication range of the existing group. This parameter depends on the geographic mobility model, the link-layer characteristics of the wireless technology (e.g., expressed by a communication radius), and the criterion on 'eligibility' to act as cluster node, e.g., the max hop-count H of the multi-hop connection. The second parameter, β, is the rate with which eligible service nodes leave the connectivity range of the replica set; β is influenced by the same three factors as stated above for α. The third parameter, γ, is the rate with which the state of the application service changes. This change rate obviously depends on the application type and the service usage scenario, hence may be influenced by the number of client nodes. The fourth parameter, δ, is the rate that represents the network and processing delay of an update message between replica nodes.

There are four main places in the Petri net; the two most important ones are labeled *IC* and *CO*. *IC* and *CO* denote the number of inconsistent and consistent nodes in the group, respectively. The top place *GS* is initially marked with a number of tokens corresponding to the network size *n*, i.e., the maximum number of nodes of the network. The initial marking of the place *CG* specifies the desired number of replica in the group (*k*). The place *X* is a utility place that moves all tokens from *CO* to *IC* and *CG* when the γ transition fires i.e., when the original data are updated. When place *X* gets marked, we remove all the tokens found in place *CO* by activating t_2. When *CO* is empty, we remove all the tokens placed in place *X* by activating t_1. Transitions t_1 and t_2 are instantaneous whereas all the other transitions are exponentially distributed timed transitions. It is important to note that the firing rates

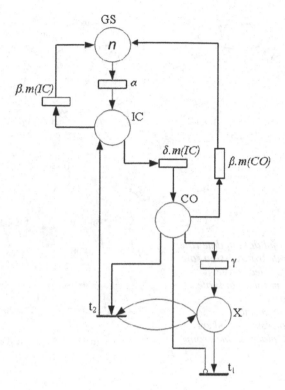

Fig. 2. GSPN model of replication group with $n=k$

of transitions (δ) and (β) are weighted by the marking $m(IC)$ and $m(CO)$ of the input places IC and CO, respectively.

The GSPN model of Fig.1 can be simplified when $n=k$. This is illustrated in Fig. 2.

3.2 Markov Model Derived from GSPN

The Markov models describing the evolution of replica group members and their consistency are derived automatically from the corresponding GSPN models. For example, the Markov model derived from the GSPN model depicted in Fig.3 with $n=k$ is given in Fig.4.

The Markov chain depicted in Fig.3 reflects an increasing number of replica group members when moving to the right within the columns. The number of *consistent* group members is depicted in the rows, increasing from top to bottom. Note that for illustration purposes, a 3-dimensional state-space labeling is used; the third component, the number of 'free' places in the replica set, is actually fully determined by the first two components.

The state in the lower right hand side is the optimal state of the replica group, as the maximum number n of consistent replica nodes is present. Fully consistent replica groups (of not necessarily maximal size) are represented by the whole lower diagonal.

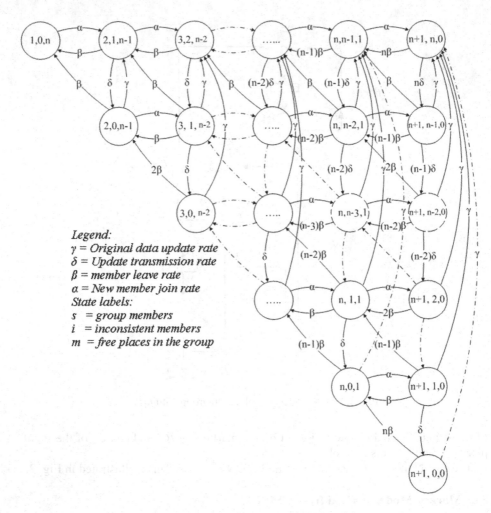

Fig. 3. Markov model of the GSPN model

The GSPN model of Fig.2 is generic and can be used to automatically generate the Markov chain associated with any (*n*) group size. As an example, Fig.4 shows the Markov chain representing replication consistency with *n=k=2* as group size. The arrow labels represent the rate of the corresponding transition; for instance, an arrow labeled "β" represents the leaving rate of a node from a group, regardless of whether this node is leaving because of a crash failure or another cause.

In the Markov model of Fig. 3, each state is labeled with three parameters (*s, i, m*) where *s* denotes the group size, *i* denotes the number of inconsistent members and *m* denotes the number of free places in the group, i.e., the number of members that can still join the group. We distinguish three main sets of states:

- The states labeled "*i=0*" denote those where all members of group at certain time are consistent.

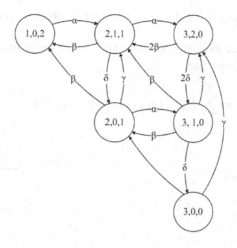

Fig. 4. Markov model of the GSPN model for $n=2$

- The states labeled "$s=n+1$, $m=0$" represented in the last column denote those where the system has no more free places and there are "$s-i$" members which are consistent.
- The state labeled "$n+1$, 0, 0" denote that the system is saturated with the maximum number of members and all are consistent.

From this model some interesting formulas can be derived; namely the probability of all existing group members being consistent. In the figure, this is the probability of the Markov chain being in any of the states in the lower diagonal of states. Using the regular structure of the Markov chain, this probability can be found by the expression:

$$P(cons) = \frac{1}{\sum_{j=0}^{n}\left(\frac{\alpha^j \beta^{(n-j)}}{j!}\right)} \sum_{i=1}^{n} \frac{(\alpha\delta)^{(n-i+1)} \beta^{(i-1)}}{\prod_{k=1}^{n-i+1}(k(\beta+\delta)+\gamma)} \tag{1}$$

The behavior of the size of the replica set (expressed by the first component, s, of the state-space) is actually fully determined by the rates of arrivals and departures from the group (α and β respectively). As this is a birth-death process, the probability of a certain replica size is equivalent to the queue-length probability of an M/M/n/n queuing system, which can be found in any standard queuing theory book to be [16]:

$$P(n, \beta, \alpha) = \frac{\alpha^n}{n! \beta^n \sum_{i=0}^{n} \frac{1}{i!}\left(\frac{\alpha}{\beta}\right)^i} = \frac{1}{\sum_{i=0}^{n} i! C_i^n \left(\frac{\beta}{\alpha}\right)^i} \tag{2}$$

Hereby, $C_i^n = \frac{n!}{i!.(n-i)!}$ denotes the binomial coefficients. Note that although Equation (2) can be derived directly from a simple M/M/n/n model, this is not the case any more for the more complex 2-dimensional Markov chain structure that lead to the derivation of Eq. (1).

In Eq. (3) the service availability is calculated given that a specific user perceives a specific server with the availability A_s.

$$A = \sum_{i=1}^{k} P(i,\beta,\alpha) \cdot (1 - (1 - A_s)^i)$$ (3)

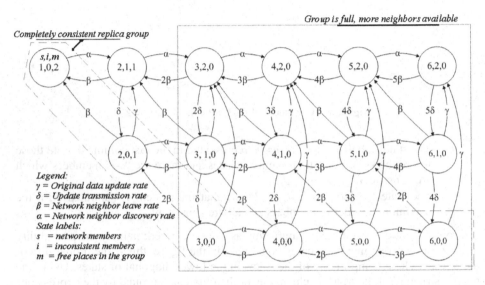

Fig. 5. Markov model with network size $n=5$ and replica group $k=2$

Fig. 5 shows another example with $n=5$ and $k=2$. The number of reachable neighbors is given by $(n-k)$. In the first part of the figure, the group is being established by nodes entering the network. The part marked as the group being full is added to make the model reflect better the dynamics of a fixed maximum size group, being maintained in a variable size connected vehicular ad-hoc network. In this part of the model nodes from the known neighborhood of the replica group are used as replacements when a node leaves the group.

4   Results

This section presents some numerical results for sensitivity analysis for the probabilities derived in Eq. (1), Eq. (2) and Eq. (3). We first discuss the values assigned to the parameters of the models and then present some results illustrating the behavior of the probabilities characterizing the inconsistency among group replica, the probability of reaching the maximum group size, and the service availability.

4.1 Parameter Values

Naturally there are constraints on the rates used in the model if the resulting numbers should show results of realistic scenarios. For instance the update rate is used to represent the end-to-end delay of the network between the nodes in the group. There is a theoretical minimum to this delay which is the time it takes to transfer one update message to a link-layer neighbor. Assuming that one update message can be sent within 50ms under good conditions (one hop, no MAC delay) the corresponding update rate will be around δ=1200/minute. To analyze the impact of this parameter on the results, two different values of δ are considered: 1000 and 100 per minute. The order of magnitude of the data change rate γ depends on the considered application. Two different values of this parameter have been considered for the results presented in this section: 10 and 100 per minute, corresponding to an average time between two consecutive updates of 6 sec. and 600 msec. respectively.

As regards the rate α of meeting new cars that are able to join the group, we have also considered different values corresponding to different traffic situations. The minimum rate is zero meaning not meeting any cars at all on the road. An example of value of the rate α is 30/sec which is approximately equivalent to cars, with the length of 5 meters, driving in opposite directions with a speed of 200 km/h with little or no space between the cars. This value could be much higher when considering multi-hop communication. Various values for the leaving rate β can also be considered to reflect different behaviors of the participating nodes. This value is also difficult to estimate because it depends on several influencing factors.

Rather than focusing on the absolute values of α and β, one can analyze the results by considering the relative ratio α/β. Higher values of this ratio correspond to environments where the probability of meeting a new car is higher than the probability that a participating node will leave the network. In a freeway scenario where cars join and leave the road via on and off-ramps and cars travel with a mean speed of 130 km/h excluding trucks the rate of cars joining the group is quite low because the cars travel with approximately the same speed. Assuming three cars joining the group per minute gives a join rate of 3/minute. With an assumption that each car stays in the group on average for 3 minutes the actual leave rate is β=0.33/minute. Accordingly the ratio α/β will be around 10. Much higher values can be obtained for other scenarios.

To summarize the settings of the parameters α, β, δ, and γ that represent the range of values expected to be found using measurements from vehicular networks would be as presented in Table 1.

Table 1. The maximum and minimum values for each parameter

Parameter	α	β	γ	δ
Min	0	0	10	100
Max	10000	10000	100	1000

4.2 Sensitivity Analyses for Replica Consistency

Fig. 6 plots some numerical results obtained by Eq. (2). As expected, it is shown that it is harder to reach the maximum group size for larger groups. If more members are needed to form a full group it is more difficult to do that given a constant arrival of new possible group members. The probability plotted in Fig.6 is only affected by the values of α and β that characterize the dynamics of the network; the higher the value of the ratio α/β, the closer the probability of reaching the maximum group size gets to the value 1. Also, it can be seen that this probability is very sensitive to the value of α/β when this ratio is relatively low (less than 10^2 in the example setting).

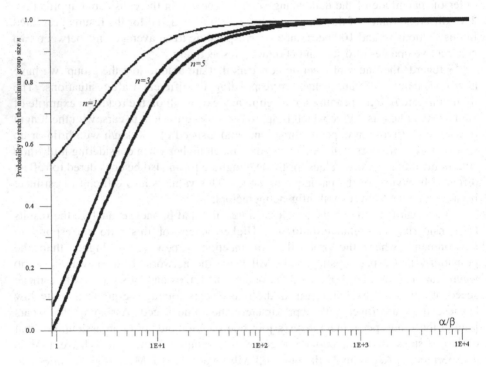

Fig. 6. Probability of presence of maximum group size $n=k$

As regards the replicas consistency, Figure 7 shows that the probability of a consistent replica set converges rather fast to a limit value for increasing α/β. This limit value depends strongly on the relation of the application state change, γ, and the network delay rate, δ. This is intuitive too, since timely updates are needed to achieve consistent replica groups.

Figure 7 shows the combined impact of parameters γ and δ on the consistency probabilities. It can be seen that a decrease of δ of one order of magnitude (from 1000 to 100), could lead to a degradation of the consistency probability in the order of 4 to 9 times, depending on the considered values for the ratio α/β and the value of γ. Also, for α/β values higher than 10, the higher the ratio δ/γ, the higher the consistency probability.

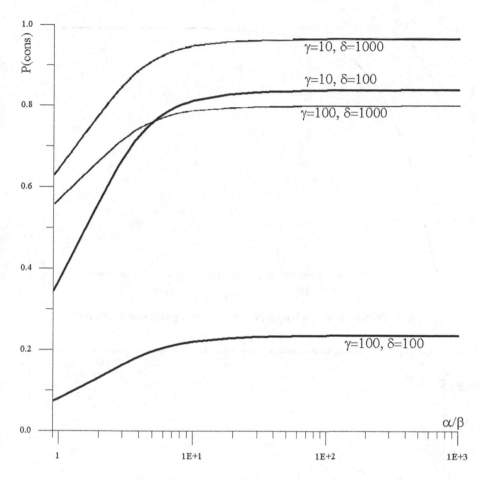

Fig. 7. Probability of having a fully consistent group for $n=k=5$

Considering the behavior of the consistency probability as a function of the replica group size, Fig.8 shows that for traffic situations corresponding to small values of the ratio α/β (e.g., in highway systems) the probability of achieving a full replica group is reduced significantly when the desired group size grows. For the desired group size of $k=7$ in a network with $n=7$ nodes the ratio between α and β must be larger than 3 to get a probability of more than 80% of achieving a full replica group. The above estimates of input values ($\alpha/\beta \leq 3$), the probability to fill up groups larger than $k=5$ nodes decreases.

With respect to the probability of all replicas being consistent the probability is high even with the ratio between γ and δ being as low as 10, the probability of having consistent replicas is about 80%. Citing the limits given above in Table 1, when considering the extreme high rates and the extreme low rates, the ratio between both γ and δ is equal to 10. Overall the probability of achieving consistent replica group members is high when the network is fast and not congested. Furthermore the data change rate γ must be considerably lower than the update transmission rate.

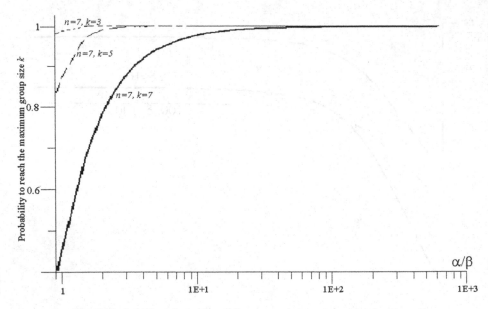

Fig. 8. Probability of reaching different maximum group size k with $n=7$

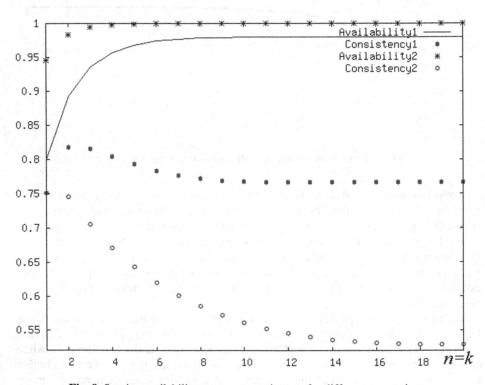

Fig. 9. Service availability vs. group consistency for different group sizes

4.3 Service Availability Analyses

Considering the analytical expression given by Eq. (3) and assuming that each server node in a group has an availability A_s=0.6. Figure 10 shows the service availability for two different settings of $\alpha, \beta, \gamma, \delta$. In the first setting, the parameters are set as follows: α=5, β=1, δ=100, γ=10. In the second setting the parameters are set as follows: α=10, β=1, δ=100, γ=20. From the figure it shows that there is a tradeoff between service availability and service correctness (here measured through data consistency). In Figure 9, $n=k$ and it goes from 1 to 20 along the x-axis. It appears that, for the considered numerical values, the best group size providing the best tradeoff between availability and correctness is 3 to 4 servers.

5 Conclusion and Outlook

In this paper, we have presented an analytical modeling study based on stochastic Petri nets and Markov chains that allowed us to analyze the behavior of a replication middleware service in ad-hoc based dynamic environments, considering quality of service and dependability related metrics. The main metrics concern the probability of having consistent replicas, the probability of reaching the maximum group size, and service availability. In particular, we carried out several sensitivity analysis studies to see how data consistency is affected in a broad range of scenarios. We can see that the probability to achieve a full group decreases significantly for group sizes with four or more replicas per group. Even though the group will not grow to its full size, the probability of having consistent replicated data is above 80% in case that the update rate is more than ten times faster than the data change rate. Recall that the data change rate represents the time between two data change events and the update rate represents the time it takes to send an update message to the replica node. With a replica group size of three the probability of reaching a full replica group is almost 50% higher when α is 100 times bigger than β.

Moreover we have shown that as service availability increases with a higher number of replicas, the service correctness starts to decrease if the group size goes beyond 4 servers.

The model presented in this paper assumes perfect replica selection and no signaling overhead when exchanging servers in the replica groups. This assumption is limiting the precision of the model but the trends shown in the results section in this paper are valid but optimistic with respect to the level of inconsistency. Another limitation of the model is that it does not consider events like network congestion. In a sense network failures and congestion events can be considered as an increase in the β parameter. The selection parameters and algorithms that should be used to select appropriate replica servers are developed in order to ensure maximum stability in the selected replica peers. The exact amount of signaling overhead involved in keeping the participating server nodes and the user nodes up to date on the current group member list is left for future studies.

186   E.V. Matthiesen et al.

References

[1] SAF, Service Availability Forum, http://www.saforum.org
[2] Artimy, M.M., Robertson, W., Phillips, W.J.: Connectivity in inter-vehicle ad hoc networks, Faculty of engineering, Dalhouse University (2004)
[3] HIDENETs, Highly Dependable ip-based networks and services, in Project Deliverable D1.2, IST-FP6-STREP-26979 (June 2003)
[4] Avizienis, A., Laprie, J.-C., Randell, B., Landwehr, C.: Basic concepts and taxonomy of dependable and secure computing. IEEE Transactions on Dependable and Secure Computing 1, 11–33 (2004)
[5] Bozinovski, M., Schwefel, H.-P., Prasad, R.: Algorithm for Controlling Transaction Consistency in SIP Session Control Systems. IEE Electronics Letters 40, 209–211 (2004)
[6] Camp, T., Boleng, J., Davies, V.: A survey of mobility models for ad hoc network research. In: Wireless Communications and Mobile Computing (WCMC) (2002)
[7] Chen, I.-R., Baoshan, G., George, S., Sheng-Tzong, C.: On failure recoverability of client-server applications in mobile wireless environments. IEEE Transactions in Reliability 54, 115–122 (2005)
[8] Matthiesen, E.V., Renier, T., Schwefel, H.-P.: A new selection metric for backup group creation in inter-vehicular networks. In: 16th IST Mobile and communications summit (2007)
[9] Chen, Z.D., Kung, H., Vlah, D.: Ad hoc relay wireless networks over moving vehicles on highways. In: MobiHoc 2001: Proceedings of the 2nd ACM international symposium on Mobile ad-hoc networking & computing, pp. 247–250. ACM Press, New York (2001)
[10] Hansen, M.B., Olsen, R.L., Schwefel, H.-P.: Probabilistic models for access strategies to dynamic information elements. Performance Evaluation (to appear)
[11] Helal, A., Heddaya, A., Bhargava, B.: Replication Techniques in Distributed Systems. Kluwer Academic Publishers, Dordrecht (1996)
[12] Olesen, R.L., Hansen, M.B., Schwefel, H.-P.: Quantitative analysis of access strategies to remote information in network services. In: Global Telecommunications Conference, GLOBECOM - IEEE (2006)
[13] Killijian, M.-O., Powell, D., Banâtre, M., Couderc, P., Roudier, Y.: Collaborative Backup for Dependable Mobile Applications. In: Proc. of 2nd Int. Workshop on Middleware for Pervasive and Ad-Hoc Computing (Middleware 2004), October 2004, pp. 146–149 (2004)
[14] Cox, D.R., Miller, H.D.: The Theory of Stochastic Processes. Chapman and Hall, Boca Raton (1965)
[15] Marsan, M.A., Balbo, G., Conte, G., Donatelli, S., Franceschinis, G.: Modeling with Generalized Stochastic Petri Nets. John Wiley & Sons, Chichester (1995)
[16] Bolch, G., Greiner, S., de Meer, H., Trivedi, K.S.: Queuing Networks and Markov Chains. Wiley, Chichester (2006)

Ten Fallacies of Availability and Reliability Analysis

Michael Grottke[1], Hairong Sun[2], Ricardo M. Fricks[3], and Kishor S. Trivedi[4]

[1] University of Erlangen-Nuremberg, Department of Statistics and Econometrics
Lange Gasse 20, D-90403 Nürnberg, Germany
Michael.Grottke@wiso.uni-erlangen.de
[2] Sun Microsystems, 500 Eldorado Blvd, Broomfield, CO 80021, USA
Hairong.Sun@sun.com
[3] Motorola Inc., 1501 West Shure Drive, Arlington Heights, IL 60004, USA
Ricardo.Fricks@motorola.com
[4] Duke University, Department of Electrical and Computer Engineering
Box 90291, Durham, NC 27708, USA
kst@ee.duke.edu

Abstract. As modern society becomes more and more dependent on computers and computer networks, vulnerability and downtime of these systems will significantly impact daily life from both social and economic point of view. Words like reliability and downtime are frequently heard on radio and television and read in newspapers and magazines. Thus reliability and availability have become popular terms. However, even professionals are in the danger of misunderstanding these basic concepts. Such misunderstandings can hinder advances in designing and deploying high-availability and high-reliability systems.

This paper delves into ten fallacious yet popular notions in availability and reliability. While the discussions on the first five fallacies clarify some misconceptions among reliability engineers working on modeling and analysis, the remaining five fallacies provide important insights to system engineers and companies focusing on system level integration.

1 Prologue

It is hard to discuss the reliability and availability concepts without first considering the lifetime of components and systems. We will mainly refer to systems in the explanation to follow but the same concepts will equally apply to components or units. In this section we review basic definitions that baseline our presentation to follow.

1.1 Basic Probability Theory Definitions

The lifetime or time to failure of a system can usually be represented by a random variable due to the intrinsic probabilistic nature of events that lead to system malfunction. Let the random variable X represent the lifetime or time to failure

T. Nanya et al. (Eds.): ISAS 2008, LNCS 5017, pp. 187–206, 2008.

of a system. The continuous random variable X can be characterized by the (cumulative) distribution function (CDF) $F(t)$, the (probability) density function (PDF) $f(t)$, or the hazard (rate) function $h(t)$, also known as the instantaneous failure rate. The CDF represents the probability that the system will fail before a given time t, i.e.,

$$F(t) = \Pr(X \leq t). \tag{1}$$

The PDF describes the rate of change of the CDF, i.e.,

$$f(t) = \frac{dF(t)}{dt} = \lim_{\Delta t \to 0} \frac{\Pr(t < X \leq t + \Delta t)}{\Delta t}. \tag{2}$$

Hence, $f(t)\Delta t$ is the limiting (unconditional) probability that a system will fail in the interval $(t, t + \Delta t]$. However, if we have observed the system functioning up to some time t, we expect the conditional probability in the interval to be different from $f(t)\Delta t$. This leads us to the notion of the instantaneous failure rate, or the hazard rate function,

$$h(t) = \lim_{\Delta t \to 0} \frac{\Pr(t < X \leq t + \Delta t \mid X > t)}{\Delta t} = \frac{f(t)}{1 - F(t)}. \tag{3}$$

Thus, $h(t)\Delta t$ represents the conditional probability that a system surviving to age t will fail in the interval $(t, t + \Delta t]$. Applied to a large population of systems, this conditional probability is the proportion of the survivors at time t that die during the immediately following small interval of time Δt.

The three functions $F(t)$, $f(t)$ and $h(t)$ are interrelated as shown in Table 1.

Table 1. Interrelationships between functions related to the lifetime distribution

$f(t)$	$\frac{dF(t)}{dt}$	$h(t)e^{-\int_0^t h(\tau)d\tau}$
$\int_0^t f(\tau)d\tau$	$F(t)$	$1 - e^{-\int_0^t h(\tau)d\tau}$
$\frac{f(t)}{\int_t^\infty f(\tau)d\tau}$	$\frac{dF(t)/dt}{1 - F(t)}$	$h(t)$

Any of these three functions can uniquely describe the lifetime distribution. For instance, if the time to failure of a system follows an exponential distribution with parameter λ then

$$F(t) = 1 - e^{-\lambda t}, \tag{4}$$

$$f(t) = \frac{d}{dt}\left(1 - e^{-\lambda t}\right) = \lambda e^{-\lambda t}, \tag{5}$$

$$h(t) = \frac{\lambda e^{-\lambda t}}{1 - [1 - e^{-\lambda t}]} = \lambda \tag{6}$$

for $t \geq 0$. Observe that the hazard rate function $h(t)$ shows that the exponential lifetime distribution is characterized by the age-independent failure rate λ. As a matter of fact, the exponential distribution is the only continuous probability distribution having a hazard function that does not change over time.

Therefore, whenever people refer to a lifetime distribution with constant failure rate, they are implicitly establishing the exponential distribution for the system lifetime.

1.2   Reliability Definitions

Recommendation E.800 of the International Telecommunications Union (ITU-T) defines reliability as the "ability of an item to perform a required function under given conditions for a given time interval." Therefore, for any time interval $(z, z + t]$ reliability $R(t \mid z)$ is the probability that the system does not fail in this interval, assuming that it is working at time z. Of specific interest are the intervals starting at time $z = 0$; reliability $R(t) := R(t \mid 0)$ denotes the probability that the system continues to function until time t. If the random variable X represents the time to system failure as before, then

$$R(t) = \Pr(X > t) = 1 - F(t), \tag{7}$$

where $F(t)$ is the system lifetime CDF.

Closely related to the reliability $R(t)$ is the definition of mean time to failure (MTTF). System MTTF is the expected time that a system will operate before the first failure occurs; i.e., on the average, a system will operate for MTTF hours and then encounter its first failure. The average of the system's lifetime distribution $E[X]$ is

$$E[X] = \int_0^\infty t f(t) dt = \int_0^\infty R(t) dt, \tag{8}$$

provided this integral is finite. If the right-hand side is not absolutely convergent, then $E[X]$ does not exist. Therefore, system MTTF can be computed by first determining its corresponding reliability function $R(t)$ and then applying (8). For example, if the system lifetime is exponentially distributed with failure rate λ then

$$R(t) = 1 - \left(1 - e^{-\lambda t}\right) = e^{-\lambda t} \tag{9}$$

and

$$\text{MTTF} = \int_0^\infty e^{-\lambda t} dt = \frac{1}{\lambda}. \tag{10}$$

1.3   Availability Definitions

Availability is closely related to reliability, and is defined in ITU-T Recommendation E.800 as the "ability of an item to be in a state to perform a required function at a given instant of time or at any instant of time within a given time interval, assuming that the external resources, if required, are provided."

An important difference between reliability and availability is that reliability refers to failure-free operation of the system during an interval, while availability refers to failure-free operation of the system at a given instant of time.

Like in the case of reliability, we can restate the availability definition with the assistance of random variables. Let $Y(t) = 1$ if the system is operating at time t, and 0 otherwise. The most straightforward measure of system availability is the instantaneous availability $A(t)$, which is the probability that the system is operating correctly and is available to perform its functions at a specified time t, i.e.,

$$A(t) = \Pr(Y(t) = 1) = E[Y(t)].\tag{11}$$

The instantaneous availability is always greater than or equal to the reliability; and in the absence of repairs or replacements, the instantaneous availability $A(t)$ is simply equal to the reliability $R(t)$ of the system.

Given $A(t)$ we can define the (steady-state) availability A of the system as

$$A = \lim_{t \to \infty} A(t).\tag{12}$$

The steady-state availability, or simply availability, represents the long-term probability that the system is available. It can be shown that the steady-state availability is given by

$$A = \frac{\text{MTTF}}{\text{MTTF} + \text{MTTR}},\tag{13}$$

where the system mean time to repair (MTTR) is the average time required to repair system failures, including any time required to detect that there is a failure, to repair it, and to place the system back into an operational state; i.e., once the failure has occurred, the system will then require MTTR hours on the average to restore operation. It is known that the limiting availability depends only on the mean time to failure and the mean time to repair, and not on the nature of the distributions of failure times and repair times. There is an implied assumption in this model that repairs can always be performed which will restore the system to its best condition ("as good as new").

If the system lifetime is exponential with failure rate λ, and the time-to-repair distribution of the system is exponential with (repair) rate μ, then (13) can be rewritten as

$$A = \frac{\mu}{\lambda + \mu}.\tag{14}$$

Another concept of interest is the interval (or average) availability $A_I(t)$ of the system given by

$$A_I(t) = \frac{1}{t} \int_0^t A(\tau) d\tau.\tag{15}$$

The interval availability $A_I(t)$ is the expected proportion of time the system is operational during the period $(0, t]$. A property that can easily be verified if we represent the total amount of system uptime during $(0, t]$ by the random variable $U(t)$ is the following one:

$$A_I(t) = \frac{1}{t} \int_0^t E[Y(\tau)] d\tau = \frac{1}{t} E[U(t)].\tag{16}$$

The *limiting average availability* A_I is the expected fraction of time that the system is operating:

$$A_I = \lim_{t\to\infty} A_I(t). \tag{17}$$

If the limit exists, then the steady-state and the limiting average availabilities are the same [1,2]; i.e.,

$$A_I = \lim_{t\to\infty} \frac{1}{t} \int_0^t A(\tau)d\tau = A. \tag{18}$$

2 Fallacies

2.1 "Fault Tolerance Is an Availability Feature and Not a Reliability Feature"

This fallacy comes from the misunderstanding of the reliability definition. The statement "the system continues to function throughout the interval $(0,t]$" does not imply the absence of internal system faults or error conditions during the interval $(0,t]$. Failure and recovery at component level is allowed as long as the system continues to function throughout the interval $(0,t]$. A simple example is Redundant Array of Independent (or Inexpensive) Disks (RAID) [3]. For RAID 1-5, it stores redundant data in different places on multiple hard disks. By placing data on multiple disks, I/O operations can overlap in a balanced way, improving performance and also increasing fault-tolerance.

Figure 1 is the state-transition diagram of a continuous-time Markov chain (CTMC) modeling the failure/repair behavior of a RAID 5 system. State 0 represents the state that all the N disks in the parity group are working, state 1 represents the failure of one disk. The parity group fails (data is lost) when there are double disk failures. The failure rate and repair rate for a disk are λ and μ, respectively.

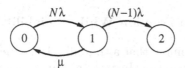

Fig. 1. CTMC for RAID 5 with N disks

Solving the CTMC model, it can be shown that the system reliability in the interval $(0,t]$ is given by [4]

$$R(t) = \frac{N(N-1)\lambda^2}{\alpha_1 - \alpha_2} \left(\frac{e^{-\alpha_2 t}}{\alpha_2} - \frac{e^{-\alpha_1 t}}{\alpha_1} \right), \tag{19}$$

where

$$\alpha_1, \alpha_2 = \frac{(2N-1)\lambda + \mu \pm \sqrt{\lambda^2 + 2(2N-1)\lambda\mu + \mu^2}}{2}. \tag{20}$$

From these expressions, the mean time to reach the absorbing state 2 (i.e., the system MTTF) is derived as

$$\text{MTTF} = \frac{2N - 1}{N(N - 1)\lambda} + \frac{\mu}{N(N - 1)\lambda^2}. \tag{21}$$

If the MTTF of a disk is $\lambda^{-1} = 20$ years [5], and the MTTR is $\mu^{-1} = 20$ hours, using RAID 5 to add parity in a rotating way, the MTTF of the parity group with $N = 6$ disks will be $5,847.333$ years.

In a system without repair (i.e., $\mu = 0$) the time to failure follows a two-stage hypoexponential distribution with transition rates $N\lambda$ and $(N-1)\lambda$. The reliability function is then

$$R(t) = \frac{N(N - 1)\lambda^2}{N\lambda - (N - 1)\lambda} \left(\frac{e^{-(N-1)\lambda t}}{(N - 1)\lambda} - \frac{e^{-N\lambda t}}{N\lambda} \right)$$
$$= Ne^{-(N-1)\lambda t} - (N - 1)e^{-N\lambda t}, \tag{22}$$

and the MTTF amounts to

$$\text{MTTF} = \frac{1}{N\lambda} - \frac{1}{(N - 1)\lambda} = \frac{2N - 1}{N(N - 1)\lambda}. \tag{23}$$

For our RAID 5 example with parameter values given above follows a system MTTF of about 7.333 years, which is considerably less than the system MTTF in the presence of repair, and it is even less than the MTTF of a single disk; this stresses the importance of combining redundancy with effective and efficient repair.

However, we have seen that in the presence of adequate repair fault tolerance can improve system reliability. It is thus not only an availability feature, but also a reliability feature.

2.2   "Availability Is a Fraction While Reliability Is Statistical"

This statement seems to imply that availability is a deterministic concept, while reliability is a random quantity. In fact, as can be seen from (7), for a given time t reliability $R(t)$ is a fixed probability that depends on the distribution of the time to failure. Of course, the parameters of this distribution - or even the type of distribution - may be unknown; then the reliability needs to be estimated from measured data. For example, assume that we observe m new (or "as good as new") copies of the same system throughout the time interval $(0, t]$. If x_t of these copies do not fail during the observation period, then we can give a point estimate of $R(t)$ as the fraction x_t/m. Note that the number of non-failing copies X_t is random; therefore, the estimator $\hat{R}(t) = X_t/m$ is also a random variable. As a consequence, the point estimate x_t/m can be far from the true reliability $R(t)$; instead of merely calculating such a point estimate, it is therefore advisable to derive a confidence interval. Based on the fact that X_t

follows a binomial distribution with size m and success probability $R(t)$, it can be shown [6] that

$$\left[\left(1 + \frac{m - x_t + 1}{x_t f_{2x_t, 2(m-x_t+1);\alpha}}\right)^{-1}; 1\right] \qquad (24)$$

is the realized upper one-sided $100(1 - \alpha)\%$ confidence interval for $R(t)$, where the expression $f_{2x_t, 2(m-x_t+1);\alpha}$ denotes the (lower) $100\alpha\%$-quantile of the F-distribution with $2x_t$ numerator degrees of freedom and $2(m - x_t + 1)$ denominator degrees of freedom. This means that if we repeat the experiment (of observing the number of non-failing systems among a set of m until time t) very often, then about $100(1 - \alpha)\%$ of the confidence intervals constructed based on the respective measured values of x_t will contain the true but unknown reliability $R(t)$. Note that the estimator and the confidence interval given above are valid regardless of the distribution of the time to failure. As an example, assume that we observe 100 new copies of a system for 10 hours each. If one of them fails, then we estimate the reliability in the time interval $(0; 10 \text{ hr}]$ to be 0.99, while the realized upper one-sided 95% confidence interval is given by $[0.9534; 1]$.

Similarly, the steady-state availability A can be estimated as follows. We can for example measure n consecutive times to failure $(Y_1, \ldots, Y_n)$ and times to repair $(Z_1, \ldots, Z_n)$ of a system in steady-state. All times to failure and times to repair, as well as the total up-time $U_n = \sum_{i=1}^n Y_i$ and the total downtime $D_n = \sum_{i=1}^n Z_i$ are random variables. Based on the values u_n and d_n actually observed, an obvious choice for a point estimate of steady-state availability is $\hat{A} = u_n/(u_n + d_n)$. Again, it is possible to derive a confidence interval. If all Y_i and Z_i are exponentially distributed with rate λ and μ, respectively, then $2\lambda U_n/(2\mu D_n)$ follows an F-distribution with $2n$ numerator degrees of freedom and $2n$ denominator degrees of freedom. Therefore, the realized upper one-sided $100(1 - \alpha)\%$ confidence interval for steady-state availability A is given by [4]

$$\left[\left(1 + \frac{d_n}{u_n f_{2n, 2n;\alpha}}\right)^{-1}; 1\right]. \qquad (25)$$

For example, if we have 10 samples of failures and repairs, and the total up time and total down time are 9990 hours and 10 hours, respectively, then the point estimate of availability is 0.999. Assuming that both the time to failure and the time to repair follow exponential distributions, the realized upper one-sided 95% confidence interval is $[0.9979; 1]$.

This availability inference process is not always feasible since the system MTTF of commercial systems such as the ones supporting most computing and communications systems is of the order of months to years. So, a more practical approach aims at estimating the interval availability $A_I(t)$ for the interval $(0, t]$ with fixed length t (e.g., a week or a month) instead. One possible approach is to observe m statistically identical new (or "as good as new") copies of the system during the time interval $(0, t]$. For each copy $i = 1, \ldots, m$, the total down-time $d_i(t)$ (realization of the random variable $D_i(t)$) in the observation interval is recorded. Alternatively, we could observe the same system for m periods of fixed duration t, provided that it is as good as new at the beginning of each of these periods. The random variables $D_i(t)$ would then represent the downtime of the system in the ith observation period, while $d_i(t)$ is the actual downtime experienced in this period.

Since the individual downtimes $D_i(t)$ are identically distributed random variables, the sample mean

$$\bar{D}(t) = \frac{1}{m} \sum_{i=1}^{m} D_i(t) \qquad (26)$$

has an expected value that is equal to the true but unknown expected downtime in the interval $(0, t]$. We can therefore use the average of the observed downtimes to compute a point estimate of the system interval availability $A_I(t)$:

$$\hat{A}_I(t) = \frac{t - \frac{1}{m} \sum_{i=1}^{m} d_i(t)}{t} = 1 - \frac{\sum_{i=1}^{m} d_i(t)}{m \cdot t}. \qquad (27)$$

If the individual downtimes $D_i(t)$ are independent, then the Central Limit Theorem [4] guarantees that for large sample sizes m the sample mean $\bar{D}(t)$, (26), approximately follows a normal distribution. This fact can be used for deriving an approximate confidence interval to the interval availability estimate.

As the observation period t increases, the interval availability estimated using (27) will eventually converge to the true steady-state availability A of the system, i.e.,

$$\lim_{t \to \infty} \hat{A}_I(t) = A. \qquad (28)$$

Simulation experiments in [7] show that it is possible to produce a steady-state availability estimate with an efficient confidence interval based on a temporal sequence of interval availability estimates. This technique does not depend on the nature of the failure and repair time distributions.

All this shows the similarities between reliability and availability from a stochastic point of view: Both reliability and availability are fixed but unknown values; they can be estimated by fractions; the estimators are random variables; and based on the distributions of these random variables, we can come up with expressions for constructing confidence intervals.

2.3   "The Term 'Software Reliability Growth' Is Unfortunate: Reliability Is Always a Non-increasing Function of Time"

This fallacy is caused by the fact that reliability $R(t \mid z)$, the probability of no failure in the time interval $(z, z + t]$, can be considered as a function of interval length t, or as a function of interval start time z.

The latter aspect is often forgotten due to the importance of the reliability function $R(t) := R(t \mid 0)$ referring to the reliability in the interval $(0, t]$. By integrating both sides of (3) we get

$$\int_0^t h(\tau)d\tau = \int_0^t \frac{f(\tau)}{1 - F(\tau)}d\tau = \int_0^t \frac{-\partial R(\tau)/\partial \tau}{R(\tau)}d\tau; \qquad (29)$$

using the boundary condition $R(0) = 1$, this yields [4]

$$R(t) = e^{-\int_0^t h(\tau)d\tau}. \tag{30}$$

Since the hazard function $h(t)$ is larger than or equal to zero for all $t > 0$, $R(t)$ is always a non-increasing function of t. This result is reasonable: If the time interval examined is extended, then the probability of experiencing a failure may be higher, but it cannot be lower.

However, if the interval length t considered is set to a fixed value, say t_0, while the interval start time z is allowed to vary, then reliability $R(t_0 \mid z)$ can be a decreasing, constant, or increasing function of z. Software reliability growth models describe how the failure generating process evolves as testing and debugging proceed. Almost all of them assume that $R(t_0 \mid z)$ will eventually be a non-decreasing function of z; hence the term "software reliability growth."

For example, in the important class of non-homogeneous Poisson process models, the instantaneous failure rate of the software is a mere function of time and does not depend on the number of faults discovered so far, etc. It can be shown that according to these models the reliability $R(t \mid z)$ is given by [8]

$$R(t \mid z) = e^{-\int_z^{z+t} h(\tau)d\tau}; \tag{31}$$

in this context, the function $h(t)$ is often called "program hazard rate." Obviously, (31) includes (30) as the special case $z = 0$. Regardless of the value of z, $R(t \mid z)$ is always a non-increasing function of t, starting out at $R(0 \mid z) = 1$. However, there will eventually be software reliability growth in the sense described above if and only if the instantaneous failure rate is eventually a non-increasing function of time. Figure 2 illustrates these aspects based on a so-called S-shaped software reliability growth model, featuring an instantaneous failure rate that is first increasing (e.g., due to learning effects on part of the testers) and then decreasing (because the software quality improves). The strictly decreasing function $R(t \mid 0)$ is depicted in the left diagram. For the arbitrarily chosen interval length t_0, the right diagram shows that $R(t_0 \mid z)$ as a function of z first decreases and then increases.

Thus, the term "software reliability growth" is correct, as it refers to the fact that the probability of no failure occurrence in a time interval of fixed length tends to be higher if the interval start time is increased.

2.4 "MTTF Is the Whole Story about Reliability"

This misconception is probably due to the fact that simple system reliability and availability (R&A) models often assume that the time to failure of individual components follows an exponential distribution. As we have seen in Section 1.1, the only parameter of this distribution is the constant failure rate λ, which according to (10) is the reciprocal value of the MTTF. Therefore, if we know that the time to failure is exponentially distributed, then this piece of information plus the MTTF indeed completely describe the distribution of the time to failure

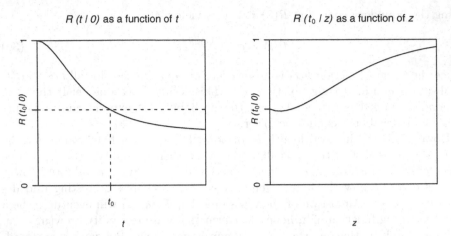

Fig. 2. Reliability $R(t \mid z)$ as functions of t and z

and hence the reliability function $R(t)$. However, it needs to be stressed that the distribution of the time to failure is never fully specified by its expected value, the MTTF, alone; we always need at least additional information about the type of distribution. Unfortunately, the exponential distribution assumption is sometimes not stated explicitly.

Even if the time to failure is assumed to follow a more complex distribution, the MTTF can suffice as an additional piece of information. For example, a two-stage Erlang distribution [4] features an increasing failure rate, but like the exponential distribution it only has one parameter, λ. From a given MTTF, the value of this parameter can be derived as $\lambda = \frac{2}{\text{MTTF}}$.

Note that for distributions with more than one parameter, information on the type of distribution and the MTTF will not be enough for completely specifying the distribution - information about additional moments of the distribution (or about its additional parameters) will be needed. For example, if the time to failure is known to follow a k-stage Erlang distribution (where k is unknown), then in addition to the MTTF we would require further information, like the variance of the time-to-failure distribution Var.TTF, in order to derive the two model parameters $\lambda = \frac{\text{MTTF}}{\text{Var.TTF}}$ and $k = \text{MTTF} \cdot \lambda = \frac{\text{MTTF}^2}{\text{Var.TTF}}$.

The fact that the MTTF by itself does not completely specify the time-to-failure distribution also means that decisions based on the MTTF alone can be wrong. As an illustration, consider the analysis of triple modular redundant (TMR) systems. The TMR technique is widely adopted in the design of high-reliability systems. Since two of the three components present in a TMR system need to function properly for the system to work, the reliability of such a system is [4]

$$R(t) = 3R_u^2(t) - 2R_u^3(t), \tag{32}$$

where $R_u(t)$ represents the reliability of any of the three statistically identical components. If the time to failure of each component follows an exponential distribution with reliability function given by (9), then we get

$$R(t) = 3e^{-\lambda t} - 2e^{-\lambda t}. \tag{33}$$

It can be shown that $R(t) > R_u(t)$ for $t < t_0 \equiv \ln(2)/\lambda$. Therefore, the TMR type of redundancy clearly improves reliability for a mission time that is shorter than t_0. However, the MTTF of the TMR system,

$$\text{MTTF} = \int_0^\infty 3e^{-\lambda t}dt - \int_0^\infty 2e^{-\lambda t}dt = \frac{3}{2\lambda} - \frac{2}{3\lambda} = \frac{5}{6\lambda}, \tag{34}$$

is smaller than $1/\lambda$, the component MTTF. Based on the MTTF alone, a system designer would always favor the single component over the TMR system; as we have seen, this decision is wrong if the mission time is shorter than t_0.

Therefore, MTTF is not the whole story about reliability. It does not suffice to fully specify the time-to-failure distribution; decisions based on the MTTF alone can thus be wrong.

2.5 "The Presence of Non-exponential Lifetime or Time-to-Repair Distributions Precludes Analytical Solution of State-Space Based R&A Models"

One common misconception is that analytic solutions of state-space based R&A models are only feasible if all modeled distributions are exponential or geometric in nature; if that is not the case, simulation modeling is the only viable alternative. This assertion could not be further from the truth given the rich theory of non-Markovian modeling.

Markov models have often been used for software and hardware performance and dependability assessment. Reasons for the popularity of Markov models include the ability to capture various dependencies, the equal ease with which steady-state, transient, and cumulative transient measures can be computed, and the extension to Markov reward models useful in performability analysis [9]. For example, Markov modeling is quite useful when modeling systems with dependent failure and repair modes, as well as when components behave in a statistically independent manner. Furthermore, it can handle the modeling of multi-state devices and common-cause failures without any conceptual difficulty.

Markov modeling allows the solution of stochastic problems enjoying the property: the probability of any particular future behavior of the process, when its current state is known exactly, is not altered by additional knowledge concerning its past behavior. For a homogeneous Markov process, the past history of the process is completely summarized in the current state. Otherwise, the exact characterization of the present state needs the associated time information, and the process is said to be non-homogeneous. Non-homogeneity extends the applicability of Markov chains by allowing time-dependent rates or probabilities to be associated to the models. For instance, in case of a non-homogeneous CTMC, the infinitesimal generator matrix $Q(t) = [q_{ij}(t)]$ is a function of time. This implies that the transition rates $q_{ij}(t)$ and $q_{ii}(t) = -\sum_{j \neq i} q_{ij}(t)$ are also functions of t.

A wide range of real dependability and performance modeling problems fall in the class of Markov models (both homogeneous and non-homogeneous). However, some important aspects of system behavior in stochastic models cannot be easily captured through a Markov model. The common characteristic these problems share is that the Markov property is not valid (if valid at all) at all time instants. This category of problems is jointly referred to as non-Markovian models and include, for instance, modeling using phase-type expansions, supplementary variables, semi-Markov processes (SMPs), and Markov regenerative processes (MRGPs). For a recent survey, see [10].

Thus, state-space based R&A models can be solved analytically, even if lifetime or time-to-repair distributions are non-exponential.

2.6 "Availability Will Always Be Increased with More Redundancy"

In a perfect world, availability increases with the degree of redundancy. However, if coverage ratio and reconfiguration delay are considered, availability does not necessarily increase with redundancy [11].

Assume there are n processors in a system and that at least one of them is needed for the system being up. Each processor fails at rate λ and is repaired at rate μ. The coverage probability (i.e., the probability that the failure of one processor can be detected and the system can be reconfigured successfully) is c. The average reconfiguration delay after a covered failure is $1/\delta$, and the average reboot time after an uncovered failure is $1/\beta$. In the CTMC model in Fig. 3 state i means there are i processors working, state D_i stands for the case that there are i processors working, the failure of a processor has been detected and the system is under reconfiguration, while state B_i means there are i processors working, the failure of a processor is undetected and the system is undergoing a reboot. The system is only available in states $1, 2, \ldots, n$.

According to the numerical results in Fig. 4, system availability is maximized when there are 2 processors. Therefore, availability will not always increase with more redundancy, and the coverage probability and reconfiguration delay play important roles. To realize redundancy benefits, coverage must be near perfect and reconfiguration delay must be very small.

2.7 "Using Low-Cost Components Can Always Build Highly Available Systems"

In Section 2.6, we argued that the coverage probability plays an important role for availability. From industry experience, low-cost components are usually designed with relatively poor fault management because component vendors are reluctant to increase expense to improve the quality of products. Thus, there are many cases in which low-cost components are accompanied with lower coverage probability, lower fault-detection probability, longer fault-detection time and larger no-trouble-found ratio (i.e., one cannot find where the problem is when the system fails). From Fig. 4, we can conjecture that we might not be able to build a highly-available system if the coverage probability is low and/or

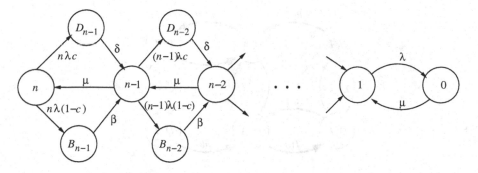

Fig. 3. CTMC model for a multi-processor system

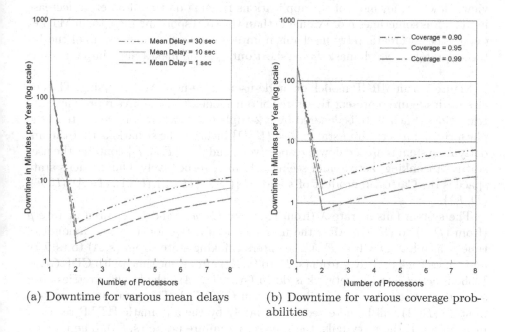

(a) Downtime for various mean delays

(b) Downtime for various coverage probabilities

Fig. 4. System downtime as a function of the number of processors used

the reconfiguration delay is long, which are the attributes that usually come with low-cost components. So before choosing a low-cost component, make sure to assess its reliability and fault coverage probability and ensure that they meet the availability goal at the system level.

2.8 "A Ten-Times Decrease in MTTR Is Just as Valuable as a Ten-Times Increase in MTTF"

Equation (13) suggests that a ten-times decrease in MTTR is just as valuable as a ten-times increase in MTTF. That is correct from system availability point of

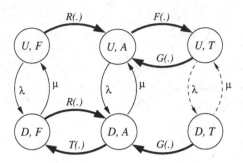

Fig. 5. MRGP Model for single-user-single-host Web browsing

view. However, for most of the applications running on the Internet, a decrease in MTTR is sometimes more valuable than the corresponding increase in MTTF, due to the automatic retry mechanism implemented at various layers of the Internet protocols which masks some short outages and makes them imperceptible [12].

Figure 5 is an MRGP model for single-user-single-host Web browsing. The circles in this figure represent the states of our model, and the arcs represent state transitions. Each state is denoted by a 2-tuple (s, u), where s is the state of the platform and u is the user status. $s = \{U, D\}$ includes the situations that the underlying system is up and down, respectively, and $u = \{T, A, F\}$ contains the user status of thinking, active, and seeing a failure, respectively. Our model's state space is the Cartesian product of s and u, $\{(U,T), (D,T), (U,A), (D,A), (U,F), (D,F)\}$.

The system fails at rate λ (from (U, u) to (D, u)), and is repaired at rate μ (from (D, u) to (U, u)). After the user has been active for a certain amount of time, which has a CDF of $F(.)$, she enters thinking state (from (s, A) to (s, T)), and comes back to active (from (s, T) to (s, A)) after some time (with CDF $G(.)$). If she is active and the network is down (state (D, A)), the browser retries after some time that follows a distribution with CDF $T(.)$. The repair of the system in state (D, A) will be detected immediately by the automatic HTTP recovery mechanism. If the retry fails, the user sees a failure (state (s, F)). The user reattempts to connect to the Web host, which is represented by transition with distribution $R(.)$. Note that transitions $F(.)$, $G(.)$, $T(.)$, and $R(.)$ have general distributions (solid thick arcs in Fig. 5); hence the model described above is not a CTMC, nor is it an SMP because of the existence of local behaviors, which are known as state changes between two consecutive regenerative points. For example, if the failure transition from (U, A) to (D, A) occurs, the user active transition $F(.)$ is not present in state (D, A). This exponential transition is known as competitive exponential transition (represented by solid thin arcs), and its firing marks a regenerative point. On the other hand, the transitions of the server going up and down in states (U, T) and (D, T) do not affect (add, remove or reset the general transitions) the user thinking process which is generally

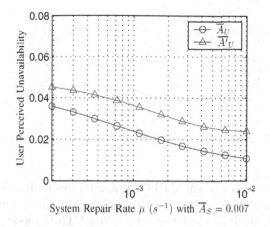

Fig. 6. User-perceived unavailability $\bar{A}_U$, $\overline{A'}_U$

distributed. They are called concurrent exponential transitions (represented by dashed thin arcs), and their occurrences are just local behaviors.

Following the methodology in [12], and using the assumptions on parameters and distributions [13], we can get the numerical results depicted in Fig. 6. For comparison purpose, we also constructed and solved the corresponding CTMC model, i.e., we replaced all the general distributions with exponential distributions with the same means.

We denoted the user-perceived service availability of the CTMC model by $\overline{A'}_U$. System unavailability was set to a constant 0.007, while the failure rate λ and repair rate μ varied accordingly. If we incorporate both the failure recovery behaviors of the service-supporting infrastructure and the online user behaviors and evaluate the dependency of the user-perceived unavailability on parameters including the service platform failure rate/repair rate, user retry rate, and user switching rate, we will find the user-perceived unavailability very different from the system unavailability.

For Web applications, the user-perceived availability is more sensitive to the platform repair rate; i.e., for two systems with same availability, the one with faster recovery is better than the one with higher reliability from an end user's perspective. We also found that the CTMC model overestimates the user-perceived unavailability by a significant percentage.

2.9 "Improving Component MTTR Is the Key to Improve System Availability"

This fallacy results from a common misunderstanding of the steady-state availability formula (13): If we maintain the MTTF invariant (e.g., by not investing in more reliable components) then we can still improve system availability by reducing component MTTR, right? Not necessarily, because the MTTF and MTTR parameters in the system availability formulas are related to system properties,

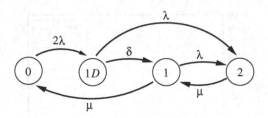

Fig. 7. CTMC model of a two-component parallel redundant system with fault recovery delay

not component ones. The system MTTR parameter in a fault-tolerant system, for instance, will also be a function of the quality of its fault management mechanism.

Consider for instance the fact that any given CTMC model can be reduced to an equivalent two-state model for the sole purpose of conducting steady-state analysis using the aggregation technique introduced in [14]. With this procedure we are collapsing all operational states into a single state, and all failed states into a single failure state. Failures in the equivalent model happen with rate λ_{eq} and are repaired with rate μ_{eq}. Therefore, we can define system MTTF or MTTF$_{eq}$ as $1/\lambda_{eq}$ and system MTTR or MTTR$_{eq}$ as $1/\mu_{eq}$ in reference to the trivial solution of a two-state availability model provided by (13). The problem is that these equivalent rates are numerical artifacts with complex formulae that most of the time cannot be physically interpreted (e.g., there is no simple relation mapping a system MTTR to component MTTR).

For example, consider a two-component parallel redundant system with a single shared-repair facility. The availability model is shown in Fig. 7. In the state transition diagram, state $1D$ represents the recovery behavior after the first fault in the system (i.e., the first component failure). All other states are labeled by the number of failed components. States $1D$ and 2 are assumed to be the system failure states in this example. The component failure and repair rates are λ and μ, respectively. Once the first system fault is triggered, the system will recover with rate δ. The time the CTMC stays in state $1D$ represents the combined time the system's fault manager needs to react to the first system fault. A second fault during this sojourn time in state $1D$ leads the system directly to the system failure represented by state 2. This event happens with rate λ.

The steady-state solution of the CTMC model in Fig. 7 results in the following state probabilities:

$$\pi_0 = \frac{\mu^2(\lambda + \delta)}{2\lambda^2(\lambda + \mu + \delta)E}, \qquad \pi_{1D} = \frac{\mu^2}{\lambda(\lambda + \mu + \delta)E}, \tag{35}$$

$$\pi_1 = \frac{\mu(\lambda + \delta)}{\lambda(\lambda + \mu + \delta)E}, \qquad \pi_2 = \frac{1}{E}, \tag{36}$$

with

$$E = 1 + \frac{\mu(\lambda + \delta)}{\lambda(\lambda + \mu + \delta)} + \frac{\mu^2}{\lambda(\lambda + \mu + \delta)} + \frac{\mu^2(\lambda + \delta)}{2\lambda^2(\lambda + \mu + \delta)}. \tag{37}$$

Equivalent system failure and repair rates can be determined applying the aggregation techniques introduced in [14]. For the system in Fig. 7 we obtain

$$\lambda_{eq} = \frac{2\lambda\pi_0 + \lambda\pi_1}{\pi_0 + \pi_1}, \tag{38}$$

$$\mu_{eq} = \frac{\delta\pi_{1D} + \mu\pi_2}{\pi_{1D} + \pi_2}, \tag{39}$$

with system availability given by (14). To better understand the impact of the equivalent rates on system availability look at the composition of λ_{eq} and μ_{eq} in (38) and (39). Take μ_{eq} as an example. A typical setting for the parameter values is: $\lambda \approx 10^{-5}$, $\mu \approx 10^{-1}$, and $\delta \approx 10^2$. Then $\delta\pi_{1D} \gg \mu\pi_2$ in the numerator of (39). This shows that the recovery rate δ, not μ, is the key to improving μ_{eq}; thus improving system availability.

This example has illustrated a case where a higher system availability can be reached much more effectively by increasing the system recovery rate rather than decreasing the component MTTR.

2.10 "High-Availability Systems Should Have No Single Point-of-Failure"

Single point-of-failure (SPOF) analysis is one of the traditional practices in reliability engineering. Naive interpretation of the topology of reliability block diagrams or other architectural diagrams may lead to the erroneous perception that the optimal improvement opportunity (without considering costs) in any high-availability architecture is always the removal of SPOFs. What the analyst may fail to realize is that the structure of the system is just one of many factors that determine the importance of a component in a high-availability system. Other determining factors are for instance the reliability/unreliability (or availability/unavailability) of the system components, the mission time, and target availability. Besides, the adoption of hierarchical modeling approaches may also lead to confusion. For instance, subsystems that appear as SPOFs in high-level diagrams may in fact correspond to highly redundant component structures.

Importance theory, a concept introduced by Birnbaum [15] in 1969, provides superior criteria than SPOFs alone for objective placement of redundancy. The reasoning behind the theory is that during the design of a system, the choice of components and their arrangement may render some components to be more critical with respect to the functioning of the system than others. The first quantitative ranking metrics proposed were the *structural importance* and *Birnbaum component importance*.

The structural importance of a component establishes the probability that the system shall fail when the component fails, i.e., the component is critical for system operation. Similar to an SPOF analysis, structural importance allows us to consider the relative importance of various components when only the structure of the system is known, but no other information is available.

When we do have additional information, improved measures such as the Birnbaum component importance provide a better framework to identify improvement opportunities to the system. For instance, when we additionally know the individual reliability of system components, we can compute the Birnbaum component importance. Semantically, this new metric represents the rate at which the system reliability improves as the reliability of a particular component improves. Another way of interpreting the Birnbaum importance metric is the probability that at a given time the system is in a state in which the component is critical for system operation. The larger the Birnbaum importance measure is, the more important the component is, in agreement with the intuition that a component that is frequently critical should be considered important.

To exemplify the distinction of both importance measures, consider the series-parallel system represented by the reliability block diagram in Fig. 8.

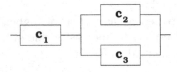

Fig. 8. Series-parallel reliability block diagram

The system is operational as long as component c_1 is functioning together with at least one of the two parallel components. Just based on the block diagram, we can determine, using the methods in [16] for instance, that the structural importance of c_1 is three times larger than those of either c_2 or c_3. This is an outcome that agrees with the intuition that series components are more fundamental to system reliability than parallel components, matching the SPOF reasoning. Now let us assume that we also know the intrinsic reliability of the system components. Suppose that the intrinsic reliability of the series component is 90% for a given mission time T, while the reliability of the parallel components are just 30% for the same mission time. Then, one can determine, using also the methods in [16] for instance, the Birnbaum importance of the components to be 0.51 for c_1, and 0.63 for the other two components. Therefore, the analysis indicates that components c_2 and c_3 should be the target of improvements (contrary to the results of a SPOF analysis) because at time T there is a 63% probability of the system being in a state that the functioning of these components is critical. For a comprehensive survey of other importance measures see [17].

3   Conclusions

Modern society and economy have been posing an increasingly imperative demand on the availability and reliability of computer systems and computer networks. The so called "24x7" (24-hours-a-day-and-7-days-a-week) requirement for these systems presents an unprecedented technical challenge. However, seemingly well-known concepts like availability and reliability are sometimes misunderstood even by professionals; such misunderstandings may eventually hinder advances in designing and deploying high-availability and high-reliability systems. This paper introduced ten fallacies existing in availability and reliability analysis and traced them back to their theoretical flaws. The first five fallacies address misconceptions related to R&A modeling and analysis, while the remaining ones provide insights for system engineers and companies focusing on system level integration.

References

1. Barlow, R.E., Proschan, F.: Statistical Theory of Reliability and Life Testing - Probability Models. Holt, Rinehart and Winston, New York (1975)
2. Leemis, L.M.: Reliability: Probability Models and Statistical Methods. Prentice-Hall, Englewood Cliffs (1995)
3. Patterson, D.A., Gibson, G.A., Katz, R.H.: A case for redundant arrays of inexpensive disks (RAID). In: Proc. SIGMOD Conference, pp. 109–116 (1988)
4. Trivedi, K.S.: Probability & Statistics with Reliability, Queueing, and Computer Science Applications, 2nd edn. John Wiley and Sons, New York (2001)
5. Schroeder, B., Gibson, G.A.: Disk failures in the real world: What does an MTTF of 1,000,000 hours mean to you? In: Proc. 5th USENIX Conference on File and Storage Technologies (2007)
6. Hald, A.: Statistical Theory with Engineering Applications. John Wiley and Sons, New York (1952)
7. Fricks, R.M., Ketcham, M.: Steady-state availability estimation using field failure data. In: Proc. Annual Reliability and Maintainability Symposium 2004, pp. 81–85 (2004)
8. Grottke, M., Trivedi, K.S.: On a method for mending time to failure distributions. In: Proc. International Conference on Dependable Systems and Networks 2005, pp. 560–569 (2005)
9. Trivedi, K.S., Muppala, J.K., Woolet, S.P., Haverkort, B.R.: Composite performance and dependability analysis. Performance Evaluation 14(3 & 4), 197–216 (1992)
10. Wang, D., Fricks, R., Trivedi, K.S.: Dealing with non-exponential distributions in dependability models. In: Kotsis, G. (ed.) Performance Evaluation - Stories and Perspectives, pp. 273–302. Österreichische Computer Gesellschaft, Wien (2003)
11. Trivedi, K.S., Sathaye, A., Ibe, O., Howe, R.: Should I add a processor? In: Proc. Twenty-third Hawaii International Conference on System Sciences, pp. 214–221 (1990)
12. Choi, H., Kulkarni, V.G., Trivedi, K.S.: Markov regenerative stochastic Petri nets. Performance Evaluation 20, 335–357 (1994)
13. Xie, W., Sun, H., Cao, Y., Trivedi, K.S.: Modeling of user perceived webserver availability. In: Proc. IEEE International Conference on Communications, vol. 3, pp. 1796–1800 (2003)
14. Lanus, M., Lin, Y., Trivedi, K.S.: Hierarchical composition and aggregation of state-based availability and performability models. IEEE Trans. Reliability 52(1), 44–52 (2003)

15. Birnbaum, Z.W.: On the importance of different components in a multicomponent system. In: Krishnaiah, P.R. (ed.) Multivariate Analysis - II, pp. 581–592. Academic Press, New York (1969)
16. Henley, E.J., Kumamoto, H.: Reliability Engineering and Risk Assessment. Prentice-Hall, Englewood Cliffs (1981)
17. Wang, D., Fricks, R.M., Trivedi, K.S.: Importance analysis with Markov chains. In: Proc. Annual Reliability and Maintainability Symposium, pp. 89–95 (2003)

Analytical Availability Assessment of IT Services

Miroslaw Malek[1], Bratislav Milic[1], and Nikola Milanovic[2]

[1] Institut für Informatik, Humboldt-Universität zu Berlin
{malek,milic}@informatik.hu-berlin.de
[2] Berlin University of Technology
nmilanov@cs.tu-berlin.de

Abstract. The often neglected problem in the service availability analysis is mapping between ICT-infrastructure and service-level availability. We present an approach which allows to map ICT-infrastructure elements to services, and to analytically assess steady-state, interval and user-perceived service availability, based on failure distributions of ICT-elements that implement a composite service. In case that full topology or all failure distributions of ICT-infrastructure elements are unknown, we provide means to estimate upper and lower availability bounds.

1 Introduction

The rapid networking expansion and convergence of computing and communication infrastructures make the availability of IT-based services (e.g., telecommunication, software or storage services) the central point in design of service-oriented IT systems. Even today, services are simply expected to be delivered on demand, and this requirement will be even more important in the near future.

Several methodologies have been established to assess service availability: analytical, quantitative and qualitative. Quantitative assessment is based on measurements. Whereas it has proven itself in several areas (e.g., hardware in form of benchmarks and testing), it is difficult to apply it to services because of the lack of adequate metrics and instrumentation (see Page 217). Qualitative availability assessment is performed informally (e.g., questionnaires and interviews) and assigns an availability class to the system (service). The qualitative results are easy to misinterpret, difficult to compare and depend heavily on the consultant performing the analysis. Analytical methods model services and calculate or simulate their availability.

Up to now, classical analytical methods have been applied to determine service availability with mixed success, partially because many approaches failed to incorporate the interdependencies between users, underlying ICT infrastructure and services. The goals of this paper are:

- Given availability definition at the ICT-level to define availability at the service-level
- Investigate functional dependency between availability at the ICT-level and service-level using an analytical model-based approach

T. Nanya et al. (Eds.): ISAS 2008, LNCS 5017, pp. 207–224, 2008.

2 Related Work

Service availability is drawing lots of attention in research community and in industry. Various methodologies are developed for building highly available systems. The Service Availability Forum (SAF) [1] is a consortium that develops high availability and management software interface specifications. Buskens and Gonzalez [2] present a high availability middleware and Immonen and Niemela [3] survey methodologies developed for reliability prediction of component based software architectures. However, these and other similar methodologies are intended for development and they are not applicable to availability evaluation of existing, already deployed services.

In [4] we carried out a detailed study of methods and tools that can be used for availability evaluation. Our conclusion is that IT service availability assessment is tackled either by the general purpose modeling methods and tools that are preferred in the research community, or by industry-oriented process management tools that support best practice frameworks such as CobiT and ITIL.

The general purpose modeling methodologies like Markov chains, Petri and Stochastic Activity Networks enable very precise availability assessment. The tools that support them are numerous: Isograph's Reliability Workbench suite [5], Moebius [6], SHARPE [7], OpenSesame [8], etc. Some of the tools specialize in a certain application area. For instance, Network Availability Program (NAP) [9] produced by Isograph is intended for availability and reliability assessment in communication networks. The NAP studies how network element failures impact the data flow between source and target nodes in the network.

Such tools and models are unable to dynamically adapt to changes in the IT infrastructure. They require experienced personnel to build and verify a model, requiring lots of man-hours for a single model. Even a minor change in the IT infrastructure requires the re-evaluation of the model, as it can be invalidated by introduced changes. The financial costs of such approach are immense and in practice it is rarely employed, apart from dedicated mission-critical systems, like flight control systems.

Industry has responded by introducing best practices that help in management of information systems. Most notable are Information Technology Infrastructure Library - ITIL [10] and Control Objectives for Information and related Technology - CobiT [11]. ITIL is technology oriented and provides a detailed description for a number of important IT practices, tasks and procedures. CobiT is of higher importance for managerial purposes as it bridges the gap between business and IT, and explains interrelations.

The process management tools support ITIL and CobiT frameworks. They are focused on direct measurement and checking of infrastructure status – which systems are operational and which are not, is there an overload situation in the network, etc. Typically they include a Configuration Management Database (CMDB) system as well, that keeps track of assets in the infrastructure and their configuration. Notable process management tools are IBM's Tivoli [12], HP's Mercury [13], Fujitsu's Interstage [14]. Their main drawback is that they are only measurement based. As the availability is user perceived and network topology dependant (as shown in Section 4), it can happen that the monitoring application indicates high availability while the real clients are actually experiencing low service availability.

In the research community, service availability was treated either broadly or in a very specialized fashion. Dahlin et al. [15] investigate the service availability in WAN networks. They assume that service is available as soon as the client and server are able to communicate and ignore other requirements that a service has to fulfill beside the connectivity. Bulka [16] analyzes reliability of optical (FDDI) token ring networks using fault trees completely ignoring the services deployed in such networks. Jiang and Schulzrinne [17] evaluate availability of voice over IP service with regard to several metrics (call success rate, call abortion rate, etc.) but their approach cannot be generalized to other types of services.

Wang and Trivedi [18] increase detail of study of service availability by precisely modeling both system and user behavior and apply the method on a VoIP system. The model is detailed, but it is developed by hand and it ignores client availability, network topology and availability.

3 Reference Architecture and Fault Model

We use the standard 3-layered architecture, such as presented in [19], to address the mapping between ICT- and service-level availability properties. In this section we briefly describe the architecture and then present the fault model.

The architecture comprises ICT-infrastructure, service and business process (BP) levels (Fig. 1). BP consists of a set of activities that are performed in coordination in an organizational and technical environment. The activities jointly realize a business goal. The coordination between activities is achieved by an explicit process representation using execution constraints. BP is described using a workflow, while BP activities are enacted by services. Services are elements of workflows. The most general definition of a service is that an IT-service is a meaningful activity (e.g., computing a well-defined task) that a software or hardware element performs on request of another software element, hardware element or a human user [20]. We will adopt a more technical definition where IT-service is characterized by three parts: offered functionality, input and output messages, and interface address or port reference [21]. A service is visible to the outside world through its interface description, which forms a contract between the client and the service itself [22]. A contract describes service requirements (preconditions) and service deliverables (postconditions). A contract (also known as service level agreement – SLA) may not include only functional (e.g., parameter) constraints, but also non-functional properties such as availability, security, timeliness. In order to perform their functions, services rely (are based on) mostly on the ICT-infrastructure (possibly also on people). ICT represents convergence of computational and communication infrastructures and is represented by hardware (such as computers and networks) and heterogeneous applications using that hardware. While there are numerous possibilities to describe or model ICT infrastructure with respect to a given property, several

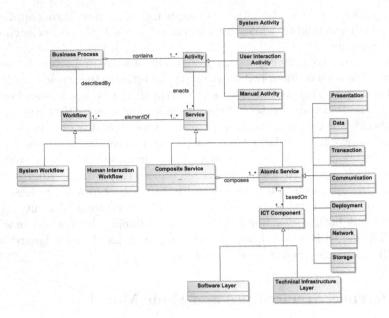

Fig. 1. Reference Architecture

modeling approaches have already been established for modeling availability, such as reliability block diagrams, fault trees, Markov chains or Petri nets.

We focus on the relationship between ICT-infrastructure and service availability and do not consider business process availability. Hence we define the following fault model.

Correct service is delivered when the service implements the required system function [23]. A service failure is an event that occurs when delivered service deviates from correct service. A service fails either because it does not comply with its contract (functional and non-functional specification) or because the specification did not adequately describe the service function. The period of incorrect delivery is service outage. The transition from incorrect service to correct service is service restoration. While service availability can be defined for abstract services (process descriptions) it can be calculated for service instances only, that is, for services which are bound to concrete ICT elements. Service behavior is defined as composite (transactional) behavior of the ICT-elements a service is based on. The deviation from correct service may assume different forms or service failure modes. We identify the following failure modes of a service:

- Temporal: a service did not meet a deadline. A service will not respond on time if 1) a subset of ICT-elements it is based on does not respond on time; 2) all ICT-elements respond on time, but synchronization exceeds the deadline; 3) there is a deadlock in synchronization.
- Value: a service responded with incorrect value. A service will respond with incorrect value if 1) a subset of ICT-elements it is based on delivers incorrect

values; 2) data and control flow between ICT-elements are faulty, e.g., a wrong parameter value has been passed to the ICT-element.

Using the failure modes, availability (understood as readiness for correct service) can be defined at the following three levels:

- Interval service availability is the number of correct service invocations over a number of total service invocations for a given time interval (e.g., one hour or one day).
- Steady-state service availability is the expected availability of a service over its lifetime and is defined as service uptime over service lifetime, for all users.
- User-perceived availability is the number of correct service invocations over a number of total service invocations, for a given time interval (interval user-perceived availability) or over service's lifetime (steady-state user-perceived availability) invoked by a particular user. It is highly correlated with service load (distribution of user requests over time).

Furthermore, we define required availability, which represents target service availability that ICT infrastructure has to deliver/match, and provided availability, which is given availability of the particular ICT infrastructure. One of the benefits of the proposed solution is the ability to match provided and required availability for services deployed on a given infrastructure.

Based on these preliminaries, the following section presents an approach to analytically determine service availability based on the failure distributions of the ICT-elements a service is based on.

4   Service Availability Assessment

Services are based on the ICT components from the software and technical infrastructure layer. The following properties characterize ICT-to-service interaction:

- Services can be arbitrarily complex. In order to describe the functionality of a real-world service, a human is required to extract service description from specification or standards.
- Large set of services, such as e-mail, web, database access is standardized in enterprise environments.
- Infrastructure on which services are deployed, like network topology, quality of equipment, skill of maintenance personnel, environmental impacts (e.g., quality of air conditioning or power supply), differ greatly from one enterprise to another.

Our proposal is to describe services using an existing process modeling language (e.g., BPMN [19]) and then to map it to the provided ICT-infrastructure, which is managed using a configuration management database (CMDB) tool such as ECDB [24]. This is illustrated in Figure 2: e-mail service always includes the same steps that have to be performed, but different enterprises have different infrastructures that determine the actual service availability.

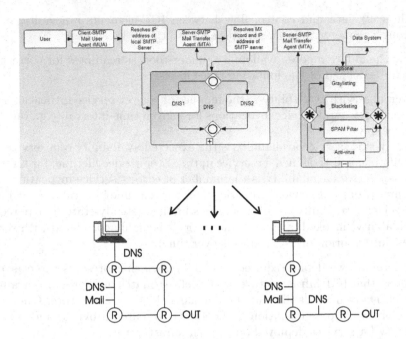

Fig. 2. E-mail Service Deployed in Different Infrastructures

4.1   ICT-Service Mapping

The proposed methodology for mapping services to the ICT building blocks of an enterprise is created in such manner that it can be integrated into a tool (details are in Section 5) that afterwards performs online availability assessment. Most of the steps are automated, so the tool can adapt to the changes in infrastructure or service functionality and calculate availability that represents the actual state of the infrastructure/network without need for human intervention. The mapping consists of the following steps:

1. Services of importance for the enterprise are identified. Their required availability is defined. The information is taken from qualitative analysis (CobiT, ITIL) or defined by the technical management.
2. A service is described in a high-level language (e.g., BPMN). Descriptions of standardized services are supported by default in the tool that we are developing. The overhead introduced by this step is limited, because the human effort is required only for the first description of a service and only in case that the service is unknown to the tool. Important benefit of the approach is that the maintenance personnel does not have to learn the sophisticated modeling techniques and languages nor to update the model each time the ICT infrastructure changes.
3. A CMDB system is responsible to collect the infrastructure data: equipment and atomic services present in network and their availability statistics. For

instance, in ECDB that is responsibility of Nmap and Nagios tools. As the output, CMDB provides an infrastructure graph (see Figure 3, left).

4. An infrastructure graph is transformed into a connectivity graph. It integrates computing and communication infrastructure by adding communication links to the computing nodes (Figure 3, right).

5. Steps of service execution (BPMN activities) from service description are mapped to the connectivity graph. Each step in execution has its source S (that initiates the step) and destination D (that performs it) in the connectivity graph and we have to find all paths between S and D. The individual source-destination paths are transformed to Boolean equations by applying & (AND) operator between nodes that belong to the same path. Multiple paths between S and D are joined using operator || (OR). The resulting Boolean equations are minimized before they are transformed to an availability model. Existing tools, such as Mathematica [25], can be used for this purpose. For instance, let us assume that mail server is deployed on host *mail.enterprise.com*, the client *client.enterprise.com* can access it using the routers R1 and R2 or using router R3. That gives us: $client\&(R1\&R2)\&mail||client\&R3\&mail = client\&((R1\&R2)||R3)\&mail$.

6. The mapped service description is transformed to a formal model (this paper demonstrates the usage of Fault Trees and Reliability Block Diagrams).[1]

7. A dedicated (third party) simulator/solver computes the formal model, calculates provided availability which is compared with the required availability. If required availability is not met, the person in charge is notified. This step closes the cycle by returning the actual availability information to the technical management that initiated the whole process.

The first step is human-dependant but it will be performed only once per service, when it is added to the enterprise. The second step is optional and as the knowledge base of the tool grows it will become template-based. The steps three through seven can be automated and they will be executed online: e.g., a change in the infrastructure triggers the update of the CMDB which initiates the new availability assessment.

Step 5 in the algorithm requires identification of all paths between two nodes in a graph. The algorithm that finds them is not difficult to implement, using recursion. Its complexity and execution time depend on the graph structure – as the number of loops in the topology increases, the algorithm complexity grows. In the worst case, when a graph is the complete graph (each two vertices are connected by an edge) the time/space complexity of the algorithm reaches $O(n!)$.

In general, such complexity is prohibitive. However, the situation in real networks is computationally feasible for majority of existing intranets as they are mostly tree-like structure with limited number of loops in the topology. The loops are formed by the routers and their count in the network is limited. A moderate number of network switches are connected to the router and the numerous end-hosts are then connected to switches creating tree-like structure.

---

[1] As there exists a bijective correspondence between RBD and FT, all examples in this paper are formalized using RBD only.

Such sparse structure is favorable for the algorithm and its complexity remains polynomial (for a tree it is linear).

4.2   Calculating Availability of an E-Mail Service

We will demonstrate the approach proposed in the Section 4.1 using e-mail service as an example to calculate steady state user-perceived availability. The example is based on the SMTP protocol defined in RFC 2821 [26]. We have chosen e-mail since it is ubiquitous communication service and is present in every modern enterprise. The availability of e-mail service is evaluated for two users in order to show that availability is not only the function of component availability but also of infrastructure topology and user location within the topology.

The first step in availability estimation is to define the service of interest and its required availability. Let us assume that management has determined that availability of the e-mail service should be 0.9985.

The next step is to provide abstract service description. We will use service description given in Figure 2. Service description is then mapped to the existing infrastructure elements. CMDB provides the infrastructure graph and component availability statistics (Table 1). The next step is to transform the infrastructure graph to the connectivity graph. If CMDB provides sufficient detail level, there is no need for this transformation – the data from CMDB can be directly used. Figure 3 shows both representations of the infrastructure.

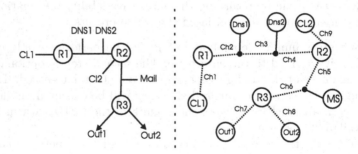

Fig. 3. Infrastructure Graph (Extracted from CMDB) and Transformation to Connectivity Graph

The abbreviations have the following meaning: Client i – CLi, Mail Server – MS, Routers – Ri, Channel – CHi, Out1 and Out2 are connections to Internet Service Providers of the enterprise. A channel is an abstraction that includes the switches and/or network adapters/links that are placed between routers and hosts. The channels are introduced for simplicity reasons – the goal of this section is to demonstrate the approach without going into unnecessary details. The channels are depicted in Figure 3 by dotted lines.

Based on the SMTP description from Figure 2 and connectivity graph from Figure 3, we map the service execution steps to paths in the connectivity graph.

In order to send an e-mail, client has to resolve address of the mail server. It is common that hosts in a network use two DNS servers, primary and secondary:

$CL_1 \to DNS$:
$(CL_1 \& CH_1 \& R_1 \& CH_2 \& DNS_1) \parallel (CL_1 \& CH_1 \& R_1 \& CH_2 \& CH_3 \& DNS_2) = CL_1 \& CH_1 \& R_1 \& CH_2 \& (DNS_1 \parallel (CH_3 \& DNS_2))$
and
$CL_2 \to DNS$:
$(CL_2 \& CH_9 \& R_2 \& CH_3 \& CH_4 \& DNS_1) \parallel (CL_2 \& CH_9 \& R_2 \& CH_4 \& DNS_2) = CL_2 \& CH_9 \& R_2 \& CH_4 \& (DNS_2 \parallel (CH_3 \& DNS_1))$

The clients now establish a connection with SMTP server and send the e-mail:
$CL_1 \to MS$:
$CL_1 \& CH_1 \& R_1 \& CH_2 \& CH_3 \& CH_4 \& R_2 \& CH_5 \& MS$
$CL_2 \to MS$:
$CL_2 \& CH_9 \& R_2 \& CH_5 \& MS$

In case that e-mail recipient is within the enterprise, the following steps would not be performed: the e-mail would be stored directly to disk system by the SMTP server, waiting there for local client to access it. In this example, we assume that recipient is outside the enterprise and local SMTP server has to determine the forward SMTP server. This requires a DNS query:

$MS \to DNS$:
$(MS \& CH_5 \& R_2 \& CH_4 \& DNS_2) \parallel (MS \& CH_5 \& R_2 \& CH_4 \& CH_3 \& DNS_1) = MS \& CH_5 \& R_2 \& CH_4 \& (DNS_2 \parallel CH_3 \& DNS_1)$

The last step is to dispatch the e-mail to the outside server. Since we can neither measure nor influence the availability of the Internet and outgoing (receiving) SMTP server, we evaluate availability up to the point where e-mail leaves the network of the enterprise:

$MS \to OUT$:
$(MS \& CH_6 \& R_3 \& CH_7 \& OUT_1) \parallel (MS \& CH_6 \& R_3 \& CH_8 \& OUT_2) = MS \& CH_6 \& R_3 \& (CH_7 \& OUT_1 \parallel CH_8 \& OUT_2)$

For the successful e-mail service execution, all these steps must be performed in series. The resulting expressions are simplified by applying the idempotence, associativity and distributivity rules of operators $\&$ and $\parallel$:

$CL_1 : (CL \to DNS) \& (CL \to MS) \& (MS \to DNS) \& (MS \to OUT) = CL_1 \& MS \& R_1 \& R_2 \& R_3 \& CH_1 \& CH_2 \& CH_3 \& CH_4 \& CH_5 \& CH_6 \& (DNS_1 \parallel DNS_2) \& (CH_7 \& OUT_1 \parallel CH_8 \& OUT_2)$
$CL_2 : (CL_2 \to DNS) \& (CL_2 \to MS) \& (MS \to DNS) \& (MS \to OUT) = CL_2 \& MS \& R_2 \& R_3 \& CH_9 \& CH_4 \& CH_5 \& CH_6 \& (CH_3 \& DNS_1 \parallel DNS_2) \& (CH_7 \& OUT_1 \parallel CH_8 \& OUT_2)$

The obtained expressions can be directly transformed into Fault Trees (FT) or to Reliability Block Diagrams (RBD). For demonstration purpose, we have chosen to use RBD (Figure 4). RBD methodology can calculate the steady state availability, but if interval availability is required as the evaluation result, a

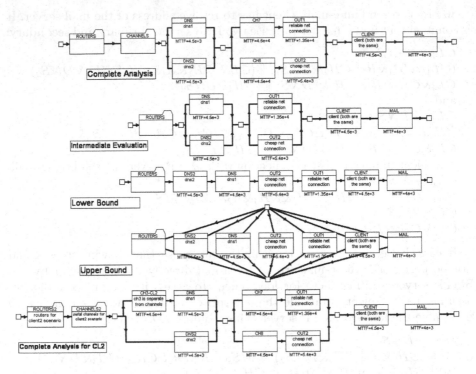

Fig. 4. Reliability Block Diagrams for the e-mail Service

Table 1. Evaluation Parameters

	Router	Channel	DNS	Mail	Client	Out1	Out2
MTTF	9000	45000	4500	4000	4500	13500	5400
MTTR	1	3	2	2	2	4	6

different formal model is required. The evaluation parameters are in Table 1. The model was solved in Isograph's Reliability Workbench and it assumes exponential distributions for failure and repair processes. The failure (λ) and repair (μ) rates are constant. Failure and repair rates are calculated from MTTF and MTTR as $\lambda = \frac{1}{MTTF}$ and $\mu = \frac{1}{MTTR}$. The evaluation results are in Table 2.

Required and user-perceived provided availability can be now compared. The provided availability of Client 1 (calculated as $1 - Unavailability$) is 0.99834, and provided availability of Client 2 is 0.99858. As our required availability is 0,9985, it is clear that e-mail service does not provide required availability to Client 1.

Since we may already be using measurement-based methods to evaluate availability of individual infrastructure elements, like routers or servers, it could be tempting to claim that the same, measurement based approach should be used for availability of services. However, as the user-perceived availability is network topology dependant and it differs from one client host to another, that implies

Table 2. Evaluation Results

	Precise for CL1	Precise for CL2	Lower	Intermediate	Upper
MTTF	1060	1280	662	1240	6.1 e+22
MTTR	1.79	1.83	2.37	1.59	0.293
Unavailability	0.00166	0.00142	0.00322	0.00127	3.5 e-24

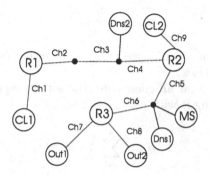

Fig. 5. Connectivity Graph After Change in the Infrastructure

that we should have to install a monitoring application on every client host in the network for every monitored service. The overhead introduced through installation of monitors on each client host, for every service the client is using, would be rather extensive and not very practical.

Furthermore, for some IT services, such as e-mail where responsibility for service execution is delegated through the network, it is not straightforward to estimate the availability by counting the success rates since measurements at individual points (on a server or on client) ignore the unavailability introduced by other elements in the infrastructure. If e-mail service success ratio is measured on client only, the availability monitor cannot detect situations where e-mail cannot leave the server because the Internet connection is not functional. Similarly, if monitor is placed on SMTP server only, it is not able to detect events when client cannot connect to the server. Therefore, precise service availability assessment through measurement requires monitoring of progress of individual e-mails through the IT infrastructure (outgoing e-mail is served once it leaves the enterprise, incoming e-mail once it reaches a client).

Our approach requires less effort for maintenance and provides additional advantage: in case of planned changes in the IT infrastructure, the impact of changes on availability can be estimated prior to implementation. For instance, if we move $DNS1$ server so that it is in the same subnetwork as the mail server (Figure 5), the availability measure for the first client remains the same but the availability of the second client increases to 0.99865. Purely measurement based approach is not able to predict the impact of infrastructure changes on availability.

4.3   Total Service Availability

The user-perceived availability of each client is not equivalent to the total service availability. Given that we have already calculated steady state or interval service availability A_i for each client i, we investigate how to derive total service availability.

Service availability is the mean value of the user perceived availabilities (for all clients):

$$A_S = \frac{\sum_{i=1}^{n} A_i}{n} \tag{1}$$

where n is the number of clients (users) and A_i are either steady state or interval user-perceived availabilities.

Equation 1 assumes that all clients use the service equally. It can be made more precise by weighing it with usage factors:

$$A_S = \sum_{i=1}^{n} A_i \cdot u_i \tag{2}$$

Usage factor u_i, for a client i, is the number of service invocations made by the client i over the total number of service invocations. From its definition, it holds that the sum of usage factors for all users (clients) is equal to one.

For steady-state service availability, A_i is steady state user-perceived availability. Parameters u_i are calculated during the service's lifetime. In practical terms, this means that it is determined using statistical methods over a longer period of time.

If Equation 2 is used to calculate interval service availability, A_i represents interval user-perceived availability. For interval availability, u_i is recorded for the observed interval, within which service availability is to be derived.

The impact of parameter selection to total availability is illustrated in Table 3. As the usage factor of CL_1 is increased, service availability decreases since client 1 has lower steady state user-perceived availability. This demonstrates how usage factors balance total service availability in case where clients don't invoke the service and access underlying resources evenly.

Table 3. E-mail Service Availability in the Enterprise for Different Values of Parameter u_i. $A_{CL1} = 0.99834$, $A_{CL2} = 0.99858$

u_1	u_2	A_s
0.5	0.5	0.99846
0.6	0.4	0.998436
0.9	0.1	0,998364
0.1	0.9	0,998556

4.4   Working with Incomplete Data

An implicit assumption of the proposed method is that complete network topology, as well as availability of individual components, are known. Although many methods for determining service availability make this assumption, in practice this is frequently not the case. The following cases of incomplete data can be distinguished:

Incomplete service description or network topology. In case that service description (functionality) or the network topology are unknown, but the ICT-components on which the service depends are known as well as their availabilities, the lower availability bound can be determined assuming that all components are placed in series:

$$LOWER : CL\&MS\&DNS_1\&DNS_2\&R_1\&R_2\&R_3\&OUT_1\&OUT_2$$

This model is unaware of communication channels and it does not include them. Similarly, the upper availability bound can be estimated assuming that all elements are placed in parallel:

$$UPPER : CL \parallel MS \parallel DNS_1 \parallel DNS_2 \parallel R_1 \parallel R_2 \parallel R_3 \parallel OUT_1 \parallel OUT_2$$

Finally, if the service description and component availabilities are known, but the exact topology of the network is unknown, availability can be estimated as:

$$INTERMEDIATE : CL\&MS\&(DNS_1 \parallel DNS_2)\&R_1\&R_2\&R_3\&(OUT_1 \parallel OUT_2)$$

The approximate service availabilities are in Table 2. The upper availability bound is of no practical use since it is very close to one. Lower bound is considerably lower than the actual availability, as expected. Intermediate model slightly overestimates the availability but it is very close to the precise value, considering that it does not utilize the network topology information. Still, this particular intermediate model example should be taken with caution since the difference is topology-dependent and may be much larger for other infrastructure configurations.

The amount of knowledge that we have about the network and the service influences other metrics of importance, apart from availability estimation. The Fussell-Vesely [27] metric determines the probability that particular component has contributed to the system failure, given that the system has failed. The metric is important since it provides guidelines to the network administrator where to incorporate the potential improvements in order to obtain the largest availability increase. Table 4 shows the differences observed in Fussell-Vesely metric for different levels of system knowledge:

- If complete information is known, according to FV metric, the administrator should improve availability of components in the following order: mail server, client, channels, routers. Other elements have minor impact on the availability.

Table 4. Fussel-Vesely Metric for different levels of system knowledge

	CL	MS	DNS1	DNS2	OUT1	OUT2	R1	R2	R3	CH1-CH6	CH7	CH8
Complete	0.266	0.3	11.7e-4	11.7e-4	15.8e-4	18.3e-4	0.067	0.067	0.067	0.0388	3.74e-5	1.3e-5
Lower	0.133	0.149	0.133	0.133	0.0818	0.271	0.033	0.033	0.033	/	/	/
Intermediate	0.347	0.39	15.3e-4	15.3e-4	19.3e-4	19.3e-4	0.087	0.087	0.087	/	/	/

- If service description is known but network topology is unknown, according to FV metric, the administrator should work in the following order: mail server, client, routers. The fit between this and the precise evaluation is good and cannot mislead administrator.
- If neither service nor topology of the network are known, based on the lower-bound assessment, the administrator should make improvements in the following order: internet connection 2, mail server, DNS servers, client, routers, internet connection 1. In this case, the metric is completely misleading and can distract the administrator from the real cause of the problem: precise analysis has shown that DNS and outbound connections have minor impact on the e-mail service availability, yet the metric recommends that both of them should be checked with high priority.

Unknown availability of some components in the network. In case that it is not possible to determine availability of one or more components in a network that are used by the evaluated service, clearly, the exact service availability cannot be calculated. Assuming that availability is unknown for n components, the availability can be observed as an n-variable function and it can be evaluated in n-dimensional space. It is necessary to assume the component availability distribution type or to take a distribution based on previous experience (e.g., if the availability distribution for one router type is known, in absence of better data it is to expect that the new router from same producer will have similar behavior), to vary the distribution parameters and to observe the availability. This approach is applicable to precise and approximative models from Sections 4.2 and 4.4 but it is highly dependant on human experience and actual behavior of unknown components.

Quantitative data on system does not exist. It is sometimes required to make availability assessment even if we are unable to determine/measure IT component availabilities, services are not described and network topology is unknown. In such extreme conditions, our and other analytical or simulation based approaches are not applicable. One possibility is to use qualitative assessment, based on the best-practice guides like CobiT [11], ITIL [10], BITCOM [28]. The best practices cover various aspects of IT management, therefore it is necessary to extract segments that are of importance for the availability, clearly define questions, interview the personnel in the enterprise and finally interpret the answers. The interpretation can be quantitative or qualitative. For instance:

- **Quantitative:** [28] lists the expected downtime per year in data centers as function of environmental factors. For example, if a data center has no redundant power supplies for equipment and air-conditioning, and no power generator, it can be expected that it may experience more than 72 hours of unplanned downtime per year. Another example is the CobiT process DS1 (Deliver and Support) that defines a metric that gives the percent of users satisfied with service delivery levels. As the CobiT specification does not define how to measure this percentage, the metric requires careful interpretation.

- **Qualitative:** Existence of formally defined RACI (Responsible, Accountable, Consulted, Informed) charts [11] clearly improves information flow in an enterprise and increases service availability. However, it is not possible to quantify the availability improvement.

Best practices can be promptly implemented, providing coarse guidelines where to aim for availability improvement. Still, they are imprecise in comparison with analytical and simulation methodologies.

5 Tool Prototype

In order to support the mapping process described in Section 4, we are developing a tool which enables to map elements from the ICT level to services and calculate service availability. For that purpose, we use a model-based approach based on Meta Object Facility (MOF) [29]. The concepts of failure modes, availability and necessary transformations are described at the metamodel (MOF M2) level, while the instances are described at the model (MOF M1) level. MOF levels are shown in Figure 6.

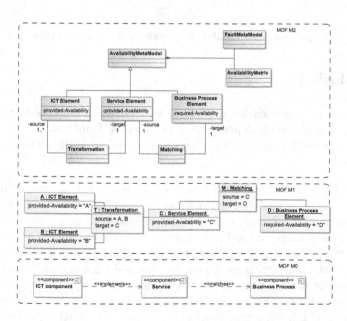

Fig. 6. MOF-based architecture for tool development

The tool architecture is shown in Figure 7. As an input, it accepts service description given in high-level process language (currently BPMN) and infrastructure data collected from a CMDB (currently ECDB). This requires graphical BPMN editor and ECDB installation. The main tool is realized using Eclipse Modeling Framework (EMF) plugin. It generates infrastructure graph, and enables (graphical) mapping of service description to the ICT infrastructure elements, which results in a connectivity graph. An XSLT transformation is performed on the connectivity graph, transforming it into formal model description. Currently, we support transformations to reliability block diagrams and fault trees. The resulting model is then used as an input to an existing solver (currently Isograph Reliability Workbench), which computes provided service availability. Required and provided service availability are then matched, and if discrepancies are found, adequate action can be taken (e.g., notification of management that initiates the modification of ICT infrastructure).

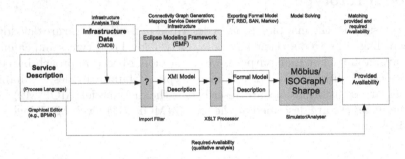

Fig. 7. Service availability assessment tool architecture

6   Conclusion

We presented an approach for analytical service availability assessment, with special focus on mapping dependencies between ICT infrastructure elements, users and services. The main advantages, compared with the existing surveyed solutions, are:

- Independence from the formal model used for analytical availability assessment. A service is modeled at the abstract level, its elements are matched to the infrastructure elements and the description is then automatically transformed to the target formal model (currently a reliability block diagram or a fault tree). The important aspect of this approach is flexibility and learning curve: the underlying model can be changed transparently, while the end user does not have to have intimate knowledge of complex mathematical formalisms used for modeling and solving/simulation. Furthermore, separation of service and infrastructure description enables automatic updates of service availability in case the infrastructure changes: it triggers new transformation and availability evaluation process.

- Support for user-perceived and overall service availability. We showed how overall service availability differs from the user-perceived availability, as it depends on the infrastructure topology, user's location and priority.
- Quantification of availability improvement. The presented framework can be used to quantify and compare availability of different implementations of a system (e.g., implementation of a system that uses the SAF HA interface specifications versus the implementation that does not support it).

We are, however, aware of the following drawbacks of the proposed solution. Modeling, in general, is not scalable. Although we remove the necessity that formal models (such as Markov chains, Petri nets or fault trees) be directly developed, it is still problematic how to describe large systems, that is, services with hundreds of states and infrastructures with thousands of nodes. Our current work focuses on the possibility to marry the three approaches that were mentioned in the Introduction, namely, to integrate qualitative, quantitative and analytical definitions, methods, and metrics. This is a non-trivial task, as it is at present unclear how to develop a unified system that can reasonably well represent measurement results, interview answers and availability values obtained by solving a formal model. One possible direction is given is Section 4, where qualitative methods (e.g., CobiT analysis) are used to define required service availability. Apart from scalability, the issue of transformation to target formal model is, in our opinion, still not satisfactorily solved. The models we use do not enable us to describe time-dependent events and to analyze history (state transition). We are currently investigating transformations to other model classes, such as Markov chains and stochastic activity networks. Regardless of the mentioned drawbacks, we consider the question of mapping services to ICT-infrastructure elements and users, and the ability to analytically calculate service availability based on information thus obtained, an important step in understanding the overall problems of availability of service-based IT systems. Finally, the ability to analytically determine service availability is a crucial step in developing of methods and tools for assessing business process availability of an enterprise (see Figure 1), a problem which has not been addressed up to now. We see an opportunity to connect business process definition with infrastructure topologies and user profiles using the service layer, based on methods that are analogous to ones proposed in this work. This could enable us to analytically determine business process availability.

References

1. Service Availability Forum (2007), http://www.saforum.org/
2. Buskens, R., Gonzalez, O.: Model-Centric Development of Highly Available Software Systems. In: Model-Centric Development of Highly Available Software Systems, pp. 163–187. Springer, Heidelberg (2007)
3. Immonen, A., Niemela, E.: Survey of reliability and availability prediction methods from the viewpoint of software architecture. Software and System Modeling 7, 49–65 (2007)

4. Malek, M., Hoffmann, G., Milanovic, N., Bruening, S., Meyer, R., Milic, B.: Methoden und Werkzeuge zur Verfgbarkeitsermittlung. Technical Report 219, Humboldt University Berlin (2007)
5. Reliability workbench (2007), http://www.isograph-software.com/rwbover.htm
6. Sanders, W.: Moebius Manual (2007)
7. Trivedi, K.: SHARPE 2000 GUI Manual (1999)
8. Walter, M.: OpenSESAME - Simple but Extensive Structured Availability Modeling Environment
9. Network Availability Program (NAP) v1.0 Technical Specification (2005), http://www.isograph-software.com/techspecs/nap32techspec.pdf
10. IT Infrastructure Library (2007), http://www.itil-officialsite.com
11. Cobit 4.1. IT Governance Institute (2007)
12. IBM Tivoli Availability Process Manager (2007), http://www-306.ibm.com/software/tivoli/products/availability-process-mgr/
13. Mercury Business Technology Optimization Enterprise (2007), http://www.mercury.com/us/products/
14. Fujitsu Interstage Business Process Manager (2007), http://www.fujitsu.com/global/services/software/interstage/bpm/index.html
15. Dahlin, M., Chandra, B.B.V., Gao, L., Nayate, A.: End-to-end WAN service availability. IEEE/ACM Trans. Netw. 11(2), 300–313 (2003)
16. Bulka, D.: Fault Tree Models for Reliablitiy Analysis of an FDDI Token Ring Network. In: Proceedings of the 30th annual Southeast regional conference (1992)
17. Jiang, W., Schulzrinne, H.: Assessment of VoIP service availability in the current internet. In: Proceedings of the Passive and Active Measurement Workshop (2003)
18. Wang, D., Trivedi, K.S.: Modeling user-perceived service availability. In: Malek, M., Nett, E., Suri, N. (eds.) ISAS 2005. LNCS, vol. 3694, pp. 107–122. Springer, Heidelberg (2005)
19. Weske, M.: Business Process Management: Concepts, Languages, Architectures. Springer, Heidelberg (2007)
20. Krafzig, D., Banke, K., Slama, D.: Enteprise SOA. Prentice-Hall, Englewood Cliffs (2004)
21. Vogels, W.: Web services are not distributed objects. IEEE Internet Computing (2003)
22. Milanovic, N.: Contract-based Web Service Composition. PhD Dissertation, Humboldt University Berlin (2006)
23. Avizienis, A., Laprie, J., Randell, B., Landwehr, C.: Basic concepts and taxonomy of dependable and secure computing. IEEE Trans. Dependable Sec. Comput. (2004)
24. ECDB: An Open Source Approach to Configuration Management (2007), http://www.cmdb.info
25. Wolfram, S.: The Mathematica Book. Wolfram Media, Incorporated (2003)
26. Klensin, J.: Simple mail transfer protocol. RFC 2821 (2001)
27. Fussell, J.: How to calculate system reliability and safety characteristics. IEEE Transact. Reliab. 24(3), 169–174 (1975)
28. Betriebssichere rechnenzentren. BITKOM Consortium (2006)
29. OMG: Meta Object Facility (MOF) 2.0 Core Specification (2004), http://www.omg.org/cgi-bin/apps/doc?ptc/03-10-04.pdf

Author Index

Baldoni, Roberto   1

Ciardo, Gianfranco   20

Dasarathy, Balakrishnan   20
Dohi, Tadashi   26, 110

Fricks, Ricardo M.   187
Fuligni, Stefano   1

Grottke, Michael   20, 187

Hamou-Lhadj, Abdelwahab   155
Hamouda, Ossama   171
Herrmann, Frédéric   142
Horstmann, Ulrich   142

Johansson, Andréas   90

Kaâniche, Mohamed   171
Kanso, Ali   155
Kato, Kazuhiko   129
Khendek, Ferhat   155
Kleber, Ulrich   142

Malek, Miroslaw   17, 207
Maruyama, Hiroshi   13
Matias, Rivalino   20
Matthiesen, Erling V.   171
Mecella, Massimo   1

Milanovic, Nikola   207
Milic, Bratislav   207

Nanya, Takashi   59
Nassu, Bogdan Tomoyuki   59

Okamura, Hiroyuki   110

Parkin, Simon Edward   43
Potter, Richard   129

Rindos, Andy   20

Sârbu, Constantin   90
Schwefel, Hans-Peter   171
Sugiki, Akiyoshi   129
Sun, Hairong   187
Suri, Neeraj   90

Toeroe, Maria   155
Tokuno, Koichi   75
Tortorelli, Francesco   1
Trivedi, Kishor S.   20, 187

Uemura, Toshikazu   26

van Moorsel, Aad   43
Vashaw, Bart   20

Yamada, Shigeru   75
Yamatozaki, Kei   129
Yassin Kassab, Rouaa   43

Lecture Notes in Computer Science

Sublibrary 3: Information Systems and Application, incl. Internet/Web and HCI

For information about Vols. 1– 4577
please contact your bookseller or Springer

Vol. 5017: T. Nanya, F. Maruyama, A. Pataricza, M. Malek (Eds.), Service Availability. XII, 225 pages. 2008.

Vol. 5013: J. Indulska, D.J. Patterson, T. Rodden, M. Ott (Eds.), Pervasive Computing. XIV, 315 pages. 2008.

Vol. 5006: R. Kowalczyk, M. Huhns, M. Klusch, Z. Maamar, Q.B. Vo (Eds.), Service-Oriented Computing: Agents, Semantics, and Engineering. X, 154 pages. 2008.

Vol. 4997: B. Monien, U.-P. Schroeder (Eds.), Algorithmic Game Theory. XI, 363 pages. 2008.

Vol. 4976: Y. Zhang, G. Yu, E. Bertino, G. Xu (Eds.), Progress in WWW Research and Development. XVIII, 699 pages. 2008.

Vol. 4956: C. Macdonald, I. Ounis, V. Plachouras, I. Ruthven, R.W. White (Eds.), Advances in Information Retrieval. XXI, 719 pages. 2008.

Vol. 4952: C. Floerkemeier, M. Langheinrich, E. Fleisch, F. Mattern, S.E. Sarma (Eds.), The Internet of Things. XIII, 378 pages. 2008.

Vol. 4947: J.R. Haritsa, R. Kotagiri, V. Pudi (Eds.), Database Systems for Advanced Applications. XXII, 713 pages. 2008.

Vol. 4936: W. Aiello, A. Broder, J. Janssen, E.. Milios (Eds.), Algorithms and Models for the Web-Graph. X, 167 pages. 2008.

Vol. 4932: S. Hartmann, G. Kern-Isberner (Eds.), Foundations of Information and Knowledge Systems. XII, 397 pages. 2008.

Vol. 4928: A.H.M. ter Hofstede, B. Benatallah, H.-Y. Paik (Eds.), Business Process Management Workshops. XIII, 518 pages. 2008.

Vol. 4903: S. Satoh, F. Nack, M. Etoh (Eds.), Advances in Multimedia Modeling. XIX, 510 pages. 2008.

Vol. 4900: S. Spaccapietra (Ed.), Journal on Data Semantics X. XIII, 265 pages. 2008.

Vol. 4892: A. Popescu-Belis, S. Renals, H. Bourlard (Eds.), Machine Learning for Multimodal Interaction. XI, 308 pages. 2008.

Vol. 4882: T. Janowski, H. Mohanty (Eds.), Distributed Computing and Internet Technology. XIII, 346 pages. 2007.

Vol. 4881: H. Yin, P. Tino, E. Corchado, W. Byrne, X. Yao (Eds.), Intelligent Data Engineering and Automated Learning - IDEAL 2007. XX, 1174 pages. 2007.

Vol. 4877: C. Thanos, F. Borri, L. Candela (Eds.), Digital Libraries: Research and Development. XII, 350 pages. 2007.

Vol. 4872: D. Mery, L. Rueda (Eds.), Advances in Image and Video Technology. XXI, 961 pages. 2007.

Vol. 4871: M. Cavazza, S. Donikian (Eds.), Virtual Storytelling. XIII, 219 pages. 2007.

Vol. 4858: X. Deng, F.C. Graham (Eds.), Internet and Network Economics. XVI, 598 pages. 2007.

Vol. 4857: J.M. Ware, G.E. Taylor (Eds.), Web and Wireless Geographical Information Systems. XI, 293 pages. 2007.

Vol. 4853: F. Fonseca, M.A. Rodríguez, S. Levashkin (Eds.), GeoSpatial Semantics. X, 289 pages. 2007.

Vol. 4836: H. Ichikawa, W.-D. Cho, I. Satoh, H.Y. Youn (Eds.), Ubiquitous Computing Systems. XIII, 307 pages. 2007.

Vol. 4832: M. Weske, M.-S. Hacid, C. Godart (Eds.), Web Information Systems Engineering – WISE 2007 Workshops. XV, 518 pages. 2007.

Vol. 4831: B. Benatallah, F. Casati, D. Georgakopoulos, C. Bartolini, W. Sadiq, C. Godart (Eds.), Web Information Systems Engineering – WISE 2007. XVI, 675 pages. 2007.

Vol. 4825: K. Aberer, K.-S. Choi, N. Noy, D. Allemang, K.-I. Lee, L. Nixon, J. Golbeck, P. Mika, D. Maynard, R. Mizoguchi, G. Schreiber, P. Cudré-Mauroux (Eds.), The Semantic Web. XXVII, 973 pages. 2007.

Vol. 4823: H. Leung, F. Li, R. Lau, Q. Li (Eds.), Advances in Web Based Learning – ICWL 2007. XIV, 654 pages. 2008.

Vol. 4822: D.H.-L. Goh, T.H. Cao, I.T. Sølvberg, E. Rasmussen (Eds.), Asian Digital Libraries. XVII, 519 pages. 2007.

Vol. 4820: T.G. Wyeld, S. Kenderdine, M. Docherty (Eds.), Virtual Systems and Multimedia. XII, 215 pages. 2008.

Vol. 4816: B. Falcidieno, M. Spagnuolo, Y. Avrithis, I. Kompatsiaris, P. Buitelaar (Eds.), Semantic Multimedia. XII, 306 pages. 2007.

Vol. 4813: I. Oakley, S.A. Brewster (Eds.), Haptic and Audio Interaction Design. XIV, 145 pages. 2007.

Vol. 4810: H.H.-S. Ip, O.C. Au, H. Leung, M.-T. Sun, W.-Y. Ma, S.-M. Hu (Eds.), Advances in Multimedia Information Processing – PCM 2007. XXI, 834 pages. 2007.

Vol. 4809: M.K. Denko, C.-s. Shih, K.-C. Li, S.-L. Tsao, Q.-A. Zeng, S.H. Park, Y.-B. Ko, S.-H. Hung, J.-H. Park (Eds.), Emerging Directions in Embedded and Ubiquitous Computing. XXXV, 823 pages. 2007.

Vol. 4808: T.-W. Kuo, E. Sha, M. Guo, L.T. Yang, Z. Shao (Eds.), Embedded and Ubiquitous Computing. XXI, 769 pages. 2007.

Vol. 4806: R. Meersman, Z. Tari, P. Herrero (Eds.), On the Move to Meaningful Internet Systems 2007: OTM 2007 Workshops, Part II. XXXIV, 611 pages. 2007.

Vol. 4805: R. Meersman, Z. Tari, P. Herrero (Eds.), On the Move to Meaningful Internet Systems 2007: OTM 2007 Workshops, Part I. XXXIV, 757 pages. 2007.

Vol. 4804: R. Meersman, Z. Tari (Eds.), On the Move to Meaningful Internet Systems 2007: CoopIS, DOA, ODBASE, GADA, and IS, Part II. XXIX, 683 pages. 2007.

Vol. 4803: R. Meersman, Z. Tari (Eds.), On the Move to Meaningful Internet Systems 2007: CoopIS, DOA, ODBASE, GADA, and IS, Part I. XXIX, 1173 pages. 2007.

Vol. 4802: J.-L. Hainaut, E.A. Rundensteiner, M. Kirchberg, M. Bertolotto, M. Brochhausen, Y.-P.P. Chen, S.S.-S. Cherfi, M. Doerr, H. Han, S. Hartmann, J. Parsons, G. Poels, C. Rolland, J. Trujillo, E. Yu, E. Zimányie (Eds.), Advances in Conceptual Modeling – Foundations and Applications. XIX, 420 pages. 2007.

Vol. 4801: C. Parent, K.-D. Schewe, V.C. Storey, B. Thalheim (Eds.), Conceptual Modeling - ER 2007. XVI, 616 pages. 2007.

Vol. 4797: M. Arenas, M.I. Schwartzbach (Eds.), Database Programming Languages. VIII, 261 pages. 2007.

Vol. 4796: M. Lew, N. Sebe, T.S. Huang, E.M. Bakker (Eds.), Human–Computer Interaction. X, 157 pages. 2007.

Vol. 4794: B. Schiele, A.K. Dey, H. Gellersen, B. de Ruyter, M. Tscheligi, R. Wichert, E. Aarts, A. Buchmann (Eds.), Ambient Intelligence. XV, 375 pages. 2007.

Vol. 4777: S. Bhalla (Ed.), Databases in Networked Information Systems. X, 329 pages. 2007.

Vol. 4761: R. Obermaisser, Y. Nah, P. Puschner, F.J. Rammig (Eds.), Software Technologies for Embedded and Ubiquitous Systems. XIV, 563 pages. 2007.

Vol. 4747: S. Džeroski, J. Struyf (Eds.), Knowledge Discovery in Inductive Databases. X, 301 pages. 2007.

Vol. 4744: Y. de Kort, W. IJsselsteijn, C. Midden, B. Eggen, B.J. Fogg (Eds.), Persuasive Technology. XIV, 316 pages. 2007.

Vol. 4740: L. Ma, M. Rauterberg, R. Nakatsu (Eds.), Entertainment Computing – ICEC 2007. XXX, 480 pages. 2007.

Vol. 4730: C. Peters, P. Clough, F.C. Gey, J. Karlgren, B. Magnini, D.W. Oard, M. de Rijke, M. Stempfhuber (Eds.), Evaluation of Multilingual and Multi-modal Information Retrieval. XXIV, 998 pages. 2007.

Vol. 4723: M. R. Berthold, J. Shawe-Taylor, N. Lavrač (Eds.), Advances in Intelligent Data Analysis VII. XIV, 380 pages. 2007.

Vol. 4721: W. Jonker, M. Petković (Eds.), Secure Data Management. X, 213 pages. 2007.

Vol. 4718: J. Hightower, B. Schiele, T. Strang (Eds.), Location- and Context-Awareness. X, 297 pages. 2007.

Vol. 4717: J. Krumm, G.D. Abowd, A. Seneviratne, T. Strang (Eds.), UbiComp 2007: Ubiquitous Computing. XIX, 520 pages. 2007.

Vol. 4715: J.M. Haake, S.F. Ochoa, A. Cechich (Eds.), Groupware: Design, Implementation, and Use. XIII, 355 pages. 2007.

Vol. 4714: G. Alonso, P. Dadam, M. Rosemann (Eds.), Business Process Management. XIII, 418 pages. 2007.

Vol. 4704: D. Barbosa, A. Bonifati, Z. Bellahsène, E. Hunt, R. Unland (Eds.), Database and XML Technologies. X, 141 pages. 2007.

Vol. 4690: Y. Ioannidis, B. Novikov, B. Rachev (Eds.), Advances in Databases and Information Systems. XIII, 377 pages. 2007.

Vol. 4675: L. Kovács, N. Fuhr, C. Meghini (Eds.), Research and Advanced Technology for Digital Libraries. XVII, 585 pages. 2007.

Vol. 4674: Y. Luo (Ed.), Cooperative Design, Visualization, and Engineering. XIII, 431 pages. 2007.

Vol. 4663: C. Baranauskas, P. Palanque, J. Abascal, S.D.J. Barbosa (Eds.), Human-Computer Interaction – INTERACT 2007, Part II. XXXIII, 735 pages. 2007.

Vol. 4662: C. Baranauskas, P. Palanque, J. Abascal, S.D.J. Barbosa (Eds.), Human-Computer Interaction – INTERACT 2007, Part I. XXXIII, 637 pages. 2007.

Vol. 4658: T. Enokido, L. Barolli, M. Takizawa (Eds.), Network-Based Information Systems. XIII, 544 pages. 2007.

Vol. 4656: M.A. Wimmer, J. Scholl, Å. Grönlund (Eds.), Electronic Government. XIV, 450 pages. 2007.

Vol. 4655: G. Psaila, R. Wagner (Eds.), E-Commerce and Web Technologies. VII, 229 pages. 2007.

Vol. 4654: I.-Y. Song, J. Eder, T.M. Nguyen (Eds.), Data Warehousing and Knowledge Discovery. XVI, 482 pages. 2007.

Vol. 4653: R. Wagner, N. Revell, G. Pernul (Eds.), Database and Expert Systems Applications. XXII, 907 pages. 2007.

Vol. 4636: G. Antoniou, U. Aßmann, C. Baroglio, S. Decker, N. Henze, P.-L. Patranjan, R. Tolksdorf (Eds.), Reasoning Web. IX, 345 pages. 2007.

Vol. 4611: J. Indulska, J. Ma, L.T. Yang, T. Ungerer, J. Cao (Eds.), Ubiquitous Intelligence and Computing. XXIII, 1257 pages. 2007.

Vol. 4607: L. Baresi, P. Fraternali, G.-J. Houben (Eds.), Web Engineering. XVI, 576 pages. 2007.

Vol. 4606: A. Pras, M. van Sinderen (Eds.), Dependable and Adaptable Networks and Services. XIV, 149 pages. 2007.

Vol. 4605: D. Papadias, D. Zhang, G. Kollios (Eds.), Advances in Spatial and Temporal Databases. X, 479 pages. 2007.

Vol. 4602: S. Barker, G.-J. Ahn (Eds.), Data and Applications Security XXI. X, 291 pages. 2007.

Vol. 4601: S. Spaccapietra, P. Atzeni, F. Fages, M.-S. Hacid, M. Kifer, J. Mylopoulos, B. Pernici, P. Shvaiko, J. Trujillo, I. Zaihrayeu (Eds.), Journal on Data Semantics IX. XV, 197 pages. 2007.

Vol. 4592: Z. Kedad, N. Lammari, E. Métais, F. Meziane, Y. Rezgui (Eds.), Natural Language Processing and Information Systems. XIV, 442 pages. 2007.

Vol. 4587: R. Cooper, J. Kennedy (Eds.), Data Management. XIII, 259 pages. 2007.